Scratch 2.0 Game Development HOTSHT

10 engaging projects that will teach you how to build exciting games with the easy-to-use Scratch 2.0 environment

Sergio van Pul

Jessica Chiang

[PACKT]
PUBLISHING

BIRMINGHAM - MUMBAI

Scratch 2.0 Game Development HOTSH⊕T

First published: February 2014

Production Reference: 1140214

Published by Packt Publishing Ltd.
Livery Place
35 Livery Street
Birmingham B3 2PB, UK.

ISBN 978-1-84969-756-9

www.packtpub.com

Cover Image by Sergio van Pul (sergiovanpul@msn.com)

Credits

Authors

Sergio van Pul

Jessica Chiang

Reviewers

Michael Badger

Joshua Madara

Mehul Shukla

Joy Suliman

Acquisition Editors

Saleem Ahmed

Erol Staveley

Rebecca Youe

Content Development Editor

Ankita Shashi

Technical Editors

Mario D'Souza

Novina Kewalramani

Humera Shaikh

Ritika Singh

Project Coordinator

Amey Sawant

Copy Editors

Sayanee Mukherjee

Deepa Nambiar

Alfida Paiva

Proofreaders

Simran Bhogal

Ameesha Green

Indexers

Mariammal Chettiyar

Rekha Nair

Graphics

Yuvraj Mannari

Production Coordinator

Nitesh Thakur

Cover Work

Nitesh Thakur

About the Authors

Sergio van Pul is a game designer and artist interested in making interactive media entertainment. He has built games and interactive applications using Flash ActionScript. He has also worked on web designs and stylesheets, using a basic text/script editor to write raw HTML and CSS, as well as using the Drupal CMS to assemble a website. He is also familiar with visual editing tools such as Photoshop and Première.

Sergio has worked as a freelance designer and programmer on a variety of projects, many of which involved interaction and education. During this time, he met people from Scratch Web Foundation, a Dutch organization that promotes digital design and programming knowledge in primary education.

Sergio started using Scratch to teach children about programming and game design. Occasionally, he also uses Scratch as a quick and easy prototyping tool to test game interaction concepts. He likes experimenting with the program and building tutorials, examples, and complete game projects. Some of his material was printed and tested during workshop sessions for Scratch Web Foundation. This book is his first official publication.

I'd like to thank the people from Scratch Web Foundation. In particular, I'd like to thank Joek van Montfort and Helen Fermate for working with me and giving me the drive and opportunity to develop engaging Scratch projects. Some of the projects offered in this book started out as little thought experiments and workshops for Scratch Web. I'd also like to thank Jan-Pieter van Seventer, one of my game-design teachers, for notifying me about an interesting workshop assignment for children. This assignment solidified my interest in Scratch as a teaching tool for interactive media education. His brief note set me on the path that eventually led to the publication of this book. Finally, I'd also like to thank my co-author Jessica Chiang for stepping in and taking some of the burden from me of writing a whole book worth of engaging Scratch projects.

Jessica Chiang is a senior software engineer, online educator, and technology enthusiast.

She has worked with a wide range of interesting and cutting-edge technologies including nuclear detector and unmanned aircraft-control system. Not only an inquisitive learner, she also loves to teach in class as well as online through her website (`shallwelearn.com`) and YouTube channel (`http://www.youtube.com/user/kookoodoll`).

Jessica has self-published an e-book titled *Shall We Learn Scratch Programming: E for Everyone*. This book has been requested by many schools to supplement their computer science and education curriculum; one such school is Jessica's alma mater, the University of California, San Diego.

I would like to thank my husband Dr. Greg Chen for his loving patience and encouragement during the whole writing process. I also want to thank both of my sons, Matt and Vincent, for being the game beta testers. Finally, I want to thank my parents for fostering in me a spirit of curiosity and adventure. Without them, I would have neither started nor completed this book.

About the Reviewers

Michael Badger has written several books for Packt Publishing including *Beginner's Guide for Scratch 1.4 and Scratch 2.0*. He writes a regular Scratch programming column for *Raspberry Pi Geek* magazine and frequently facilitates Scratch workshops for both parents and kids. To learn more, visit www.scratchguide.com.

Joshua Madara is a digital and electronic artist living in Seattle, Washington, where he enjoys doing esoteric things with computers. He has introduced Scratch to people of all ages through community centers, makerspaces, and online classes.

Mehul Shukla is one of the PlayStation® Mobile specialists in the SCEE R&D Developer Services Team. The Developer Services Team provides front line engineering support for all game developers, large or small, on all PlayStation platforms. On a daily basis he provides technical support and performance advice for developers all over the globe on the PSM community forums.

Mehul has also given technical talks about PlayStation®Mobile development at a number of Games Industry conferences and academic events.

Mehul joined SCEE R&D straight from University and has a Master's degree in Games Programming and a Bachelor's degree in Computer Systems Engineering.

Mehul has also worked on books titled *PlayStation® Mobile Development Cookbook* and *Mobile Game Design Essentials*, both published by Packt Publishing.

Joy Suliman is an educator and community facilitator who specializes in creating dynamic learning workshops with a creative technology focus for children and young people. Joy brings together her strong online skills with her diverse experience in learning technology, workshop facilitation, research, professional development training, online collections, regional outreach, and youth work to develop innovative, integrated learning programs, professional development workshops, and community engagement strategies for informal learning settings.

She has worked at Queensland University of Technology, the Powerhouse Museum in Sydney, Arab Council in Australia, ABC local radio, and the University of Wollongong.

www.PacktPub.com

Support files, eBooks, discount offers and more

You might want to visit www.PacktPub.com for support files and downloads related to your book.

Did you know that Packt offers eBook versions of every book published, with PDF and ePub files available? You can upgrade to the eBook version at www.PacktPub.com and as a print book customer, you are entitled to a discount on the eBook copy. Get in touch with us at service@packtpub.com for more details.

At www.PacktPub.com, you can also read a collection of free technical articles, sign up for a range of free newsletters and receive exclusive discounts and offers on Packt books and eBooks.

http://PacktLib.PacktPub.com

Do you need instant solutions to your IT questions? PacktLib is Packt's online digital book library. Here, you can access, read and search across Packt's entire library of books.

- ▸ Why Subscribe?
- ▸ Fully searchable across every book published by Packt
- ▸ Copy and paste, print and bookmark content
- ▸ On demand and accessible via web browser

Free Access for Packt account holders

If you have an account with Packt at www.PacktPub.com, you can use this to access PacktLib today and view nine entirely free books. Simply use your login credentials for immediate access.

Table of Contents

Preface

Scratch offers a fun way of getting introduced to programming and interactive media design. Within minutes of starting the program, you can see the first results of your work. Visual feedback comes early and often, making high-level, abstract concepts a lot easier to understand.

Even without a specific plan in mind, it's fun to play and experiment with the software. You are always discovering and learning something new, and even failed projects can have funny or spectacular results.

Since Version 2.0, Scratch has moved from a desktop application to an online interface. Scratch 2.0 also includes many new and exciting features, which makes creating more advanced games possible.

This book presents a series of fully-realized interactive projects to work on. It will teach you how to build great games with lots of depth. The final results will be close to production level games. This book not only introduces you to the new features of Scratch 2.0, but also introduces you to interactive media design in general. You can take the lessons learned here and apply them to create games with tool sets other than Scratch.

We hope you enjoy working on the projects in this book. May they inspire you to create even better games!

What this book covers

Project 1, *Blowing Things Up!*, builds a simple game involving a cannon and some targets. You will learn about placing sprites, building scripts, and setting the game in motion.

Project 2, *Beating Back the Horde*, teaches you how to create multiple enemies and how to move them along a predefined path. You will also learn about drag-and-drop and click mouse controls.

Project 3, *Start Your Engines*, shows you how to build a keyboard controlled game. The game will showcase simple collisions between objects and how to handle them. You will also learn to create and use a timer.

Project 4, *Space Age*, shows you how to build a game that is extensive and configurable in terms of level of difficulty. This game comes complete with spaceship, shield, scoreboard, enemy, and an ample supply of ammunition.

Project 5, *Shoot 'Em Up*, shows you how to build a fast-paced action game with waves of enemies to defeat. You will learn about setting up movement patterns and speeds for both the player character and enemies.

Project 6, *Building a Worthy Boss*, shows you how to finish your side-scrolling shooter with a memorable boss encounter. You will learn to design an epic finish for a game level.

Project 7, *Creating a Level Editor*, teaches you how to create a tile editor and automatically build tile-based maps with it.

Project 8, *Dungeon Crawl*, involves you using the tile editor from the previous project to build an action RPG. You will also learn how to create multiple levels and different enemies.

Project 9, *Hunger Run*, shows you how to build a fast-paced auto-scrolling platform game. This project explains how horizontal and vertical scrolling work.

Project 10, *Sprites with Characters*, will dive into creating complex sprites using Scratch 2.0's vector editor. Piece by piece, we will build a robot and add animation scripts. The finished sprite can be imported to other Scratch projects.

Appendix, *The New Scratch Interface*, will give you an overview of the new Scratch 2.0 interface and will show you some of the new features you can play with.

What you need for this book

To complete the projects in this book, you will need one or more of the following tools:

- You will at least need the Scratch 2.0 online editor (www.scratch.mit.edu).
- Or alternatively the Scratch 2.0 offline editor (http://scratch.mit.edu/scratch2download/).
- To use the Scratch editors, you'll need Flash Player installed on your computer (http://get.adobe.com/flashplayer/).

- An image editor will come in handy when creating sprites. We can recommend a few different ones, but you can use any digital drawing tool you are comfortable with:

  - Photoshop Elements (`http://www.adobe.com/products/photoshop-elements.html`) or GIMP (`http://www.gimp.org/`).

Who this book is for

You are interested in video games. You enjoy playing games and are curious to know how games work. You have dreamed about creating your own game for some time but are not sure where to start. If you would like to become a game designer or programmer, but are not yet sure if it is the proper career for you, then this book can help you get started. With practical examples, we teach you how to build your own games. Along the way, you will learn how to design and build a video game. You will be introduced to basic programming principles and you will learn how to make digital drawings. All the steps to build the projects described are explained in detail. You will need to be somewhat comfortable with using a computer, but no expert knowledge is required.

Conventions

In this book, you will find several headings that appear frequently.

To give clear instructions of how to complete a procedure or task, we use:

Mission briefing

This section explains what you will build, with a screenshot of the completed project.

Why is it awesome?

This section explains why the project is cool, unique, exciting, and interesting. It describes what advantage the project will give you.

Your Hotshot objectives

This section explains the eight major tasks required to complete your project.

- Task 1
- Task 2
- Task 3

- ▶ Task 4
- ▶ Task 5
- ▶ Task 6
- ▶ Task 7
- ▶ Task 8

Mission checklist

This section explains any prerequisites for the project, such as resources or libraries that need to be downloaded, and so on.

Task 1

This section explains the task that you will perform.

Prepare for lift off

This section explains any preliminary work that you may need to do before beginning work on the task.

Engage thrusters

This section lists the steps required in order to complete the task.

Objective complete – mini debriefing

This section explains how the steps performed in the previous section allow us to complete the task. This section is mandatory.

Classified intel

This section provides some extra information relevant to the task.

You will also find a number of styles of text that distinguish between different kinds of information. Here are some examples of these styles, and an explanation of their meaning.

Code words in text, database table names, folder names, filenames, file extensions, pathnames, dummy URLs, user input, and Twitter handles are shown as follows: "It should be obvious that the `scoreRed` variable is meant for a red starfish."

A block of code is set as follows:

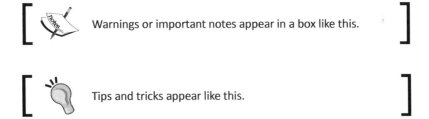

```
when I start as a clone
set my_grid_idx ▼ to new_grid_idx
set my_loc_in_grid ▼ to pick random -240 to 240
if my_grid_idx < bad_food_start_grid_idx then
    switch costume to pick random good_food_start_cos_idx to 8
else
    switch costume to pick random 1 to 8
set my_start_loc_in_grids ▼ to my_grid_idx * grid_length + my_loc_in_grid
go to x: my_start_loc_in_grids y: -120
show
```

New terms and **important words** are shown in bold. Words that you see on the screen, in menus or dialog boxes for example, appear in the text like this: "We start the program with the **when <green flag> clicked** block."

We have indicated the green flag icon that appears on the screen as a **<green flag>** tag in the entire book.

> Warnings or important notes appear in a box like this.

> Tips and tricks appear like this.

Reader feedback

Feedback from our readers is always welcome. Let us know what you think about this book—what you liked or may have disliked. Reader feedback is important for us to develop titles that you really get the most out of.

To send us general feedback, simply send an e-mail to feedback@packtpub.com, and mention the book title via the subject of your message.

If there is a topic that you have expertise in and you are interested in either writing or contributing to a book, see our author guide on www.packtpub.com/authors.

Customer support

Now that you are the proud owner of a Packt book, we have a number of things to help you to get the most from your purchase.

Downloading the example code

You can download the example code files for all Packt books you have purchased from your account at http://www.packtpub.com. If you purchased this book elsewhere, you can visit http://www.packtpub.com/support and register to have the files e-mailed directly to you.

Downloading the color images of this book

We also provide you a PDF file that has color images of the screenshots/diagrams used in this book. The color images will help you better understand the changes in the output. You can download this file from https://www.packtpub.com/sites/default/files/downloads/7569OT_Graphics.pdf

Errata

Although we have taken every care to ensure the accuracy of our content, mistakes do happen. If you find a mistake in one of our books—maybe a mistake in the text or the code—we would be grateful if you would report this to us. By doing so, you can save other readers from frustration and help us improve subsequent versions of this book. If you find any errata, please report them by visiting http://www.packtpub.com/submit-errata, selecting your book, clicking on the **errata submission form** link, and entering the details of your errata. Once your errata are verified, your submission will be accepted and the errata will be uploaded on our website, or added to any list of existing errata, under the Errata section of that title. Any existing errata can be viewed by selecting your title from http://www.packtpub.com/support.

Piracy

Piracy of copyright material on the Internet is an ongoing problem across all media. At Packt, we take the protection of our copyright and licenses very seriously. If you come across any illegal copies of our works, in any form, on the Internet, please provide us with the location address or website name immediately so that we can pursue a remedy.

Please contact us at `copyright@packtpub.com` with a link to the suspected pirated material.

We appreciate your help in protecting our authors, and our ability to bring you valuable content.

Questions

You can contact us at `questions@packtpub.com` if you are having a problem with any aspect of the book, and we will do our best to address it.

Project 1

Blowing Things Up!

Scratch is a fun-to-use program that teaches you about animating, programming, and building games. You already know this because you have been making simple games with Scratch for a while, and now you want to learn more. This project will use some of the most important Scratch tools and explain some basic game programming principles.

Mission briefing

We will make an artillery game. You might know this type of game from the very popular **Angry Birds** series, but this is actually a very old concept, dating back to the earliest computers. It was an obvious choice for imaginative programmers to turn military calculations into a game, because computers were originally used to calculate missile trajectories.

Why is it awesome?

We won't be able to guide any real missiles (luckily) with the scripts in this game. Instead of using proper mathematical calculations, we will use some simple tricks to get the desired results.

In games, it is rarely necessary to be absolutely realistic. Sometimes, bending the rules of reality creates more spectacular results; take Angry Birds, for instance:

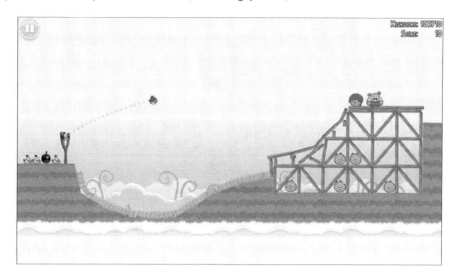

We won't build a game as sophisticated as Angry Birds straight away. Our example will be more bare bones but still fun to play. In later projects, we will look back at this first example, and you will be challenged to add new things to this game to make it more interesting.

Your Hotshot objectives

In this project we will be:

- ▸ Creating a new project
- ▸ Starting scripts
- ▸ Adding targets
- ▸ Creating a parabolic shot
- ▸ Creating a landscape

While doing this, you will learn about (among other things):

- ▸ Drawing with Scratch
- ▸ Using variables
- ▸ The xy-coordinate system
- ▸ Operators and conditions (what has to happen and when)
- ▸ The very useful cloning feature to quickly duplicate objects

Mission checklist

To get started, go to the Scratch website (scratch.mit.edu) and start a new project by clicking on the **Create** button at the top of the page. If you already have a Scratch account, it might be useful to log in first, so that you can save your work in your account. If you are new to Scratch and are unfamiliar with the interface, have a look at *Appendix*, *The New Scratch Interface*.

Creating a new project

We need to make sure that we're logged in and ready to get to work on a new project. We'll then draw some sprites and assemble our awesome cannon (and cannonballs). The Scratch menu bar gives us the option to explore the existing projects from other users (using **Explore**) or create a new project ourselves (using **Create**):

Prepare for lift off

You are presented with a new project, including the **Scratch cat** as usual. We won't use the cat, so you can right-click on the sprite, and choose **delete**. A **sprite** is the official name for a 2D computer image. Most Scratch projects are built using sprites. You can find an overview of all the sprites used in a project in the bottom-left corner of the screen, underneath the **stage**.

Engage thrusters

We will draw our own sprites for this game. Let's start with a simple cannonball!

The cannonball will be the main actor in this game because it will be the object that "blows things up". There are a few ways to add a new sprite to the stage. We can draw a sprite, select a sprite from the Scratch library, or import it from our hard drive. It's also possible to take a picture with a webcam.

To draw sprites, we perform the following steps:

1. Click on the little paintbrush icon between the stage and the sprites window. This will open the **costumes** tab.

2. Check if the editor is in **Bitmap Mode** or in **Vector Mode**. To create our drawing, we will select **Vector Mode**.

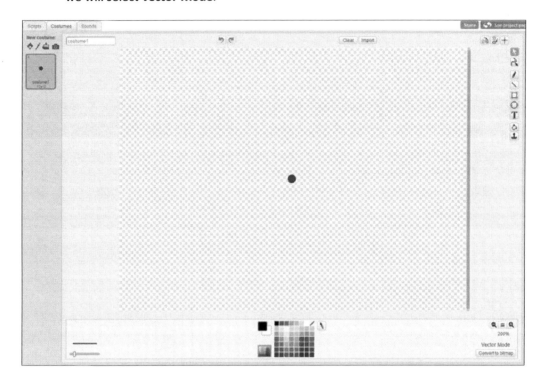

3. Select the Ellipse tool (the circle) seen on the right-hand side of the drawing canvas. Click and hold the left mouse button and drag it. You will probably end up with something that's not quite a circle.

4. Undo your drawing with the back arrow button at the top of the drawing canvas. When things go wrong, you can always go a few steps back. You can even clear the entire screen (using **Clear**) and start over.

5. To create a perfect circle, hold *Shift* while dragging the mouse. Don't make your circle too big. It has to be able to move about the stage freely without bumping into the edges all the time.

6. Next, click on the crosshair button at the bottom of the toolbar. This button lets you center your image. Now click on the center of your cannonball.

7. We name the new sprite cannonball.

Your cannonball is now done and ready for business. It will look like a simple grey dot as in this screenshot:

Let's move on to creating a cannon to shoot from. The cannon will consist of two parts: the back of the cannon, which serves as the pivot point, and the barrel. The following are the steps to create them:

1. Create a new sprite by clicking on the paintbrush icon.

2. Start again by creating a circle. This circle should be slightly larger than your cannonball.

3. Next, select the Rectangle tool that is right above the Ellipse tool.

4. Draw a rectangle that is as high as the circle but about three times as wide.

5. Click on the Select tool and drag the rectangle to overlap the right half of the circle.

6. Make sure that the center point of the cannon is placed at the center of the circular element, near the back of the cannon.

7. We name this sprite cannon.

8. Just keep in mind that the cannon consists of two separate shapes. You can color them separately, or you can color them together by first selecting both the shapes while holding the *Shift* key.

Objective complete – mini debriefing

We've now got ourselves a cannon and some ammunition to shoot with.

Starting scripts

Let's have some fun making the cannon shoot its cannonball. It's always a good idea to script and test the interactive parts of your game as early as possible. Without scripts, it's just a bunch of pretty pictures! They might be nice to look at, but they won't keep the player entertained for long.

Engage thrusters

We have two objects to script. **Object** is an official programmer word that means something that performs an action in a program.

In this case the objects are visible. Our sprites are our objects. We have a cannonball and a cannon. The player will be able to control the direction of the cannon. The cannonball will fly away in a certain direction based on which way the cannon is pointing. So the way things are controlled is:

player → cannon → cannonball

Let's create a short script for the cannon. This script will save the direction the cannon is pointing to, so that the cannonball will know in which direction to fly.

We have to create a **variable** to store the direction of the cannon. If you're unfamiliar with variables, read the information box on the following page. To create a variable, follow these steps:

1. Click on the **Data** category. This is where you can create variables.

2. We will now click on the **Make a Variable** button.

3. Name the variable `direction` and make it available **for all sprites**.

4. We start the program with the **when <green flag> clicked** block. This is the easiest way to set any program in motion.

5. Underneath it, we will place a **forever** block, because we will check the cannon's direction indefinitely.

6. If you want, you can tick the checkbox to make the variable visible on stage. Then, you can see the direction that the cannon is facing in, at all times.

7. Put a **set () to ()** block in the **forever** block and select **direction**.

8. View the **Motion** category and look down at the list of blocks to find the built-in cannon **direction** variable. Place it in the open space. It may look superfluous to send the built-in variable value to a self-made variable. We do this because Scratch can't send built-in sprite variables to other sprites directly. Our self-made variable can be used in all sprites.

This is all the scripting that has to be done for the cannon. The following is the finished script:

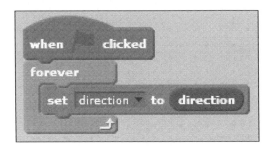

About variables

Variables are an important part of programming. They allow you to store information for later use and to transfer information between different objects. A variable consists of two things; a name by which it is recognized and the word/number/object that it stores.

The easiest way to think about it is to compare the variable to a jar of pickles in a grocery store. The store clerk is the computer. He handles this jar and all the other jars that are available in the store. The jar is a variable.

On the face of it they all look the same, like glass containers. It's hard to distinguish one jar from another. That's why every jar has a label with a word on it. This is the name of the jar/variable. Most probably, the name of the jar will say something about what's in the jar. The jar of pickles, for example, will be called "Pickles".

You move up to the counter and ask the clerk, "How many pickles are in the Pickles jar?" and the clerk checks the jar, counts the pickles, and says, "There are 9 pickles in the jar." You now know something about the content of the Pickles jar. You feel like having a snack and decide to buy two pickles. After you paid and received the pickles, you ask again, "How many pickles are in the Pickles jar?" and the clerk counts the contents of the jar again (just to make sure) and answers, "There are 7 pickles in the jar."

It's most common to store numbers in a variable, because computers like to work with numbers, but variables can also contain names or even whole objects. Scratch keeps it simple, though. Scratch variables can only contain numbers or names/words.

Perhaps, it's better to illustrate the explanation of variables with the following screenshot:

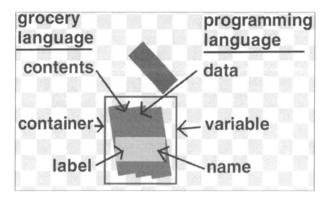

We will go on to create a script to move the cannonball:

1. Click on the cannonball sprite to open its script editor.

2. The cannonball will also be triggered with a **when <green flag> clicked** block. Its actions will also be contained inside a **forever** loop.

3. Place a **move () steps** block inside the **forever** block. That's the basic necessity to set the sprite in motion.

Now we build a few more controlling scripts, so the cannonball actually goes where we want it to go:

1. Place a **go to ()** block on top of the **move () steps** command and select **cannon**. This makes the cannonball hop back to its starting position.

2. Make the cannonball copy the cannon direction with a **point in direction ()** block and by insetting the **direction** variable. Note that this is our added variable (orange background) from the **Data** category, not the built-in (blue background) variable from the **Motion** category. The variable with the orange background is the saved cannon position. In this case, the variable with the blue background is the current direction of the cannonball, which wouldn't change anything when applied to itself.

To make the cannonball move forward, instead of constantly resetting, we use another kind of loop with a condition:

1. Put a **repeat until ()** block around the **move** command.

2. Then, place a **touching ()** condition block in the vacant space and select **edge**.

Now the cannonball will angle itself in the same direction as the cannon, and it will keep moving forward until it reaches the edge of the stage. At that point, the script repeats and the cannonball is reset to its starting position in the cannon. The following is the completed script:

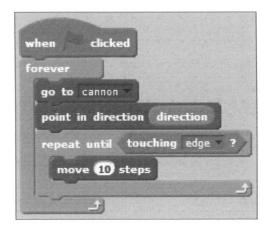

We're not building any fancy controls at this point. Click on the **i** button in the top-left corner of the sprite in the **Sprites** window:

This will switch the sprites view to the **sprite properties** screen. Here you can view and edit some information about your sprites. An important one is the sprite name; you can name the sprite here if you didn't already do so in the sprite editor during its creation. Notice the sprite name in the top field of the properties screen:

What we are really looking for at this moment is the little **direction** tool located on the right side of the window.

Objective complete – mini debriefing

Click on and drag the little blue pin to change the direction that the cannon is facing in. Try it and see how the cannonball shoots in different directions depending on the direction of the cannon.

Don't forget to click on the **green flag** at the top of the stage (if you haven't already) to activate both scripts!

Adding targets

This game will be no fun without something to shoot at and blow up. So, we are going to create some targets for the cannonball to hit. We will first draw a new sprite. Then, we are going to use a very cool new feature of **Scratch 2.0**: the ability to create copies of a base object. This can save a lot of time when you want to have multiple objects that work the same way. This is often the case in games. Think of all the enemies you've squashed or all the coins you've picked up in various action games.

Engage thrusters

We will first draw a traditional archery style target, with a circular disk of red and white rings placed on a simple wooden stand, shown as follows:

To create the target, follow these steps:

1. Create another new sprite with the Paintbrush button.

2. Select the Ellipse tool and make sure the fill color is red and the border color is white.

3. Adjust the line thickness to create a fairly thick line.

4. Draw a vertical oval shape.

Don't worry too much about the size. We will adjust the proportions later. It's easier to draw big shapes first, so you can easily see the details and relative placement. When the drawing is complete, you can scale it down to the desired size. First, we need to create two more oval shapes.

Method 1

The first method to create these shapes is as follows:

1. Click on the Ellipse tool.

2. Place your cursor over the existing oval at the top-left edge of the red fill.

3. Click on it and drag to the lower-right edge of the red fill to draw another oval. This oval will fit neatly inside the first one.

4. Repeat these steps to create a third, even smaller oval.

Method 2

The second method to create these shapes is as follows:

1. Click on the **Duplicate** button in the toolbar.

2. Click on the oval shape you have already made.

3. When you move the cursor, you will see a transparent "ghost" of the circle, moving along with the cursor.

4. Click anywhere on the drawing canvas to place a copy of the oval there.

5. Use the scaling widgets you see around the shape when it's selected, to scale the copied circles down to the right size.

6. Drag them inside each other to create the finished target disk.

Now that we have our oval shapes, we can continue building our target!

1. Click on the appropriate sample from the color swatches to change the line color to brown.

2. Click on the Line tool and draw a vertical line, about as high as the target disk.

3. Draw another line diagonally down from the upper tip of the first line.

4. The two legs of the target stand are complete.

5. Click on the Select tool and drag a box around the entire target disk. This will select all three shapes as a single object.

6. Click on and drag the **rotation pin** at the top of the selection box and rotate the disk upward.

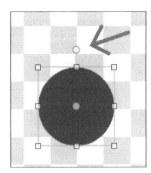

7. Click on and drag the shape over the target stand. The center of the disk should line up with the top of the stand.

About layers

Perhaps, your shapes are overlapping in the wrong way, with the stand on top of the disk, instead of underneath it. This means that the shapes are sorted in the wrong order. A Scratch drawing consists of separate layers, like sheets of transparent papers stacked on top of each other. The sheets on the top will cover the sheets underneath. This way you can create the illusion of depth, by placing objects that should be far away at the bottom of the stack.

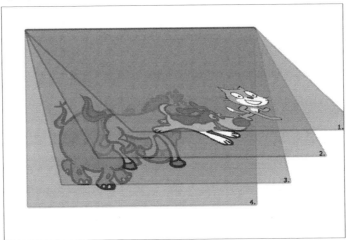

8. Change the order of shapes with the Forward a layer and Back a layer buttons, if needed.

9. Select the entire drawing by dragging a box around it with the Select tool.

10. Scale the entire drawing down to the desired size. You can scale proportionately (horizontally and vertically, evenly) if you hold a **corner widget** while dragging.

Creating multiple targets

We will write a script for the target we just drew; this script will place copies of the object at random locations on the stage. To do this we will use the new **clone** block. This is one of the most exciting new features of Scratch 2.0. Instead of manually copying your sprites N number of times, you can just use a script to do this work for you. It can save a lot of time when creating and editing objects.

1. This script will start with a **when <green flag> clicked** block, just like the earlier ones.

2. Attach a **go to x: () y: ()** block. Fill in the numbers `-100` and `0`.

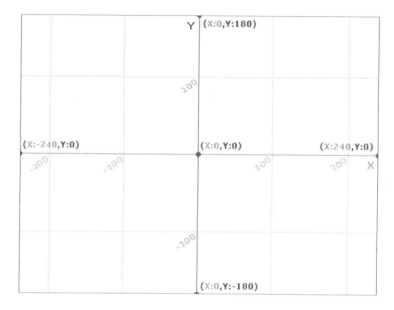

About X-Y coordinates

X stands for the horizontal position, that is, how far left or right something is. Y stands for the vertical position, that is, how high or low something is. This way the computer can easily save the position of any object on the stage. Look at the bottom-right corner of the stage. Here you will see the current position of the mouse shown as X and Y coordinates. This can be a helpful tool when deciding where you want objects to appear on stage with a script. Just point to the right place, look at the numbers, and put them at the right places in the script.

The center point of the Scratch stage has the coordinates **(X:0,Y:0)**. The horizontal positions range from **-240** to **+240**. And the vertical positions range from **-180** to **+180**. If you look at the assignment for the previous target, you will notice that the target is placed somewhat left of the center (-100) and on the center line vertically (0).

3. Next, add a **show** block. Yes, the sprite is already visible now, but at the end of the script we will make it disappear. This block makes sure it appears again in time when the script runs.

We are going to make five target clones. We will let the target sprite step right five times and create a clone of itself at each step.

1. Attach a **repeat ()** block and fill in 5.

2. Inside the **repeat ()** block place a **move () steps** block.

3. Instead of a fixed number, use a **pick random** 20 **to** 80 block to make the spots where a target will appear a little unpredictable and more interesting.

4. Then, attach the new **create clone of ()** block underneath the **move** command inside the **repeat** block. Select **myself**.

5. Finally, use the **hide** option on the original sprite. Place this block at the end, outside the loop.

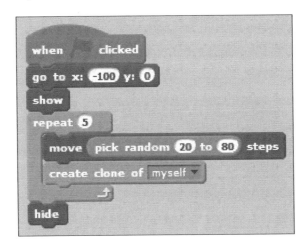

So now we have a cannon, a cannonball, a bunch of randomly created targets, but still no exciting game. The cannonball can fly through the air, but it doesn't do anything when hitting a target; it just passes right through. This can be easily fixed.

We'll continue scripting the target first. After a clone is created, you can start running a script on the clone. This is a new way of initiating a script.

1. Start a new script in the target object with a **when I start as a clone** block.

2. Attach a **wait until ()** block. This will pause the script until something happens.

3. Place a **touching ()?** condition block inside the slot. Select **cannonball**.

4. The next step is to attach a **wait () secs** block.

5. Fill in a very short time of 0.05 seconds. This might seem a little useless, but it will give the other scripts (specifically the cannonball script in this case) time to respond before the target disappears.

6. The last step is to **delete this clone**.

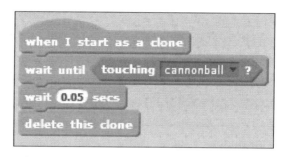

Cannonball collisions

The targets disappear when hit by the cannonball, but the cannonball can go on through multiple targets. This makes the game a bit too easy. It would be better if the cannonball is stopped by hitting a target as well. So a new cannonball has to be aimed and shot for each target.

Making the cannonball disappear on contact with a target just requires a little addition to the existing script. The cannonball is already reset to its original position when hitting the stage edge. We can use this already existing script and also check for hitting a target.

1. Click on the cannonball sprite in the **Sprites** view to see its scripting panel.

2. Grab an **() or ()** operator block.

3. Pull the **touching <edge>?** block from the script and place it in one of the **() or ()** slots. It doesn't matter which one.

4. Also get a new **touching ()?** block. Place it in the other slot and have this condition checking for target. (Have you already properly named your target sprite?)

5. Place this entire conditional structure in the now vacant condition slot in the existing script.

The cannonball gets reset when it touches the edge or a target. It doesn't matter that the target is a clone. It is still called a "target".

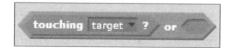

Objective complete – mini debriefing

Currently the cannonball is moving on in a straight line. In reality, a cannonball doesn't move like that (but we'll be fixing this). It is heavy, and what goes up must come down. You can try it yourself with a ball or a stone. Throw it upwards in front of you and see what happens. Just be careful with the neighbor's windows!

Creating a parabolic shot

The ball will move upwards in the direction you threw it. At some point it will start to slow down, stop, and then start falling down. The path the ball follows is called a parabola. This is what we expect of gravity. It's always around us, so we don't pay too much attention to it. If you would throw the ball in space, which has no gravity, the ball would move on forever in a straight line, as it does now in our game. On Earth, the ball will move up for a while, then slow down, and eventually fall down again. This movement path is described in the following diagram:

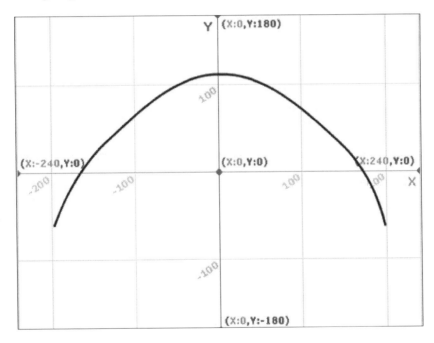

In this case, the cannon and cannonball should be on the ground, so we want to simulate some gravity. Not only will the parabola trajectory look more interesting, it will also make the game more challenging. You could try hitting a target by shooting the cannonball at a steep angle and have it hit a target as it drops down. It is very useful to shoot over the hills, which we will do in the last stage of this project.

Engage thrusters

To simulate gravity, you could use a realistic mathematical formula. But it can be hard to figure out, and in a simple game, it often isn't needed. We are going to create a good-looking parabola trajectory with just a simple calculation and some trickery.

To simulate the pull of gravity, we are going to use the built-in **timer** variable. This timer will start counting seconds when the game is started, but we can reset it to start counting again. We will be using the increasing number as a constantly increasing pull, which will eventually start dragging the cannonball downwards.

The steps to create the trajectory are as follows:

1. We select the cannonball sprite to add to its scripts.

2. After the **move () steps** command, add a **change y by ()** block. This will cause the cannonball to vertically move a bit after taking its steps.

3. Place a **() * ()** (multiplication) operator in the box.

4. Then put the **timer** variable in one of the operator slots.

5. In the other slot, fill in a number manually. Try a few numbers, just for the fun of it, and see what happens.

    In my opinion, the number **-5** has the best result. But if you disagree, you're free to choose another number. Just make sure that the number is negative, because a positive number will cause the cannonball to float ever faster upwards.

6. To reset the timer after the cannonball has hit something, add a **reset timer** block at the start of the loop.

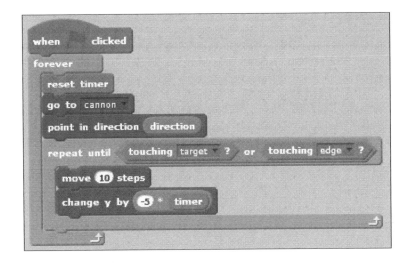

Objective complete – mini debriefing

Test the game again and turn the cannon to point at different angles. See how the parabolic trajectory of the cannonball responds.

Creating a landscape

As the final stage of this project we will create a hill for the targets to sit on. The landscape will have a diagonal slope; we have to change the parabola trajectory to shoot at different points on the hill. The finished game will look like the following screenshot:

Engage thrusters

We could manually draw landscapes as sprites. But if we want to create many different levels, it could take a lot of work. Instead, we will make a drawing tool to create the hill.

1. First, create a copy of the cannonball by right-clicking on the sprite in the **Sprites** view and choosing **duplicate**, shown as follows:

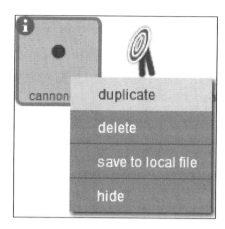

2. Click on the **i** button on the copied sprite and change its name to `drawing tool`.

3. Throw away the scripts in the copied sprite. Those are only useful for the cannonball, not for the drawing tool.

4. Switch to the **Costumes** tab and change the color of the drawing tool to dark green using the color swatches. This is mostly to make it visually different from the cannonball, so that we don't confuse the two.

5. Go back to the **Script** tab so that we can create a new script for the drawing tool.

6. We start the script again with a **when <green flag> clicked** block.

7. Attach a **pen up** block to make sure the tool doesn't draw anything while moving to its starting point.

8. Add a **clear** block. This might not look useful now, but like with the **hide** and **show** commands in the target sprite script, this will help clear the screen once we want to restart the game.

9. Move the tool to its starting point with a **go to x: () y: ()** block.

10. Fill in 240 after **x** and 0 after **y**, so the tool starts at the right edge of the stage.

11. Next, set the pen size to 5 using a **set pen size to** block. Again you might want to create a thinner or thicker line.

12. Choose a green color for a natural-looking hill in the **set pen color to ...** block.

13. Place the drawing tool on the stage with a **pen down** block. We are now ready to start drawing the landscape.

14. Then, we move the pen diagonally to the bottom edge with a **go to x:** -100 **y:** -180 block. Because the pen is down, it will draw a line between its start and end point.

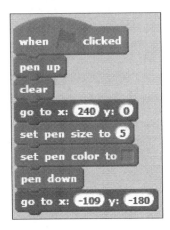

To make full use of our newly drawn landscape, we have to set the targets down on them. But how do we do that on such an uneven surface? The solution is to slowly move the targets down and use another collision test to decide when the targets have reached the landscape and should stop moving. We add the following script to the target sprite:

The steps to perform this test are as follows:

1. Click on the target sprite so you can view its scripts.

2. Add a **repeat until ()** block at the start of the clone script.

3. Inside the **repeat until** loop place a **change y by ()** block and fill in a negative number to make the targets move down.

   I filled in the number -4 for a fairly slow speed. You may take bigger steps, but then the targets could end up being stuck partly through the landscape. Not a big issue, but it might not look as nice.

4. To stop the targets from moving when they reach the landscape, add a **touching color ()?** condition to the **repeat until ()** block.

5. Click on the color box and then point and click on the green line that you've drawn.

Computers are very precise about color. Keep this in mind if your color collision doesn't work. Most likely, the actual color of the object will be slightly different from the color that you checked for. You can't see it with the naked eye, but the computer can tell the difference based on the color number. The finished script should look like the following screenshot:

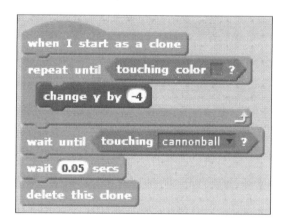

As a final step, change **y:** 0 to **y:** 180 in the other target sprite script. This will place the target at the top of the stage and make sure that it doesn't end up inside or underneath the landscape.

Now that we have another object on the stage, that is, the landscape, there is one more thing we have to do to finish the game. When the cannonball hits the ground, it should stop instead of moving straight through the landscape. This is similar to the addition we added after including the targets. Now we only need to add another collision check for the cannonball to respond to.

The following are the steps for this collision check:

1. Get another **() or ()** operator block.

2. We will check for hitting the green landscape color, just like we just did with the targets.

3. In the other slot, we will place the entire condition check, like we made earlier. So our latest **() or ()** block will become the outermost block in the construction.

4. Place the entire construction back in the **repeat until ()** slot and we're done.

The cannonball will now respond to hitting the stage edge, a target, and the landscape.

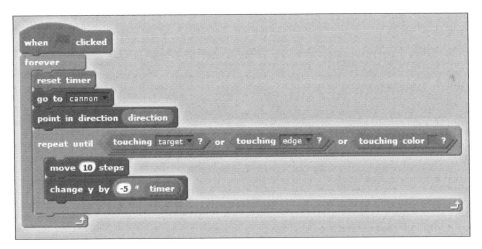

Objective complete – mini debriefing

That's it! We should now have an automatic landscape complete with a functioning cannon, firing script, and targets.

Mission accomplished

Your first game is now done, well, sort of. You learned how to draw sprites and how to add scripts to them to make them interactive. We used the new cloning feature to quickly copy the same sprite, including its functionality. We worked with collisions between objects, some variables, and simulated gravity to create a simple, but challenging game. The finished game will look like the screenshot that follows:

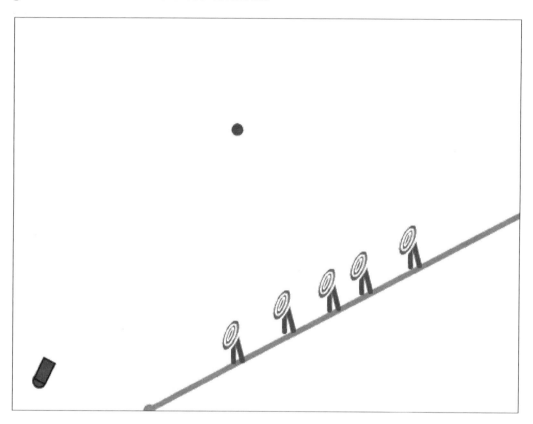

Hotshot challenges

It's still far from the Angry Birds example that we mentioned at the start, but all the basic elements are there. Test your game, and play with the numbers a bit to see how they can affect the playability! Have a go with the following tasks:

- If you increase the cannonball speed to very high, it will become very fast, but hard to control.
- Try increasing or reducing the number for the simulated gravity effect.
- Do you still know which number that is? It is somewhere in the cannonball script.
- Can you change the number so it feels like the game takes place on the moon, where gravity is not as strong as it is on Earth?

In later projects, we will look back at this game and you will be challenged to expand and improve it, based on the things you will learn in those projects. The game might not look like anything special just yet, but with some effort and imagination, you could make it into an exciting game to rival Angry Birds.

Project 2
Beating Back the Horde

In this project, we will make a game that is a bit more involved. What kind of game will we be making? We are going to make one of the classics, a **Tower Defense** game (http://old.casualcollective.com/#games/FETD2). Our game won't be as polished as the example, but it gives you a solid base to work with and develop further.

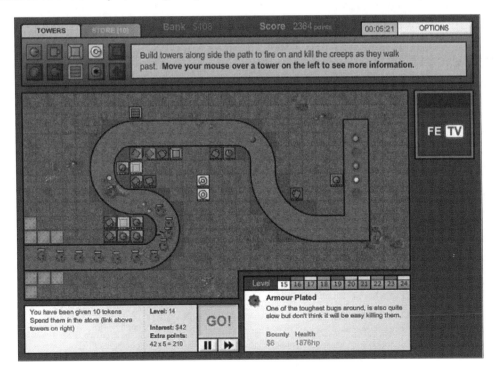

Mission briefing

We will use the cloning tools again to create hordes of enemies to fight. We will also use these tools to create cannons and cannonballs. It's easy to reuse assets from other projects in Scratch 2.0. The new **Backpack** feature allows you to easily exchange assets between projects. How this works will be demonstrated in this project.

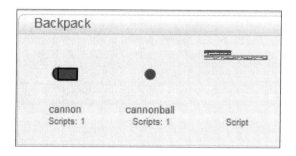

Why is it awesome?

This example is a lot more involved than the previous one. The final result will be a much more finished game that still leaves plenty of room to adapt and continue building on. While making this game, you will learn how to draw a background and how to make and use different costumes for a single sprite.

We will make full use of the cloning technique to create many copies of similar objects. We will also use more variables and another type of variable called **List** to keep track of all the things going on in the game.

You will also learn about a simple way to create movement patterns for computer-controlled objects.

Your Hotshot objectives

We will divide the project in to the following tasks based primarily on the game sprites and their behavior:

- ▸ Creating a background
- ▸ Creating enemies
- ▸ Creating cannons
- ▸ Fighting back
- ▸ Increasing the horde

- ▸ Adding a base
- ▸ Limiting resources
- ▸ Winning the game

Mission checklist

Click on the **Create** button to start a new project. Remove the Scratch cat by right-clicking on it and selecting **delete**.

Creating a background

Because the placement and the route to walk is important in this kind of game, we will start with the creation of the **background**. To the left of the **Sprites** window, you will see a separate picture. Underneath is the word **Stage** and another word, the name of the picture that's being shown. This picture is white when you start a new project because nothing is drawn on it yet. The following is an example with our background image already drawn in:

Engage thrusters

We will draw a grassy field with a winding road running through it when looked at from the top, by going through the following steps:

1. Click on the white image.
2. Next, click on the **Backdrops** tab to get to the drawing tool. This is similar to the **Costumes** tab for sprites, but the size of the drawing canvas is clearly limited to the size of the stage.

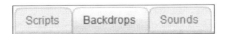

3. Choose a green color and draw a rectangle from the top left to the bottom right of the canvas.

4. Then click on the **Fill** tool and fill the rectangle with the same color to create a grassy background.

5. On top of the field, we will draw a path that the enemies will use to walk on.

6. Switch the **Fill** tool to a brown color.

7. Draw rectangles to form a curving path as shown in the following screenshot. The background is now done. Let's save our work before moving on.

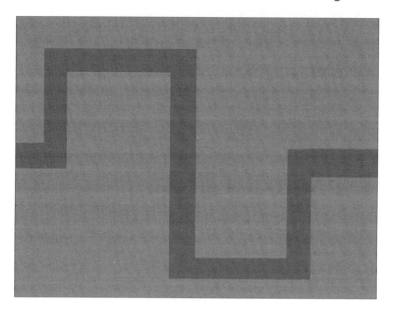

Objective complete – mini debriefing

The background is just a pretty picture with no direct functionality in the game. It tells the player what to expect in the game. It will be logical that enemies are going to follow the road that was drawn. We will also use this road as a guideline when scripting the movement path of the enemies. The open spaces between the path make it obvious where the player could place the cannons.

Creating enemies

We will quickly create an enemy sprite to make use of the background we just drew. These enemies will follow the path drawn in the background. Because the background image is fixed, we can determine exactly where the turns are. We will use a simple movement script that sends the enemies along the path from one end of the stage to the other. Like with the targets in the previous project, we will use a base object that creates clones of itself that will actually show up on stage.

Prepare for lift off

We will first draw an enemy sprite. Let's keep this simple for now. We can always add to the visual design later. The steps to draw it are as follows:

1. Click on the paintbrush icon to create a new sprite.

2. Choose a red color and draw a circle. Make sure the circle is a proper size compared to the path in the background.

3. Fill the circle with the same color.

4. We name the new sprite `enemy1`.

That's all for now! We will add more to the appearance of the enemy sprite later. The enemy sprite appears as a red circle large enough to fit the path.

Engage thrusters

Let's make it functional first with a script. We will place the base enemy sprite at the start of the path and have it create clones. Then we will program the clones to follow the path as shown in the following steps:

1. The script will start when the **when <green flag> clicked** block is clicked.

2. Place the sprite at the start of the path with a **go to x:** -240 **y:** 0 block.

3. Wait for three seconds by using the **wait ... secs** block to allow the player to get ready for the game.

4. Add a **repeat ...** block.

5. Fill in 5 to create five clones per wave.

6. Insert a **create clone of <myself>** block.

7. Then wait for two seconds by using the **wait ... secs** block so the enemy clones won't be spawned too quickly.

Before we start moving the clones, we have to determine what path they will follow. The key information here are the points where the path bends in a new direction. We can move the enemies from one bend to another in an orderly manner.

Be warned that it may take some time to complete this step. You will probably need to test and change the numbers you are going to use to move the sprites correctly. If you don't have the time to figure it all out, you can check and copy the image with the script blocks at the end of this step to get a quick result.

Do you remember how the xy-coordinate system of the stage worked from the last project? Get a piece of paper (or you can use the text editor on your computer) and get ready to take some notes. Examine the background you drew on the stage, and write down all the xy-coordinates that the path follows in order. These points will serve as waypoints.

Look at the screenshot to see the coordinates that I came up with. But remember that the numbers for your game could be different if you drew the path differently.

To move the enemy sprites, we will use the **glide ... secs to x: ... y: ...** blocks. With this block, a sprite will move fluidly to the given point in the given amount of time as shown in the following steps:

1. Start the clone script with a **when I start as a clone** block.

2. Beyond the starting point, there will be seven points to move to. So stack together seven **glide ...** blocks.

3. In the coordinate slots, fill in the coordinates you just wrote down in the correct order. Double-check this since filling in a wrong number will cause the enemies to leave the path.

   Deciding how long a sprite should take to complete a segment depends on the length of that segment. This requires a bit of guesswork since we didn't use an exact drawing method. Your most accurate information is the differences between the coordinates you used from point to point.

4. Between the starting point (-240,0) and the first waypoint (-190,0), the enemy sprite will have moved 50 pixels. Let's say we want to move 10 pixels per second. That means the sprite should move to its new position in 5 seconds.

5. The difference between the first (-190,0) and the second (-190,125) waypoint is 125. So according to the same formula, the sprite should move along this segment of the path in 12.5 seconds.

6. Continue calculating the glide speeds like this for the other blocks. These are the numbers I came up with: 5, 12.5, 17, 26.5, 15.5, 14, and 10.5, but remember that yours may be different.

[You can use the formula `new position - old position / 10 = result` to figure out the numbers you need to use.]

7. To finish off, delete the clone when it reaches the end of the path.

Test your script and see the enemies moving along the path. You might notice they are very slow and bunched together because they don't travel enough distances between spawns. Let's fix that by adding a variable speed multiplier. Not only can we easily tweak the speed of the sprites, but we can also use this later to have other enemy sprites move at different speeds, as shown in the following steps:

1. Create a variable and make sure it is for this sprite only.

2. Name it `multiplier_R`. The R stands for red, the color of this enemy.

3. Place **set <multiplier_R> to …** at the start of the **<green flag>** script.

4. Fill in `0.3` as a number for the basic enemy.

5. Take the speed numbers you filled in previously and multiply them with the multiplier.

6. Use a **…*…** operator block.

7. Place the **multiplier_R** variable in one slot.

8. Type the correct number in the other slot.

9. Place the calculation in the **glide** block instead of the fixed number. The completed scripts for enemy movement will look as follows:

Objective complete – mini debriefing

Test the game again and see how the enemies move much faster, about three times as fast if you have used 0.3 for the multiplier. You can play with the variable number a bit to see the effect. If you decrease the multiplier, the enemies will move even faster. If you increase the number, the enemies will become slower.

Creating cannons

Now that we have enemies running around our game, we need to find a way to stop them. To do this, let's use the tried and tested way of shooting them to bits. In our last game, we already made something to shoot with—the cannon and the cannonball. We can easily reuse these sprites in this game and write new scripts for them.

Prepare for lift off

To transfer sprites and scripts from one project to another easily, we can use the new Backpack feature. Look at the bottom of the Scratch window and you will see a narrow bar with the word **Backpack** on it and a small arrow pointing up. Click on the bar to open your backpack. If you haven't used this feature before (or aren't logged into your account), your backpack will be empty.

We will get the sprites from the previous project and place them in the backpack as shown in the following steps:

1. First, save your active project so you won't lose any progress that you've made.

2. To save, click on the **File** drop-down menu, and select **Save now**.

3. Look to the right of the menu bar and find the folder image with an **S** on it. This leads to the page with all your Scratch projects. Click on the folder image to go to this page.

4. Find the **Artillery game** project and open it. You can go directly into the edit mode if you click on the **See inside** button instead of the project title.

5. Once inside the project, open your backpack again by clicking on the **Backpack** bar.

6. Drag-and-drop both the cannon and the cannonball sprite into your backpack. Copies of the sprites, including their scripts, will be saved to the backpack.

7. Click on the folder image again to go back to your project page.

8. Find and open the **Tower Defense** project.

9. Open the backpack.

10. Drag-and-drop the cannon and cannonball sprites into the **Sprites** window of this project. These sprites are now copied as part of this project.

The backpack feature gives you easy access to often-used sprites and scripts. Over time, you will probably collect a standard set of objects to place in your backpack and carry with you at all times. Think of standard movements and keyboard control scripts; for example, if you build a series of games or animations, you might also reuse the same character sprites often.

Engage thrusters

Now that we have a cannon and some ammo, we can start doing something about those enemies running free. In this game, we will place cannons on the stage with a mouse click. The cannons will aim towards the cursor point. So contrary to most Tower Defense games, you will have to aim at the enemies manually by pointing the mouse at them. The cannons will fire cannonballs automatically.

Like with the targets in the Artillery Game and the enemies in this one, we will script a base object that spawns clones to multiply the cannons and cannonballs as shown in the following steps:

1. Click on the cannon sprite in the **Sprites** view and open the **Script** tab.
2. Throw away the script from the previous game by right-clicking and choosing **delete**, or drag-and-drop the entire script back into the **script block** menu.
3. Start a new script with a **when <green flag> clicked** block.
4. Attach a **forever** loop.
5. Place a **go to <mouse-pointer>** block inside. This will cause the cannon sprite to always be where the mouse cursor is pointing. If your cannon seems to be offset from the mouse pointer, check whether its center point is aligned properly.
6. Start another script with a **when this sprite clicked** block.
7. Attach a **create clone of <myself>** block.
8. That's all you need to start placing cannons on the stage.
9. Start a third script with a **when I start as a clone** block to script the created clones.
10. Attach a **go to front** block to make sure the cannons are placed on top of the other graphics.
11. Add a **forever** loop.

12. Inside the loop, place a **point towards <mouse-pointer>** block to aim the clones at the mouse cursor position at all times. That finishes our cannon scripts for now.

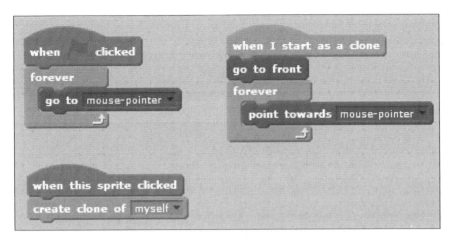

You can now place as many cannons as you want all over the stage. We will refine these scripts later to improve the game challenge. But let's script the cannonballs first so we can actually shoot enemies instead of just pointing at them menacingly.

We want to fire all the cannons we place. So the clones of the cannonball have to be placed at all cannon positions repeatedly. How do we turn one cannonball into many? And how do we keep track of what all of them will do? This might seem like a challenging problem, but actually it isn't too difficult. Moving the clones will be very similar to the Artillery Game example, minus the gravity. The challenge here is to start all clones at the right spot, this being the position of all the cannons. Because the number of cannons will increase as we place more on the stage, the number of positions to remember is variable. So the obvious conclusion is to use a variable to store the positions. But a regular variable won't suffice because that can only store one thing at a time. We will have an increasing list of things to store, so instead of using a regular variable, we will use a list to store the cannon coordinates.

We will create two lists for ease of use. One will store all the x coordinates in order. The other will store all the y coordinates. We will use these lists as a combined pair. Keep that in mind and be careful that you don't switch around the sorting order of either of them, because that will make a mess of your stored data and cause unpredictable results. The following are the steps required to create the lists:

1. Select the **Data** category in the **Scripts** tab.
2. Use **Make a List** and call it cannon-x.

3. Use **Make a List** again and call it `cannon-y`.

4. The lists should be empty at the start of the game. To ensure this is the case, we will add a script to the **Stage** that empties the list.

5. Start a new script in the **Stage** with a **when <green flag> clicked** block.

6. Add a **repeat ...** loop for a limited number of repeated actions.

7. Place a **delete ... of <cannon-x>** block inside the repeat loop.

8. Select **1** or the first item in the list to be deleted. This way, the first item in the list will be stripped and the second item will become the first for the next repeat in the loop.

9. We want to repeat the loop as many times as there are items in the list. So in the number slot, place the **length of <cannon-x>** variable. This variable stores the number of items stored in the list.

10. Right-click on the **repeat** loop and choose **duplicate** to make a copy of the actions.

11. Attach the copied loop to the first one.

12. Change all references from **cannon-x** to **cannon-y** to perform the same actions on the other list.

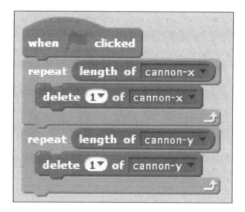

These loops will make sure both lists are emptied when we start a new game. Now we are ready to fill the lists with new coordinates. We will store the cannon coordinates when a clone is created. Then we will use these saved coordinates to place cannonball clones at all the cannon locations. To do this, follow the given steps:

1. Click on the cannon in the **Sprites** view and look at its **Scripts** tab.
2. In the **clone** script, before the **forever** loop, place two **add thing to ...** blocks.
3. Replace the word **thing** with the built-in **x-position** and **y-position** variables of the cannon.
4. Click on the small black arrows and change the selectors to **<cannon-x>** and **<cannon-y>** respectively. Make sure you connect the variables to the correct list. Switching them around will cause unpredictable results. The finished script should look as follows:

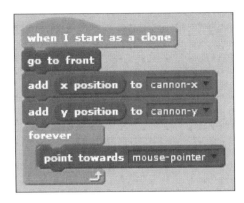

If the lists are shown on your stage (remember to select the box in front of the variable block), you can see how they are filled with coordinates as you place cannons on the stage. Try this a few times to get familiar with how lists are constructed and reset.

Now that we are properly saving the cannon coordinates, let's use them to create some cannonballs as shown in the following steps:

1. Go to the **Scripts** tab of the cannonball sprite.
2. Start a script, as usual, with a **when <green flag> clicked** block.
3. First make sure you hide the original sprite so it won't be shown when not needed.
4. Add a **forever** loop to place cannonballs for as long as the game is running.
5. Create a new **variable** named i. This is a temporary variable that we will use as a counter to step through our lists. Using the letter i (and j, k, l, and so on for <> temporary variables) is a programming standard.
6. **Set <i> to** 0 to start counting from 0.

7. Add a **repeat ...**loop, and in the slot, place the **length of <cannon-x>** variable. In this case, it won't matter which list variable you use because both lists are of equal length.

8. Then, inside the **repeat** loop, change the value of **change <i>** to 1 to start counting up.

9. Attach a **go to x:... y:...** block.

10. In the empty slot behind the x slot, place an **item** 1 **of <cannon-x>** block.

11. Place the same block in the y slot, but change the referenced list to **cannon-y**.

12. Replace the fixed numbers with the **i** variable. This will cause the script to step through the list with each repeat and increase the **i** variable.

13. Finish this script with the important step **create clone of myself**. This should still be placed inside the **repeat** loop.

14. Create another script for the created clones starting with a **when I start as a clone** block.

15. Just like we did with the cannon clones, add a **go to front** block to make sure the cannonballs are placed above the other sprites.

16. Then, we show the clone to make it visible on the stage.

17. Let them point towards the mouse pointer by using the **point towards <mouse-pointer>** block.

18. Add a **repeat** loop. The default number of 10 is fine.

19. Inside the **repeat** loop, place a **move** 10 **steps** block. You can leave the default number here as well.

20. At the end of the script, outside the **repeat** loop, place a **delete this clone** block.

21. Let's not forget to save the project again. The scripts for the cannonballs allow the them to be placed and moved across the stage.

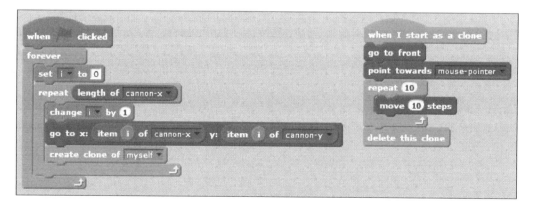

Objective complete – mini debriefing

The clone script will cause the clones to face the mouse cursor. Then, they will start moving for a limited number of steps before being destroyed. This will cause the cannons to have a limited range. If you would like a longer or shorter range, you can change the default numbers. The repeat number determines how long the cannonball will be on the stage. The move number will determine how fast the cannonball moves. Keep in mind that very fast moving cannonballs might skip over enemy positions and therefore miss, even though it will look like the cannonball moves straight through them.

Classified intel

It's generally a good idea to collect all the initialization scripts that aren't tied to a specific object in the **Stage** object. That way you will always know where to find these variables and you don't have to search through many objects and scripts. You will see that in many cases, this is used to reset the global variables such as lives, points, power-ups, and in this case, object coordinates.

Learning about list variables

Lists are a type of variable that can contain more than one value. I compared a variable to a jar containing one thing. You can compare a list to a shopping list. The list can contain things that belong together, like all of the groceries we want to get from the shop. Not only do we want to get pickles but we also need bread, butter, cheese, tomatoes, and so on. Those all go on the list. When we get an item, we can strike it from the list; thus, deleting it. Oh, we also need onions. We can add that to the list. You can add and remove things from lists as required. You can even add things in between other things by writing between the lines. But in the case of a computer, all the things that follow will just move down a bit to make room for the things that were added.

Learning about global and local variables

There are two types of variables. They work essentially in the same way, but their scope is different. **Scope** is a word that means how far their influence reaches. You have global variables that can be seen and used by all objects in a project. In Scratch, you can set this with the **For all Sprites** option, which is the default. You can change this option to **For this sprite** only to change the variable to local. That means this variable is only known to the sprite that it was created for. You can't use this variable in other sprites. This can be useful if you have similar variables that need to have a different value for each object, like a personal speed value for each enemy we use in this project.

Fighting back

So we can now place cannons that shoot cannonballs in the direction of the mouse cursor. But we still aren't hitting any enemies. Let's quickly fix that problem.

Engage thrusters

We will check when a cannonball and an enemy collide and take proper action accordingly. The steps to do it are as follows:

1. Inside the cannonball, clone **repeat**, and place an **if ... then** condition block to check collisions.

2. Check for collisions by using the **touching <enemy>** block.

3. When a cannonball touches an enemy, first wait for 0.05 seconds by using the **wait ... secs** block. This is to ensure that the enemy has time to respond to the collision as well.

4. Then we add a **delete this clone** block to delete the clone.

So cannonballs will not only expire after having traveled a certain distance, but also when they hit an enemy. You could omit this step, but that would make the game a bit too easy because cannonballs can move on and hit multiple enemies, as was the case in the Artillery Game before we fixed that.

The enemies have to respond to being hit by a cannonball as well. So let's add that condition to their script. The condition to check for the enemy is actually the same as for the cannonball, but in reverse order. So the easiest way of adding it is to copy the script segment and change the variable pieces as shown in the following steps:

1. Click-and-drag the **if** statement from the cannonball to the enemy sprite in the **Sprites** view.

2. Click on the enemy sprite in the **Sprites** view to look at the enemy scripts. You will see the segment you dragged has been copied to the enemy scripts.

3. Create a new **when I start as a clone** script.

   You can't use the other one, because that will be busy gliding the clones from point to point. These **glide** blocks are effectively worked through one at a time. So the script will pause for a short while at each step. Adding a repeated condition check would disrupt the fluid movement of the enemy sprites.

4. Add a **forever** loop.

5. Place the copied segment inside the **forever** loop to check continuously.

6. Now change the object to be checked to **cannonball**.

7. You can remove the **wait … secs** block because the enemy is allowed to respond immediately when it touches a cannonball.

8. Save the project.

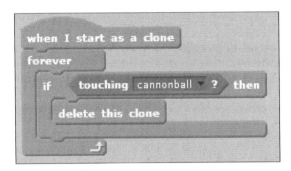

Objective complete – mini debriefing

Test your game and see how it works. The bare basics of the game are now in place. Enemies move along a given path and you can place cannons that shoot cannonballs at them to stop the horde from reaching their destination. You might also note that this game is way too easy. Cannonballs are spawned at a rapid rate and cannons can be placed anywhere on the field in large numbers. This makes it impossible for the enemies to reach the other side of the map intact, unless you decide to do nothing.

The rest of the project will focus on adding more to the basic scripts to make the game more challenging. We will slow down the spawning of cannonballs, create more enemies, and limit where and when you can place cannons.

Classified intel

At this point, cannons can be placed anywhere, including on the road. This can make the game too easy and it also looks a bit messy. Let's limit where you can place cannons. We will build a few gun platforms and place them within in the level. Cannons can only be built on these platforms, so the player has to start thinking about the cannon's range and optimal placement. It also prevents the player from putting cannons in the middle of the road. Follow these steps to create a platform:

1. Click on the paintbrush icon to create a new sprite.

2. Select the **Rectangle** tool and choose a medium gray color.

3. Draw a vertical rectangle.

4. Check the shape as it appears on the stage to determine the right size.

5. Pick a lighter color of gray and fill the rectangle with the **Fill** tool.

You can imagine this to be a raised concrete platform when looked at from the top. You can embellish the graphic if you wish, but it won't be necessary for the game. Remember to keep your drawings clear so the player can easily understand what the drawing represents.

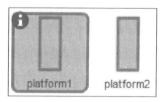

Rewriting the placement script is fairly simple. We will relocate the script that we already wrote from the cannon sprite to the platform sprite as shown in the following steps:

1. View the cannon's **Scripts** tab.

2. Drag the entire **when this sprite is clicked** script to the platform in the **Sprites** view.

3. Click on the platform sprite to see its scripts. You will find a copy of the **when this sprite is clicked** script there. If not, you have probably misplaced the script. Try again in this case.

4. Make sure that the script creates a clone of **<cannon>** and not of **<myself>**. We don't want the platforms to start copying themselves. Correct this if needed.

5. After you have copied and edited the script, delete the original script in the cannon by right-clicking on it and selecting **delete**.

6. Next, right-click on the platform sprite in the **Sprites** view and select **duplicate** to create a second platform.

7. Drag and place both platforms to the correct place on the grass between the bends in the road. They should be placed as shown in the following screenshot:

Test your script and see how you can now only place cannons on the two platforms and not on the grass or the road.

Slowing down the rapid firing of cannonballs just requires a small addition to the script. Remember how everything in "computertime" goes really fast, but you can slow it down with a **wait** command as shown in the following steps:

1. Have a look at the cannonball's **Scripts** tab.

2. See how the **forever** loop in the **<green flag>** script has no **wait** block in it at all. Cannonballs will therefore be created as fast as your computer can manage.

3. Place a **wait ... secs** block just inside the **forever** block and fill in 0.1. This will slow down the creation of cannonballs a bit. You can increase the number for an even slower spawn rate and a more challenging game.

Increasing the horde

Limiting the offensive power of the player helps to make the game a bit more challenging. But a single group of five enemies isn't much of an attack force to withstand. Let's give the player some more work to do by increasing the number of enemies and then create more enemy variants.

Engage thrusters

We will copy and edit a few scripts that we have already built to create more waves of enemies as shown in the following steps:

1. Go to the enemy's **Scripts** tab.
2. Look at the **<green flag>** script and see how we first set the enemy sprite to the correct position and then made a few clones in a limited **repeat** loop.
3. Right-click on the **wait** block just before the **repeat** loop and select **duplicate**. This will create a copy of the block and everything underneath it.
4. Drag the copy to the bottom of the script and click on it again to attach it.
5. Move the cursor back to the first **wait** command and repeat the process to create four consecutive **repeat** loops.
6. Change the numbers in the second, third, and fourth **wait** block from 3 to 10. This will increase the time between waves and makes sure one wave has moved a good distance along the road before the next wave is spawned.
7. Instead of just five enemies to defeat, we now have 20, separated in four waves. A fair challenge but still not too exciting.

Enemies currently die on the first hit they receive. This makes them very weak and also not very Tower Defense-like. The enemies in these games usually have a **healthbar**, requiring multiple hits before they go down. This not only makes the game more challenging, but it's also visually appealing as you see the cannons tracking the enemies and trying to defeat them before they move out of range. So let's create a healthbar for our enemies. Instead of going down in one hit, they will be able to take 10 hits before being defeated.

There are multiple ways to solve this problem. But the easiest way of doing it is by creating multiple costumes, each with a slightly shorter healthbar graphic. Each time an enemy gets hit, it will advance to the next costume until it reaches the last one, after which it will be destroyed. The following are the steps to create the costumes:

1. Open the enemies' **Costumes** tab.
2. We make sure that we are editing the costumes in **Vector Mode**.
3. Select a bright green color for the healthbar.
4. Click on the **Line** tool and draw a horizontal line underneath the red circle.
5. Create nine more costumes for the sprite by right-clicking on it and choosing **duplicate**.
6. Use the **Erase** tool to remove a part of the healthbar at each costume. The last costume should have no visible bar left.

At each step, the healthbar should be shortened a little. Since Scratch doesn't have a ruler in its drawing tools, you can't be pixel-perfect about it. I found the best way of doing it is to keep cutting the list of costumes in half. The first one has a full healthbar. The last one (number 10) has no healthbar left. So costume number five should have only half healthbar. Costume 2.5 (which doesn't exist, so we'll pick number 3) should have three quarters of the healthbar showing. Number 7.5 (again we pick a whole number, so 8) should only show a quarter.

Click back and forth through the costumes to visually check that you diminish the healthbar in equal steps for each costume.

Since the last costume is the enemies' dead state, we are going to reshape it to inform the player he has vanquished an enemy, as shown in the following steps:

1. Click on the last costume (number 10) in the list to select it.
2. Click on the **Reshape** tool.
3. Then click on the red circle.
4. You'll see some circular widgets show up on the edge of the circle. You can reshape a form by dragging these widgets with the mouse. Drag the points at the cardinal compass directions inwards towards the center.
5. Drag the other points out a bit.
6. This will create a cross-like shape, signifying that the enemy is dead as shown in the following screenshot:

With a script, we will step through the different costumes on each hit. This will make it appear that the hit bar shrinks and eventually the enemy is killed. The following are the steps to do it:

1. Go to the **Scripts** tab to start making use of the new costumes. We will make changes to the **clone** script.

2. Drag the collision check condition out of the script and put it aside for later use.

3. Remove the **forever** loop from the script.

4. In its place, put a **repeat until ...** block.

5. Set the collision check inside this block.

6. Get a = operator block and place it in the condition slot of the **repeat until ...** block.

7. Place the **costume#** variable from the **Looks** category in one slot of the equation.

8. Type 10 in the other slot. This will cause the script to repeat until the sprite is showing costume number 10, the dead state we just drew.

9. The clone should only be destroyed after the **repeat** condition is met. So drag the **delete this clone** block out of the **if** statement and re-attach it at the bottom of the script.

10. Instead of immediately deleting itself, the clone should advance a costume when hit by a cannonball. Place a **next costume** block inside the **if** statement to achieve this.

11. To prevent the sprite from stepping through multiple costumes on a single hit, make the loop to wait for 0.05 by using the **wait ... secs** block.

12. To prevent the sprite from immediately disappearing on receiving the last hit, and thus not showing the dead costume, we place another **wait** 0.5 **secs** block just before the **delete** command.

13. As a final step, to make sure the enemies always start at costume number 1 when the game starts, we place a **switch costume to <costume1>** block in the **<green flag>** script. Note that this is the name of the costume.

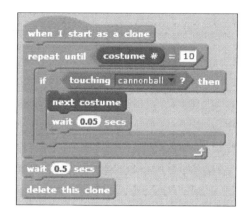

Test the game again to see that the enemies are indeed showing a healthbar and are losing health as they get shot, before disappearing after being hit 10 times. Now, we are well on our way to creating an enjoyable game.

To make things even more interesting, we will create two more enemy types. These behave in largely the same way as the first enemy. But with some minor changes to their scripts, we can make them behave quite differently. We will create a faster enemy that takes less time to travel the length of the road. We will also create a slower enemy that is harder to kill than the first enemy. Each type of enemy will be depicted in a different color.

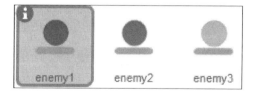

Let's start with the fast enemy, the blues. The following are the steps to create it:

1. Right-click on the enemy sprite in the **Sprites** view and select **duplicate** to make a copy of this sprite and all its scripts.

2. Go to the **Costumes** tab of the copied sprite and change its color from red to blue using the **Fill** tool. You have to recolor all the costumes.

3. Then go to the **Scripts** tab to make some changes.

4. To make this enemy faster than the red one, we need to change the multiplier value. Create a new variable called `multiplier_B` (for blue).

5. Replace all the **multiplier_R** variables in the scripts with the new **multiplier_B** variables.

6. Change the **multiplier_B** value in the **<green flag>** script to `0.15`. This will make the blue enemies twice as fast as the red ones.

We also change a few things about the wave patterns so these new enemies won't arrive at the same time as the original ones. To do this, follow the steps given:

1. Remove the last **wait** and **repeat** segments and delete them. Three waves of fast enemies are enough of a challenge.

2. Change the wait numbers to `8`, `20`, and `5` to change the pauses between waves.

3. Change the number of repeats to `3` for all **repeat** loops. This will decrease the number of enemies spawned per wave.

That's all there is to do to create fast enemies. Let's move on to the third type of enemy. Follow the steps given:

1. Again select **duplicate** to make a copy of the red enemy sprite to create a third enemy type.

2. Go to the **Costumes** tab of the new enemy and color the costumes yellow.

3. To make this enemy harder to kill, we will give it more costumes. Copy each costume once to make a total of 20 costumes. Don't make a copy of the final dead state. You only need one of those.

4. You might have to rearrange the newly created costumes to display a continuously shrinking healthbar as you move through the costumes.

5. Erase a small bit of each second costume as an in-between step for the healthbar steps you made earlier.

6. Go to the **Scripts** tab to make some changes to the script, making this enemy slower and tougher.

7. To make use of all 20 costumes, change the number to check in the **clone** script from `10` to `20`. This is all that's needed to make the enemy go through 20 hits before being destroyed.

8. To make it a bit easier for the player to destroy this enemy in time, we will make it a bit slower than the other ones.

9. Create a new variable called `multiplier_Y` and again replace all instances of **muliplier_R** with the new one.

10. Change the value of the **multiplier_Y** variable to 0.5 to make this enemy slower than the red enemy.

11. Remove the last two **repeat** segments to create only two waves of these heavy enemies.

12. Change the wait times to 18 and 10.

13. Change the number of repeats to 2 to only create two enemies per wave.

14. After this, save the project to make sure you don't lose your progress.
    The following screenshot shows the altered script for the third enemy type:

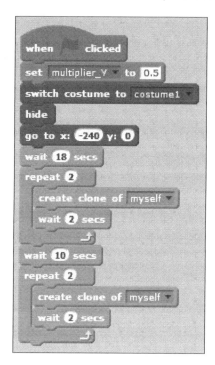

Objective complete – mini debriefing

We now have an interesting army of enemies coming our way. Test the game and see how it looks. Take special note of when the enemies spawn, how fast they move, and how they respond to incoming fire. You can play around with the numbers in the < **green flag**> scripts to make the enemies appear in different patterns.

Adding a base

Defeating the enemies is not enough. We need a solid goal to fight for. We will create this in the form of a base at the end of the road. The enemies will try to reach the base, decreasing its health with each enemy that enters it. The player must try to stop the enemies before they reach the base.

Prepare for lift off

We will draw the base with some face-like features. Things that look human help the player to empathize more with them. The following are the steps to create a base:

1. Create a new sprite by clicking on the paintbrush icon.

2. Choose a dark gray color and draw a circle. To create a perfect circle, hold *Shift* while drawing.

3. **Fill** the circle with a light gray color.

4. Decorate the base with some circles and squares to resemble an open gate. See the following screenshot for an example.

5. Like the enemies, this base will have a healthbar. Pick a bright yellow color and draw a line to the top-left of the base.

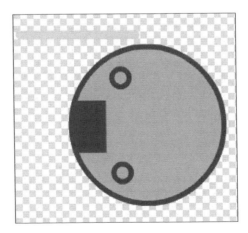

The base can be hit 20 times. So it will have 20 costumes, but don't copy them all at once. As the healthbar decreases, we will also draw some damage on the base as an extra visual indication to the player that all is not well and they should be trying harder. The following are the steps to do it:

1. First make nine copies for a total of 10 costumes.

2. Erase the healthbar to half in equal steps per costume.

3. On the tenth costume, draw a few cracks on the base. Use the dark gray color you used for the outline. With the first half of the images done; for the costumes 11 to 15, we will add some more damage.

4. Now copy this updated image five times.

5. Decrease the healthbar to a quarter of its original length.

6. Draw a few more cracks in the last image. The final quarter of costumes will show even more damage until the base is destroyed.

7. Make five more copies of the last image.

8. Decrease the healthbar to nothing.

9. Draw even more cracks on the last two images.

10. The last image is the dead/game-over state. To represent this visually, we will create a broken down base. Drawing the broken down base will take a bit more work than the previous steps, but it will look a lot better than just leaving the image as it is.

11. Select only a few parts of the base and move them a bit away from the center.

12. Select another part and move it in a different direction.

13. Notice that you will move the lines but probably not the gray circle. That's because it's bigger than your selection, and that's okay.

14. Click on the circle to select it and press *Delete* to get rid of it.

15. Pick the same light gray color you drew the circle with.

16. Click on the **Pencil** tool and increase the line thickness.

17. Create some new irregular shapes on top of the repositioned cracks to represent broken shards of the base.

18. Choose the **Select** tool and then click on one of the newly drawn shapes to select it.

19. Click on the **Back a layer** button while holding *Shift* to send the shape all the way to the bottom. This will make sure the cracks appear on top of the base shards.

20. Do this for all the shards that you've drawn. The following screenshots show the base in various stages of decay:

Engage thrusters

Go to the script tab to write the scripts that make the base move through all of its costumes and then break apart. You might think we will use a collision check like we did with the enemies, but this not the case. The enemies will keep moving some distance after they first hit the base, unlike the bullets, which are destroyed on contact. This continued contact would mean that the collision check is activated continuously, quickly going through all base costumes.

Instead of a collision check, we will use the broadcast method to make sure each hit is only counted once. In a later project, we will do more with broadcasts and explain how they work. The following are the steps to do it:

1. Start a new script on the base with a **when I receive ...** block.
2. Create a new message and name it `reached base`.
3. Attach a **next costume** block to step to the next costume when the message is received.
4. Add an **if ... then ...** block to check whether the base has reached its last costume.
5. Grab a = operator and the **costume#** variable for the base.
6. Put them together and write `20` in the open slot.
7. Inside the if statement, place a **stop <all>** block to terminate all scripts, effectively ending the game.
8. We still have to put the base in the right position. So start a new script with a **when <green flag> clicked** block.
9. Add a **go to x: ... y: ...** block.
10. Fill in the numbers to place the base at the right end of the road. I used the values `240` and `-5` for the x and y coordinates respectively. But your coordinates might be a bit different.
11. Use the **Switch costume to <base1>** block to make sure the game starts with the first (full health) image showing.

12. Then add a **go to front** block to make sure the base is the topmost sprite. This way, enemies will disappear underneath the base making it look like they are entering. Have a look at the scripts for the base sprite shown as follows:

Almost done, but there is one more thing to do. The base is waiting for the message "reached base", but no one is sending it. Let's fix that by following the steps given:

1. Click on the red enemy to see its script.
2. At the end of the clone movement, after the last **glide** block, add **broadcast <reached base>**. Now the base will receive this message when an enemy has finished its move.
3. Do the same for the blue and yellow enemies.

Objective complete – mini debriefing

As always, we added a feature so we save our work and test to see whether it all works properly.

Limiting resources

We now have a decent horde of enemies threatening our base. There is still one problem though. The player can place cannons at their leisure. So they can quickly build up an impenetrable barrage of artillery. No horde could survive that onslaught.

Engage thrusters

To really make a challenging game, we have to limit the player's options a little. To do that, we will script a resource system. The player will start the game with some "credits" to build a few cannons with. When the funds are depleted, they can't build anymore. Killing enemies will gain the player some more credits and allow them to increase their artillery battery. The following are the steps to create the credits:

1. First create a new **variable** called `funds`. This will count your credit pool.
2. Then click on the **Sounds** tab to add a sound effect.

3. Click on the **choose sound from library** icon and select the **pop** sound.

4. Click on **OK** to add it to the available sounds for the project.

5. In the stage sprite script, after emptying the lists, set funds value to 40 by using the **set < funds> to** block. This will be the starting amount of credits.

6. Go the the first platform's **Scripts** tab. We will make some additions to the script.

7. Get an **if ... else ...** block.

8. Get a **>** operator for the condition slot.

9. Place the **funds** variable on the left of the **>** operator.

10. Type in 19 on the right of the **>** operator. We will make the price of cannons 20 credits, so you need to have at least that amount in your funds.

11. Inside **if**, add a **change <funds> by** -20 block.

12. Also drag the **clone** block inside the **if** block.

13. Inside the **else** block, place a **play sound <pop>** block. When there aren't enough funds to create a cannon, this will make a sound to let the player know about it.

14. Copy the whole script to the second platform.

15. Click on **Delete** to delete the original script from the second platform. A platform script should look like the following screenshot:

The player can now spend funds. Next, let's create a way to gain funds so the player can keep building as the game progresses. The following are the steps given to do it:

1. Click on the red enemy.

2. In the enemy clone script that checks for cannonball hits, add a **change <funds> by** 2 block just before the clone is destroyed.

3. Do the same for the blue and the yellow enemy but with different values. Killing a blue enemy will reward 3 credits. Killing a yellow one will give the player 4 credits.

Objective complete – mini debriefing

These additions put a nice limit on the amount of resistance a player can build up. It builds tension as the player's offensive power will increase as the horde does.

Winning the game

Just one more thing to do to finish the game. At the moment, the enemies can win the game by destroying the base. But the player can't really win the game. There's no clear end state to kill all the enemies. To finish the game, we will determine fixed winning and losing conditions and add a game screen to clearly tell the player whether they have won or lost the game.

Prepare for lift off

Let's create the screen graphic first by following the given steps:

1. Click on the paintbrush icon to create a new sprite.

2. Choose a dark yellow color and draw a large rectangle.

3. Click on **Fill** to fill the rectangle with a light yellow color.

4. Select the **Text** tool and write the text YOU WIN! in the center of the rectangle.

5. Duplicate the costume by selecting **Duplicate**.

6. Edit the text in the second costume to read GAME OVER.

Engage thrusters

To show the game screen at the right moment and to display the proper costume, we will use a script as shown in the following steps:

1. Click on the **Scripts** tab to add some scripts to the game screen.

2. Start a new **when <green flag> clicked** script.

3. Attach a **go to x: 0 y: 0** block to place the screen at the center of the stage.

4. Then, hide it to start the game without displaying the game screen.

5. Start a second script with a **when I receive ...** block.

6. Create the new message game over.

7. Add a **switch costume to <costume 2>** block.

8. Then display the game screen by clicking on **show**.

9. Place a **stop <all>** block to stop all scripts to end the game.

Scripting for the win condition is a bit more work. When does the player win the game? When all the enemies have been killed or have entered the base while the base has not yet been destroyed. The last part of that condition is already taken care of because the scripts we have just written will put the game in the game over state as soon as the base is destroyed. If we haven't reached the game over state yet, the base must still be "alive".

So we only have to take care of counting the enemies and check whether we have reached the total yet.

First, count the total number of enemies that are spawned during the game. If you've used the numbers mentioned earlier, there should be 35 enemy clones moving through the game. Remember that number. The following are the steps to count the number of enemies:

1. Create another variable called enemies.

2. Use the **Set enemies to** 0 block at the start of the game screen **<green flag>** script.

3. We will check for the win condition at the end of the script. Add a **wait until ...** block.

4. Plug in the condition **enemies** = 35.

5. When this condition has been met, the script continues with **switch to costume <costume1>**.

6. Click on **Show** to make the sprite visible.

7. Use **stop <all>** to stop all scripts to end the game.

8. Now let's start counting so the win condition can be met.

9. Go to the red enemy's **Scripts** tab.

10. Add a **change <enemies> by** 1 block in both **clone** scripts, just before a clone is destroyed. This counts all the enemies as they are killed or when they have reached the base.

11. Also add these blocks to the blue and yellow enemies. If you forget some, the script will never count to 35 and the player can't win. The finished game screen script should look like the following screenshot:

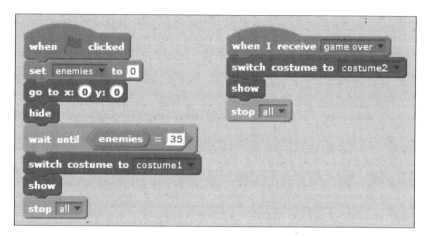

Objective complete – mini debriefing

Test the game to see whether you performed all the steps correctly. Temporarily show the enemies variable by checking the boxes to see if the counting works. Try killing all the enemies to get to the win condition. Also, test to see whether the enemies destroying the base will get the game to the game-over condition.

Mission accomplished

We created a very solid base for a Tower Defense game. This example showed how you can make an interesting, seemingly complex game if you just take it one step at a time. By working on one game object, thinking about what it should be doing, how you can achieve that, and then building the scripts, you can create stunning results without the need to have a grand overview of the game before you start. Many games allow incremental changes and additions, making the game more complex and interesting with each step. Our finished game shows a colorful parade of enemies as seen in the following screenshot. We better stop them from reaching their destination.

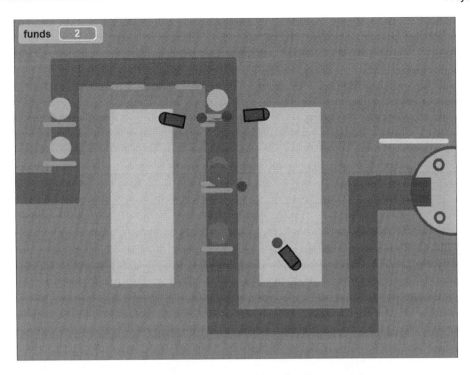

Hotshot challenges

That concludes this tutorial. But there are still many more things you can do with this game.

First of all, you can play endlessly with the variables to create a different game challenge, change the number of enemy waves, change the number of enemies in the game, or how they behave. You can change and test building funds to find the perfect difficulty level.

You can improve the graphics by adding more color and texture to the sprites. You could draw creepy faces on the enemies to make them look more like creatures.

And then, you could also add more levels in the game, change the background, and relocate the platforms and the base. Of course you have to achieve this with scripts since each level requires an update of placements and walking routes.

Project 3

Start Your Engines

In this project, you will learn that things are not always as they appear. Sometimes, it's useful to separate the code and functionality of the game from the pretty graphics. In the project that we will build here, we will separate a player-controlled object from the sprite that represents it. We will also use an invisible collision mask to give the program a much clearer feedback than a regular image.

Mission briefing

With this project, we will recreate a much-loved game series. At the end of the project, you will be able to invite a friend and enjoy the game you've built together. We're going to do a remake of **Mario Kart** and it will include a **multiplayer** feature.

Why is it awesome?

We will look into a very effective and efficient way of separating graphics from programming. Computer code should be as clear as possible. With fancy decorative graphics, this is not always possible. Therefore, we create fancy graphics for the player to see while they're playing, and we'll create another set of simpler graphics for the computer to work with. With only a few scripts, we can tie these graphics together to create a unified experience.

Your Hotshot objectives

We will start by creating some graphics so that we can see what we are doing. Then we will get into some scripting, and eventually tie all the bits and pieces together to create a finished game. In this project, we will deal with the following steps:

- Drawing a racetrack
- Creating a kart
- Building keyboard controls
- Using a collision mask
- Dealing with collision events
- Adding a second player
- Finishing the game

Mission checklist

We will use some existing **bitmap images** for this project. We need to edit these images, so an image editing program might be useful. This program could be **Adobe Photoshop** (`http://www.adobe.com/downloads/`), **GIMP** (`http://www.gimp.org/`), or even **MS Paint**. It doesn't really matter, as long as you feel comfortable using it.

The following screenshot shows the GIMP editor:

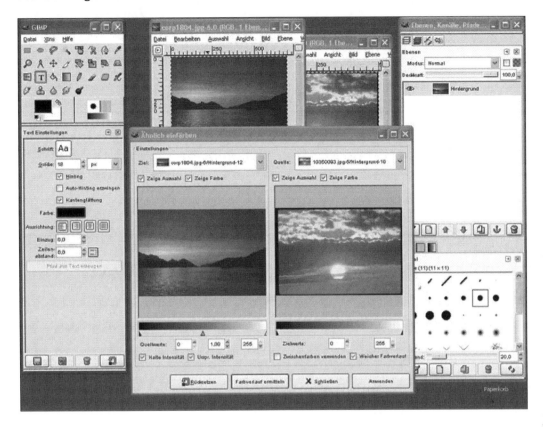

Drawing a racetrack

We will start by adding a racetrack to the **Stage backdrops**. This way, we have some guidelines for the rest of our program. We know how the road is shaped and where the curves, corners, and walls are.

Prepare for lift off

For the background, we will use an original Mario Kart map. You can find game images such as these all over the Internet. What's important to remember here is that the image you choose should fit your game screen. In this case, the game screen is 480 pixels wide and 360 pixels high, so a background image should be at least that size.

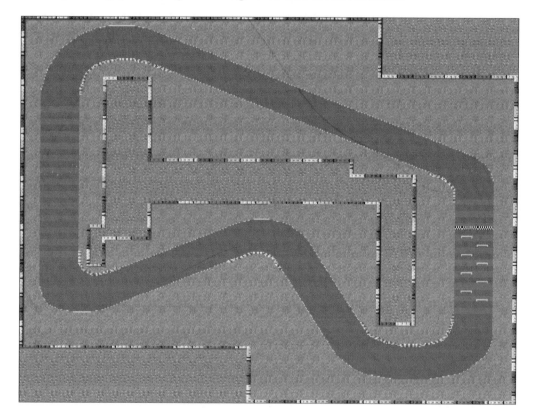

Another thing to note is that although these images may be freely available, it doesn't mean that they are completely free. The original artists put time and effort in creating them. Also the game studio and/or producer (**Nintendo**, in this case) invested money to promote and sell their game.

Engage thrusters

We will get a good-looking race map and place it as a background image in the **Stage** sprite:

1. Find a Mario Kart map online or use the image file that comes with this project. Download the image to your computer if you're looking for an image on your own.

2. Start a new Scratch project and remove the cat sprite.

3. Click on the folder icon underneath the **Stage** thumbnail. This will open the **file browser** of your computer.

4. Navigate to the folder where you saved your map image.

5. Click on the image and select **Open**. This image will now be loaded as a backdrop.

The image will be shown in the **Backdrops** editor in its actual size or as big as possible if it's bigger than the stage area.

Your image might have different proportions than the stage area. In this case, you'll have to resize the image to fit the entire screen. To do this, follow these steps:

1. Click on the Select tool, then on the image. You'll see the **scaling widgets** show up around the edges of the image.

2. Pull the scaling widgets to fit the image to the screen. Take note that this will stretch the image, somewhat changing the shape of the track. But this shouldn't be too much of a problem.

3. Perhaps you also need to clean the image, removing any unwanted details, such as coins and question blocks. You can do this in the Scratch editor, but this is where an external image editor might also be useful.

Objective complete – mini debriefing

When we're done editing the image, we'll have a racetrack which fills the entire stage. The track contains a well-defined road, some sandy areas around it, and some colorful borders and grass that a kart won't be able to cross. These different elements will become important later in the project. That's why we're taking note of them.

Creating a kart

Now that we have a racetrack, the next important thing to create is a race kart. Again, we will use images from the original Mario Kart game.

Prepare for lift off

Go online and find a Mario Kart **sprite sheet** depicting Mario in his race kart. A sprite sheet is a special type of image that's often used in professional 2D games. It collects all of the costumes that belong together into a single image. That way, an image only has to be loaded once. The game program only shows a small part of the sprite sheet at any given time. With scripts, the window through which you view the sprite sheet can be moved. This has an effect similar to changing costumes in Scratch; it creates animation.

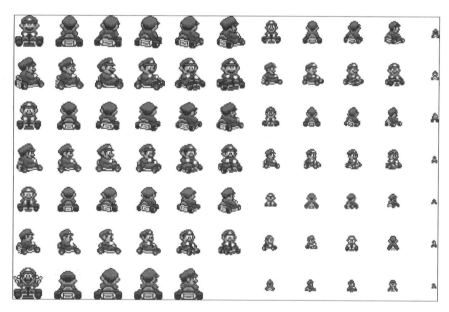

We will assemble a row of costumes that shows the character in his kart from all angles. By moving through the costumes, the sprite will appear to rotate by a full circle. We will use these costumes later to indicate the direction the character is facing in the game.

For this stage, an external image editor will be very useful because we want to load all the different images as separate costumes. You can do it in Scratch, but you'll be doing a lot of erasing to only leave one image per costume. You'll also see that most sprite sheets only show images facing in one direction. We want to have separate images for both directions, so we will need to mirror most of them to face the other side as well.

Engage thrusters

Let's first look at the method that uses an external editor:

1. Start your preferred editor and load the sprite sheet.

2. Cut out each sprite that you want to use and save it separately. Make sure that the area around the sprite is transparent, so you don't end up with a colored box surrounding your character sprite.

3. If needed, make mirrored copies of all the images facing in the other direction. This will be necessary for all of the images that aren't facing straight up or down.

4. Double-check to make sure that your collection of separated sprites describe a full circle in approximately equal steps.

With the images ready to be loaded, we can start adding them to Scratch by using the following steps:

1. In Scratch, create a new sprite and name it kart1.

2. Click on the **New costume** link to open the drop-down menu.

3. Select the **Import** option.

4. Select and import the first sprite costume.

5. Click on the **Set Costume Center** icon and place the center point at the bottom of the image between the wheels; see the following screenshot:

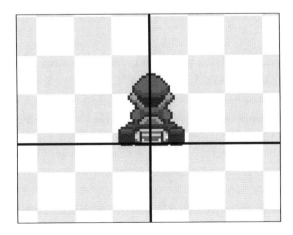

6. Repeat the process for all the other costumes.

7. If your costumes aren't sorted properly, fix them by dragging them around.

That's one method to get your images into Scratch. Now for the other method:

1. Create a new sprite and name it `kart1`.

2. Click on the **New Costume** link and choose **Import** from the drop-down menu.

3. Select the entire sprite sheet to load it as a new costume.

4. Duplicate the sprite sheet costume as many times as there are costumes in a full circle (our example uses 22 costumes).

5. Now, start editing the first costume. Pick one image from the sprite sheet that you want to save and erase all of the rest. Use the Fill tool with the transparent color to remove any background color surrounding the selected image.

6. Place the center point at the bottom of the image, between the wheels.

7. Repeat this process for all of the images that you need to create a full-circle animation.

As I mentioned, the second method does take some endurance, but it works.

Objective complete – mini debriefing

We now have a kart sprite with a series of costumes that allow the sprite to rotate in all of the directions. We will script these costumes in the next project.

Classified intel

You might want to test whether your rotating animation looks nice. That's easy to do and just requires adding the following small script to the sprite:

1. Start with a **set size to () %** block and fill in 1000. We will overscale the image so that you can clearly see all the details.

2. Attach a **forever** loop.

3. Inside the loop, place a **next costume** loop to endlessly cycle through all of the costumes that we added.

4. Also add a **wait () secs** block to slow the animation down a bit; fill in the value 0.1.

The following screenshot shows the final script:

Move your sprite to the center of the stage and click on the script we just made to activate it. The sprite will scale up and start animating. Does the sprite move in a fluid circle? If the rotation is jumpy or seems to move against direction, you might need to switch a few costumes around. Does the image seem to wiggle or hop up and down? Then you probably didn't place the center point correctly. You can tweak and test your animation cycle until it looks just right.

Building keyboard controls

Let's get that kart moving! In the previous project, we learned how to control a game using the mouse. In this section, we will control the game using the **keyboard**.

Prepare for lift off

The controls for this game will be divided between the kart sprite and a separate **control sprite**. The kart sprite will be attached to this control sprite. The kart sprite will only concern itself with displaying a pretty and logical image. It tells the player where the kart is on the track and in which direction it is facing. The control sprite will manage all things "under the hood", such as movement speed and collision checks.

Separating these two functions allows us to have the imagery behave somewhat independently from the game rules and mechanics. It allows more room for animation and special effects without hindering the continuation of the game. It also allows easy replacement of the graphics altogether. One controller could "wear" different sprite costumes at any given time; for example, to represent a different character in the game.

Engage thrusters

Let's first create the control object. This is a sprite just like any other:

1. Create a new sprite with the Paintbrush icon.
2. Name the sprite `player1`.
3. Draw a small red circle with the Ellipse tool. Remember to hold *Shift* for a perfect circle.

We'll write a script for the control sprite next:

1. Start with a **when <green flag> clicked** block.
2. Attach a **set size to () %** block. Fill in the value `20` to make the circle very small. We should barely be able to see it, as long as the computer can still check collisions with it later.

3. Next, add the **set <ghost> effect to () %** block (with the value 100) to make the control sprite completely transparent. It is still there and will interact with all of the other objects on the stage. It has just become invisible.

4. Place the control sprite at its starting position with a **go to x: () y: ()** block. Aim for the first starting bracket at the right side of the track. I used the values 192 and -27 respectively.

5. Insert a **point in direction ()** block with value 0 or straight up. The control sprite is now ready to start moving. To move forward, we will use a speed variable that will make the kart move automatically.

6. Navigate to **Make a variable** and make a variable named speed1.

7. Grab a **forever** block and place it underneath the script we already wrote.

8. Inside the loop, place an **if () then** block. We will use this to check if we have reached top speed.

9. Inside the condition slot, place a **speed1 < ()** block (with the value 4).

10. If the speed is not yet 4, we will increase it using the **change <speed1> by ()** block (with the value 0.2).

11. Attach a **move () steps** block underneath the **if () then** block and place the speed1 variable in the vacant slot to set the kart in motion.

12. Add a **wait () secs** block (with the value 0.1) to keep the kart under control. It responds way too fast if the script is not reduced by a bit.

The following screenshot shows the final script:

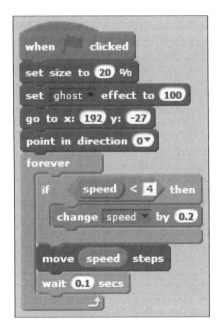

The player will be able to steer left and right with the keyboard keys:

1. Get two **key () pressed** blocks and place them next to each other.
2. Select the **d** key for one block.
3. Underneath it, attach a **turn <clockwise> () degrees** block; fill in the value 6.
4. Select the **a** key for the other block.
5. Attach a **turn <counterclockwise> () degrees** block to it; fill in the value 6.

The following screenshot shows the final script:

That's all you need to do to make the control sprite turn left and right. Now, we need to attach the kart sprite, so we can actually see where the control sprite is going:

1. Drag-and-drop both key control scripts onto the kart sprite to copy them there.
2. Click on the kart sprite to see its **Scripts** view.
3. Before we go on with the scripts, we need to change a sprite property, so we press the **i** icon on the sprite.
4. We change the **rotation style** to no rotation; this option is shown as a blue dot.

5. This makes sure the sprite isn't responding directly to our rotation input. Instead of actually rotating the sprite, we are going to change its costume to correspond with the current angle.
6. Next to the key control scripts, start a new script with **when <green flag> clicked**.
7. Attach the **Set size to () %** block and fill in 50.
8. Now add the **point in direction ()** block with value 0 or up. This synchronizes the kart sprite direction with the control sprite direction.
9. Add a **forever** loop.
10. Make the kart sprite go to `player1` using **go to <player1>**. As long as the loop runs, the kart sprite will follow the control sprite around.

We need a formula to calculate which costume to show. Each costume should correspond to a certain range in direction. We can convert the number for each direction into the number for each costume as follows:

1. Place a **switch costume to ()** block inside the **forever** loop.

2. Put a **() + ()** operator in the slot; the second empty slot of the operator block has to be filled in with 1.

3. The first empty slot of the operator block is filled with another operator: **() / ()**.

4. Place the **direction** variable from the **Motion** category in the left slot.

5. Type the number 17.14286 in the right slot. This is approximately 360 degrees divided by 21 or the range in degrees that each costume should occupy.

The following screenshot shows the final script:

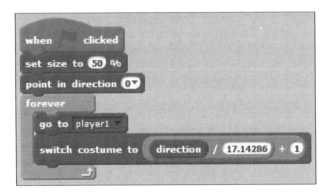

Objective complete – mini debriefing

We now have a controllable game character. Start the game by clicking on <green flag> and see the kart move forward. Steer the kart around the stage with the *A* and *D* keys. If you set up the scripts correctly, the kart sprite will change costumes as you change direction. Drive around the map to check whether the sprite animates properly.

Classified intel

Note the difference between using the ghost effect and hiding a sprite. When you use the ghost effect, a sprite is invisible but present. It will still interact with the other sprites on the stage. So, you can check collisions with an invisible ghost object.

When you hide a sprite, it is actually removed from the stage. Other objects can't collide with it anymore. This might be useful if you need an object only in a part of your program. You can show it when it's needed, and when it's not needed, you hide it to prevent it from interrupting any other processes.

Using a collision mask

Although our kart can move freely about the stage, it isn't in any way restricted to the road. This doesn't make for much of a game. We need a way to check where the kart is driving, and if it hits the sandbox or a wall, we should see some effect on the kart.

This means that we should start checking collision events. What do we check against? The background image describes the shape of the racetrack, but it's a single object filling the stage, so we can't check against the background by name. The kart drives on top of it, so it always hits the background.

We could check for color, but the background is a detailed image. This means that we would have to check for many different colors that would produce the same effect. It's hard to determine if similar-looking colors are, in fact, equal. Computers are very precise about this.

So what we will do is create a simplified map to check the collision. We will draw all of the important shapes, but leave out the details. Collision checks will be a lot less confusing this way. This **collision mask** will be hidden from view, but the scripts will work with it. In this way, it relates to the background in a way similar to how the control sprite relates to the kart sprite.

Prepare for lift off

For this step, it will be really useful to have an external image editor. That would make it much easier to work with complicated shapes, such as the curves in the road. You can draw the collision mask in the Scratch editor too, but it will probably be less precise.

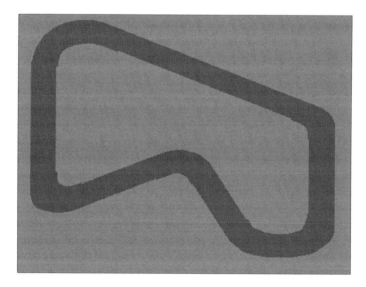

Engage thrusters

We will draw the collision mask in the Scratch **Costumes** editor. Let's see how to do so:

1. Click on the Folder icon in the **Sprites** menu to import the background image as a sprite. We will use the original image as a base and paint over it.

2. Let's make sure that we are working in **Vector Mode**. We can toggle between **Vector Mode** and **Bitmap Mode** in the lower-right corner of the **Costumes** tab.

3. Ensure that the image fills the entire stage. It should be the same size as the **Backdrop** image. Use the Select tool to rescale the image, if necessary.

4. Choose a green color and select the Rectangle tool.

5. Draw green rectangles on top of all the grassy areas. Also include the blocked borders surrounding the grass. Be as precise as possible.

6. Next, we switch over to a brown color.

7. Paint over all of the sandy areas. Don't worry about being too neat. Once the entire sandy area is covered, we will push this layer to the back of the image with the Back a layer button. Hold *Shift* to send the layer all the way to the back with one click.

8. Lastly, choose a gray color and set the **Pencil** size to the biggest size.

9. In a fluid movement, follow the inner edge of the circuit.

10. Click on the Reshape tool to make the circular reshape widgets appear on the line we just drew.

11. Move the widgets around to fit the line around the curves as neatly as possible.

12. You can add widgets to the line if you click on an empty place in the line.

13. Draw another curved line for the outer border of the road.

14. In case there are still some gaps left in the middle, we will fill those up too.

15. When we're done with the drawing, we select the original background image with the Select tool and press *Delete* to remove it. This will make our brown background appear.

The following screenshot shows the road in the process of being shaped with the Reshape tool:

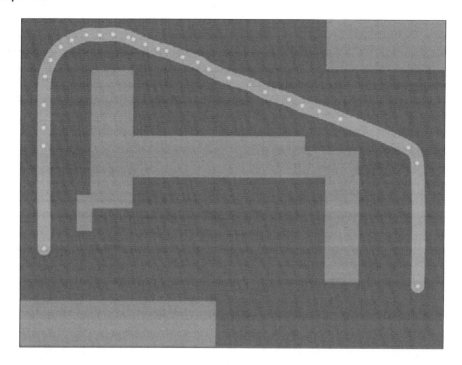

Once all of the shapes are in the proper place to be a simplified copy of the background image, our collision mask is complete.

We will add a small script to the mask to properly place it and make it invisible. The scripts that we add soon will still respond to the collision mask, but the players will see the much better-looking **Backdrop** image:

1. Go to the **Scripts** tab of the collision mask.
2. Start the script with a **when <green flag> clicked** block.
3. Place the mask at the center of the stage with a **go to x: () y: ()** block; fill in the value 0 for both the empty slots. If the placement looks off center after running the script, also check whether the center point of the sprite is placed at the absolute center of the image.
4. Add a **go back () layers** block; fill in the value 100. We use a high number to make sure that the collision mask is moved to the bottom.
5. As a final step, add the **set <ghost> effect to ()** block with value 100 to make the mask invisible.

The finished script will look like the following screenshot:

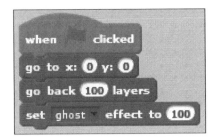

Objective complete – mini debriefing

This step is simply in preparation for the next scripting step. We just drew a simplified copy of the background by hand, using whichever drawing skills and tools we had available.

It can be a bit tricky, depending on how accustomed you are with digital drawing tools. However, it is very worthwhile to spend some time on it. With each effort you will improve your drawing skills, and these skills will be very useful for all kinds of digital creations, from games to animation. You might even learn a bit about how to edit your holiday pictures.

Dealing with collision events

Now that we have a collision mask, we can have our kart respond differently, depending on where it is driving. When on the road, the kart will increase throttle up to full speed. When hitting the sandbox it will be slowed down, and hitting the walls is even worse. The kart will bounce back and completely lose momentum.

Let's build these responses with a few scripts.

Engage thrusters

We will add a series of script instructions to the player1 sprite. We will assemble the instructions first, then place the script segment at the right spot in the existing script:

1. Start with an **if () then** block.

2. For the condition, we will check **touching color ()?**.

3. Click on the color box and then on the sandy color of your collision mask with the eyedropper icon.

4. Inside the **if () then** block, place a **set <speed1> to ()** block.

When the kart drives through sand, we will slow it down. We do this by multiplying its current speed with a number smaller than 1 using these following steps:

1. Place a **() * ()** operator block in the vacant slot.

2. Fill the left slot of the operator with the `speed1` variable.

3. Type in `0.8` in the right slot of the operator.

4. To add the instructions for hitting the borders, copy the entire **if () then** statement and attach it to the original.

5. Change the color to check for the green color that you used on the collision mask.

When hitting the border, the kart should bounce back. We do this by multiplying the speed with a negative number:

1. Change `0.8` to `-0.6`.

2. Grab the entire script and drag it to the existing **when <green flag> clicked** script. Place it between the **if () then** statement that checks for maximum speed and the **move** instruction.

This is all that you need to do for the bouncing-off-walls effect.

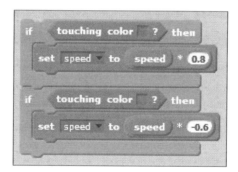

Objective complete – mini debriefing

Test the script and see how the kart responds to hitting the sandbox or the walls. It will no longer be possible to drive carefree across the stage. If you leave the road, the kart will come to a grinding halt giving your opponent an advantage.

Adding a second player

Driving around the circuit on your own is fun but not very challenging. It would be much better if you could invite a friend to compete against. In this step, we will introduce a second player character. Both characters will be visible on the same screen and will be controlled with one keyboard. We're effectively building a simple form of multiplayer.

Engage thrusters

To create a second player, we mainly have to copy the work we've done already. We need a second control sprite and a second kart sprite. We already added a Mario sprite to the game, so let's bring in his brother Luigi as the second player:

1. Right-click on the control sprite named `player1` and choose **duplicate**.
2. The copy will be called `player2` automatically. If that's not the case, change the name manually.
3. Go to the `player2` **Scripts** tab.
4. Change the **key pressed** controls from **a** and **d** to **left arrow** and **right arrow** respectively.

The other script works exactly the same as for the `player1` sprite.

Copying the sprite can cause some trouble with the variables. So let's make a new speed variable to be used for the second player sprite. We will name this `speed2`.

We also need another kart costume set. Instead of a guy in red, let's make the second player a guy in green:

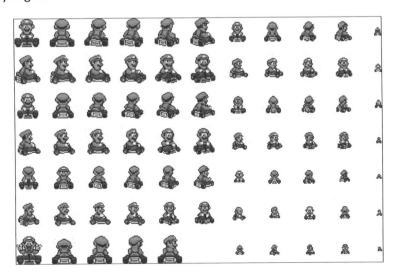

Find a Luigi sprite sheet. Most of these sheets come in sets for a single game. So if you found a Mario sprite sheet, the Luigi version shouldn't be far off. You can also use the sprite sheet that comes with this project.

1. First, make a copy of the `kart1` sprite to easily get a second kart sprite with all of the scripts attached.

2. Instead of following the `player1` sprite, this sprite has to follow `player2` (using **go to <player2>**).

3. We also need to change the **key pressed** controls from **a/d** to **left/right**.

4. The hard work comes with changing the costumes. We need to follow the same procedure we used earlier to create a series of Luigi sprites. Replace all of the Mario costumes with the equivalent Luigi costumes.

5. Once we're done with the images, we can check the animation with the small test script that loops through all of the costumes.

6. Make the necessary changes, if needed.

Objective complete – mini debriefing

We now have two player characters that are controlled with different keys. You should grab a friend now and test the game together. Just adding another player to play the game with adds a lot of fun to the activity, even though we haven't scripted a way to clearly win the game yet.

Classified intel

We could leave it at that; but, after driving a few rounds together, you'll notice that both the racers are able to pass through each other. This looks somewhat unrealistic; however, we can fix it easily. We are going to add a collision check. When a player hits his/her competitor, he/she will bounce back, just like when hitting a wall.

1. Check the script of control sprite `player1`. Take note of the part where we check for collisions with walls.

2. Pull the **touching color <green>?** block out of the slot and set it aside.

3. Instead, place an **or** operator block in the slot of the **if () then** condition.

4. Replace the **touching color <green>?** block to the left of the **or** block.

5. Place a **touching <kart2>** block in the slot right of the **or** operator. Note how we check for the kart and not the control sprite. This is because the kart sprites are a lot bigger than the control sprites. So, they are easier to hit.

6. Player one will now not only bounce back when hitting a wall, but also when hitting his/her opponent. Of course, we need to do the same for player two, or the game would be a bit unfair.

7. Make sure to have control sprite `player2` respond in the same way to hitting `kart1`.

Turning players into obstacles that slow each other down also adds a tactical element to the game. Players can now actively try to run each other off the road.

Finishing the game

Two players can now race each other around the circuit, which is already a lot of fun. But it would be even better if the game has a clear end state and a notification about who won the game.

Engage thrusters

We will add some more scripts to the control sprites `player1` and `player2`. We will first build one complete instruction set, which we can then easily copy to the second sprite.

To determine whether a player has completed a round, we need to add a finish line. This can be a simple additional sprite laid across the track:

1. Click on the Paintbrush icon to create a new sprite.

2. Select the Line tool and draw a horizontal line. Make sure that the line is wide enough to stretch across the road and the sandy areas next to it.

3. Drag the line to the position of the finish line on the backdrop image.

4. Name the new sprite `finish`.

5. Go to the **Scripts** tab of the `finish` sprite.

6. Add a **when <green flag> clicked** block.

7. Attach a **set <ghost> effect to ()** block to make the line invisible; fill in the value `100`.

8. Then, we go to the **Scripts** tab of `player1` to add to the script there.

9. We create two more variables named `lap` and `touchFinish`. Both variables should apply only to this sprite (using **only to this sprite**).

10. Click on the check box for the `lap` variable to make it visible on stage. Drag the display to the top-right corner of the stage.

We will check for collisions with the finish line and increase the lap variable accordingly to count the number of laps the players have driven:

1. Get an **if () then () else ()** block to form the basic structure of the script. This block will check when a kart is or isn't touching the finish line and set the appropriate variable correspondingly.

2. Inside the **if** slot, place an **if () then** block (*without an "else"*). With this block, we will count the number of laps completed.

3. Inside the **if () then** block, add **change \<lap\> by ()**; fill in the value 1.

4. Also add **set \<touchFinish\> to ()** with the value 1.

5. Inside the **else** slot, place a **set \<touchFinish\> to ()** block with the value 0.

Let's write the conditions for the **if** statement next:

1. The slot in the **if () then () else ()** block should be filled with a **touching \<finish\>?** condition check.

2. In the **if () then** block, we place a **() = ()** operator.

3. On the left side of the equation, we place the `touchFinish` variable.

4. To the right, we fill in 0.

Crossing the finish line usually takes the kart sprite longer than one loop through the script. With the previous check, we prevent the lap counter to increase multiple times while the kart is crossing the line.

We also need to do something special when the player has completed three laps to indicate that they finished the race.

1. Place yet another **if () then** block inside the second **if** statement.

2. Put a **() = ()** operator in the condition slot.

3. Put the `lap` variable to the left of the equation.

4. Insert 3 to the right of the equation.

5. When the player has finished three laps, add **say timer** to show how long it took the player to finish the race.

6. We also need this stack of instructions for `player2`. So, let's first drag it over the `player2` sprite to copy the script there.

7. Then drag the stack to the **when \<green flag\> clicked** script. Place it just underneath the other **if () then** collision checks.

8. Click on the `player2` sprite to view its **Scripts** tab and place the copied script segment in the same place as we did for `player1`.

9. Also make the `lap` variable for `player2` visible by clicking on the check box.

10. Drag the display to the top-right corner of the stage and place it underneath the `player1` lap display.

The script should look like the following screenshot:

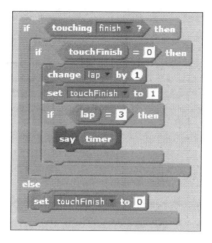

Lastly, we need to set the lap variables to their starting values when the game starts.

Place a **set <lap> to ()** block at the start of the **when <green flag> clicked** script; fill in the value -1. Do this for both control sprites.

We use -1 and not 0 because the karts will drive over the finish line as soon as they start racing, activating the script we just wrote and increasing the lap number. So we can explain -1 as "the race has not started yet" and 0 as "the race has begun, but no lap has been completed yet".

Objective complete – mini debriefing

That completes our kart racing game. Two players can now compete against each other to race three laps in record time. Gather some friends and have a racing competition. Playing against the computer is good entertainment, but playing with friends and family is even more enjoyable. You can also show off your hard work!

Classified intel

You may have noticed that we keep switching the value of the touchFinish variable with an **if () else** statement. You can compare it with flipping a light switch. This is a special kind of variable called **Boolean**. It only has two meaningful numbers. It can be either 0 (off) or 1 (on). Any other numbers will be counted as 1.

This kind of variable is often used in games to check whether something is active. We use it here to check if we are still touching the finish line after first hitting it. Without this check, the lap variable would be increased with each script loop, which as you may remember, is very fast. We only want to have the collision registered once, after which the kart has to completely pass over the line before a collision may be checked again.

Mission accomplished

While building this game, we learned about separating game logic from graphics. This makes it easier to edit specific parts of the game. A simple Scratch game is often made by a single person. But in a professional game development studio, many different people will work on different parts of a game. In those circumstances, it's very useful if each part can be developed separately without seriously breaking the game as a whole.

We explored some options to create better graphics both with the Scratch tools and with other image editors. We only scratched the surface though; this is a subject worthy of a separate book.

We also created a simple form of a multiplayer game. Games are always more enjoyable if you can share them with a friend. Perhaps you noticed how the game experience changed when you added the second player and started testing the game together with someone else. If you haven't done that yet, I strongly encourage you to do so.

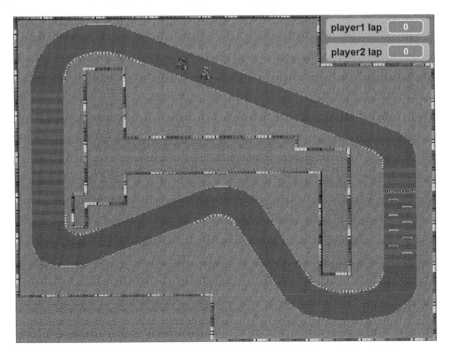

Hotshot challenges

There is more that you could add to this game. Let me give you some ideas for inspiration:

- ▸ You could add even more players to create even more fun and chaos on the circuit. It will become quite crowded around the keyboard, but that is part of the fun.

- ▸ You can improve the endgame. Instead of the text bubbles, you could include the "YOU WIN!" display that we created in the previous project. Use **Backpack** to copy the sprite and then adapt the costumes and scripts.

- ▸ Of course, you can also include more race tracks. You might even try to build a level select menu, so players can choose which track to use before the race begins.

Project 4

Space Age

In this project, we will create a first-person shooter game called **Space Age**. We will learn how to utilize several Scratch 2.0 features to create this multilevel, fun-filled game. Let's start!

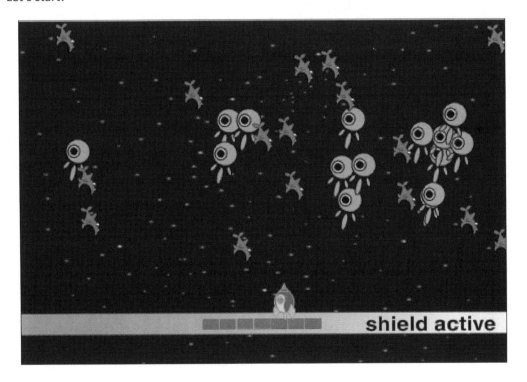

Mission briefing

This is the year 3001, and the situation is dire. Your planet is under attack and is in imminent danger of complete destruction. Alien invaders from the planet of Gor are coming in waves. You and other six fighters are the last and only hope your planet has. You may not have chosen this mission but the mission has chosen you.

Why is it awesome?

We will build a multiple-level game, which contains a scoreboard, game manager, and different enemies for each level. This game is also configurable, so you can adjust the level of difficulty as well as add new levels.

Moreover, we will utilize several Scratch 2.0 features including More Blocks, Cloning, and Timer.

Your Hotshot objectives

We will build the game step by step; by first creating a player character, then adding enemies, and finally adding the environment. We will be performing the following tasks in this project:

  ▸ Starting with the starter project

  ▸ Adding scripts to Spaceship

  ▸ Updating enemy sprites

  ▸ Adding scripts to Spaceship Ammo and Enemy Ammo

  ▸ Adding scripts to Shield and Shield Life

  ▸ Meeting your Game Manager

  ▸ Adding levels – three simple steps

Mission checklist

To speed up the process and allow us to focus on scripting, we will use prepackaged Scratch sprites wherever we can. Only some background sprites will be hand drawn.

Starting with the starter project

To simplify the script creation, we will start with the starter project. The starter project contains the following:

- ▶ Stage
- ▶ Global variables
- ▶ Incomplete sprites (sprites that contain incomplete costumes, variables, or scripts)
- ▶ Complete sprites (sprites that contain all the necessary parts and can be configured)

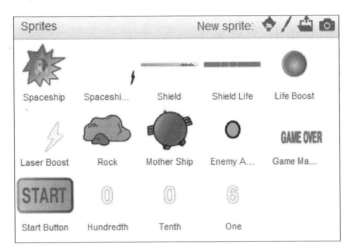

Engage thrusters

Open the starter project and check out the stage, global variables, and the sprites.

The costume stage in Space Age is imported from the Scratch media library under Space. It does not have any script and is only used for the background.

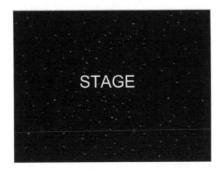

Open the starter project and check out the sprites included. The following table gives a quick overview of what each sprite does:

Sprite name	Description	Scripts included in starter project?
Spaceship	The sprite that the player controls directly	No
Spaceship Ammo		No
Shield	Protects the Spaceship against enemy crash but not against the enemy ammo	No
Shield Life	Displays the power level of the shield	No
Life Boost	Resets shield power to full	Yes
Laser Boost	Increases laser power to shoot through all enemies on the laser track	Yes
Rock	Enemy sprite that falls	Yes
Mother Ship	Enemy sprite that flies in a pattern	Yes
Enemy Ammo	Ammo fired by the enemy sprites	Yes
Game Manager	Manager's game levels and scores	Yes
Start Button	When pressed, game starts	Yes
Hundredth	Display the hundred's digit of the score	Yes
Tenth	Display the ten's digit of the score	Yes
One	Display the one's digit of the score	Yes

Global variables are variables that are shared by all sprites and local variables are variables used by one sprite only. Global variables are convenient for sprites to share information, just like a bulletin board. You may think of global variables as posts on a bulletin board for all sprites to see, and local variables as private letters just for the eyes of the owner sprite.

To create a global variable, just select the **For all sprites** radio button as shown in the following screenshot:

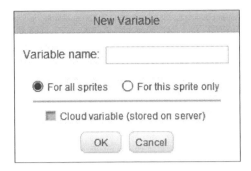

In Space Age, there are six global variables: enemy_count, frame_rate, game_level, game_score, power_boost_on, and max_game_level. Their description is given in the following table:

Global variable name	Description
current_enemy_count	Current count of enemies in game
frame_rate	The frame refresh rate; often used to pause for the costume
game_level	Current level of the game; range—1~max_game_level
game_score	Current game score; range—000~999
power_boost_on	True if spaceship's laser boost is on; false if it is off
max_game_level	Highest level in this game

Objective complete – mini debriefing

We've covered the stage, global variables, and the sprites in Space Age. After getting a quick glimpse of all the sprites, next we will complete each sprite.

Adding scripts to Spaceship

The Spaceship sprite can move and fire ammo at the enemies. To do so, we need to create codes to do the following:

▸ **Start**

▸ **Move**

▸ **Shoot**

▸ **Response**

▸ **End**

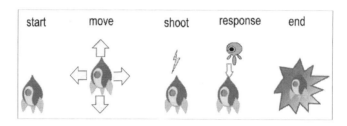

Engage thrusters

Now we are ready to equip the Spaceship with scripts, so it can be controlled.

To create the script that executes upon game initialization, perform the following steps:

1. Start with a **when I receive <game_start>** message block.
2. Move to the bottom center of the stage and enter 0 and 100 in the **go to x: () y: ()** block.
3. Switch the costume to normal using the **switch costume to <>** block.
4. Enable **go to front** and **show**.

The following screenshot shows the final script:

```
when I receive game_start ▼
go to x: 0 y: -100
switch costume to normal ▼
go to front
show
```

Horizontal movement

For movement, we will create two more blocks using **More Blocks**, one for the horizontal movement and another for the vertical movement. The **More Blocks** feature lets the users group the commonly used codes in custom blocks, making the code shorter and easier to read. In terms of computer programming languages, **More Blocks** are like methods or functions. Each **More Block** can have zero or several input parameters. Similar to the variables in a mathematical function, input parameters are plugged into **More Blocks** to produce the desired result. For example, one can have a More Block named Jump that will jump num_jump times, num_jump being the input parameter. At runtime, if num_jump holds a concrete value such as 3, then the Jump block would jump three times. For horizontal movement, we are going to create a **More Block** named Move Horizontally, which when executed, would move the Spaceship horizontally, as shown in the following screenshot:

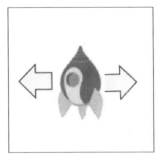

To create code for horizontal movement, perform the following steps:

1. Select the **More Blocks** tab and click on the **Make a Block** button.

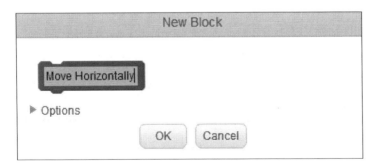

2. On the **New Block** dialog box, click inside the empty **More Block** and type `Move Horizontally`. Expand the **Options** tab and click on the **Add number input:** button.

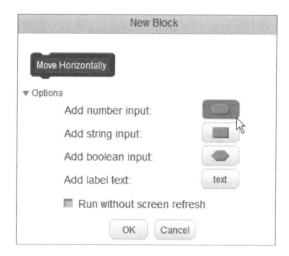

3. Then, enter the value of `direction` for the boolean input parameter. The boolean datatype has only two possible values: `0` (false) or `1` (true).

You should see the new **More Block** as shown in the following screenshot:

4. From the **Operators** tab, drag out the **<?>* <?>** block and drag the **direction** block to make the **<x position> + (<direction> * <move_steps>)** block visible.

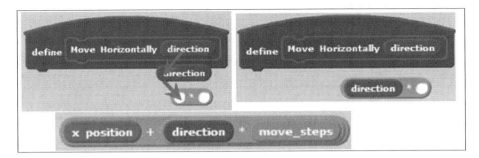

5. Build the **go to x: (<x position> + (<direction> * <move_steps>)) y: <y position>** block.

6. Add this script to define the direction using the **define Move Horizontally <direction>** block.

Let's add scripts to move the Spaceship when a user hits the right or left arrow key as follows:

1. Start with **when <right arrow> key pressed**. Move to the right via **Move Horizontally <1>**.

2. Start with **when <left arrow> key pressed**. Move to the right via **Move Horizontally <-1>**.

Vertical Movement

To write the code for the vertical movement, we will also create a custom block.

The steps to write the code for vertical movement are as follows:

1. Create a custom block named **Move Vertically**.

2. Right-click on the body of the **Move Horizontally** block and select **duplicate**.

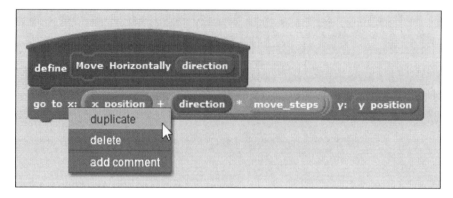

3. Update the copy so that it is **go to x: () y: ()**; the slots are filled as shown in the following screenshot:

4. Then, attach the **go to x: () y ()** block under the **Move Vertically** definition block. The resulting custom block should look like the following screenshot:

5. Start with **when <up arrow> key pressed**. Move to the right via **Move Vertically ()** with the value 1.

6. Start with **when <down arrow> key pressed**. Move to the right via **Move Vertically ()** with value -1.

The Spaceship should shoot ammo when the Space bar is pressed. To do so, when the Space bar is pressed, a clone of the Spaceship Ammo would be created to fly straight up until it hits the edge or an enemy sprite.

The steps to build the shooting code are as follows:

1. Start with the **when <space> key pressed** block.
2. To prevent the game from hanging up when the user hits the Space bar too many times, we will add a timeout between each round of firing. Let's wait for 0.05 seconds by using the **wait () secs** block.
3. Now add the code to fire the ammo by using **create clone of <Spaceship Ammo>**. Note that we still cannot shoot the Spaceship Ammo. This is not possible until we add the scripts to the Spaceship Ammo sprite later in the project.

The finished script should look like the following screenshot:

For the sake of game responsiveness, the Spaceship sprite does not continue to check whether it has collided with the enemy sprites or their ammo. Instead, the checking is done by the enemy sprites and their ammo. When notified, the Spaceship reacts to the collision by simply changing its costume.

The steps to build the script are as follows:

1. Start with the **when I receive <ship_collided>** block.
2. Then, use the **switch costume to <hit>** block.
3. Wait for 0.5 seconds for the user to see the Spaceship explode (using the **wait () secs** block).

The following screenshot shows the final script:

The Spaceship sprite terminates when it receives the game_over message.

The steps to write the code are as follows:

1. Start with the **when I received <game_over>** block.
2. Then, add the **hide** block.
3. Finally, add the **stop all** block.

The finished script should look like the following screenshot:

Objective complete – mini debriefing

Now, try testing the Spaceship sprite by moving it horizontally using the left and right arrow keys. Then, test the vertical movement using the up and down arrow keys. Additionally, you can test each script block by double-clicking on it. When a script block is being run or executed, its outline would turn faint yellow.

Classified intel

In this section, we introduce More Blocks. I hope you found creating a custom block fairly easy. However, deleting a custom block is not as intuitive. There is no "delete this custom block" available when right-clicking on the block definition. To remove a custom block, first remove all the references to it. Then, drag the definition block to the tool area in order to delete it.

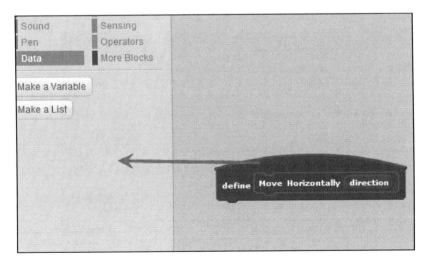

Updating enemy sprites

Space Age has four levels; for each level, a special enemy sprite is responsible for the attack and they are as follows:

- ▶ Level one: Rock
- ▶ Level two: Monster
- ▶ Level three: Robot
- ▶ Level four: Mother Ship

In the starter project, there are only two enemy sprites: Rock and Mother Ship. Both the Rock and Mother Ship have complete scripts and are ready to participate in the game. We will copy Rock to create Monster and Robot, and then tweak their local variables to increase the difficulty.

Prepare for lift off

The Rock sprite attacks by crashing and firing ammo. When created as a clone, it continues to fall down at a random speed and randomly fires rounds. The speed of falling as well as the frequency of firing the ammo are configured through `min_speed`, `max_speed`, and `shoot_random_wait`.

Before duplicating Rock to create new sprites, first test the Rock sprite by playing the game. Click on the green flag, and hit the **Start** button to start playing. If all is well, you should see the Level One information page scrolling by and the Rock clones shown as a drove. Hold the ammo, because we have yet to add scripts to the Spaceship Ammo sprite.

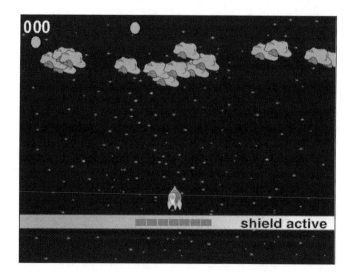

Engage thrusters

Now, let's create a Monster:

1. Right-click on **Rock** and select **duplicate** to create **Rock2**.

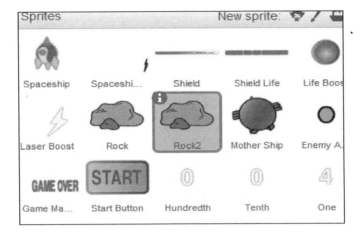

2. To change the name from **Rock2** to **Monster**, click on the round **i** icon, and change the name to Monster.

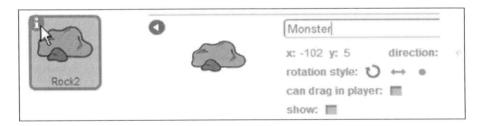

3. Next, go to the **Costumes** tab, and delete the existing costumes. Click on **Upload costume from file**, and navigate to <chap4_images_dir>\costumes\enemies\ monster, select normal.svg and hit.svg, and click on **OK**.

4. Verify whether the Monster sprite has both the normal and hit costumes as shown in the following diagram:

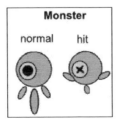

Now, let's create the Robot sprite:

1. Right-click on **Rock** and select **duplicate** to create **Rock2**.

2. To change the name from **Rock2** to **Robot,** click on the round **i** icon, and change the name to Robot.

3. Create the Robot sprite costumes by navigating to <chap4_images_dir>\ costumes\enemies\robot and then import normal_robot.svg and hit_ robot.svg.

4. Verify whether the Robot sprite has both the normal and hit costumes as shown in the following diagram:

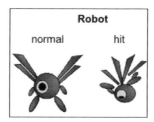

Let's make Monster and Robot faster and shoot out more ammo. To do so, we will change the min_speed, max_speed, and shoot_random_wait variables. Navigate to Monster's **Scripts** tab and change its scripts as follows:

1. Add the **when <green flag> clicked** script.

2. Use **set <min_speed> to ()** and change its value from 4 to 5.

3. Use **set <max_speed> to ()** and change its value from 8 to 10.

4. Use **set <shoot_random_wait> to ()** and change its value from 1000 to 100 (wait less, shoot more often).

The final script will look like the following screenshot:

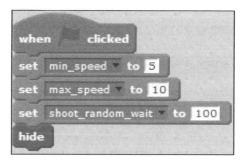

Repeat the same steps for Robot, but make it harder:

1. Find the **when <green flag> clicked** script.

2. Use **set <min_speed> to ()** and change its value from 4 to 6.

3. Use **set <max_speed> to ()** and change its value from 8 to 10.

4. Use **set <shoot_random_wait> to ()** and change its value from 1000 to 75 (wait less, shoot more often).

The final script will look like the following screenshot:

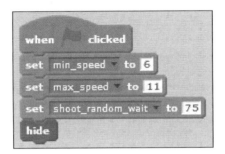

Objective complete – mini debriefing

We have created two new sprites by first making two copies of the Rock sprite and named them Monster and Robot. Then, we tweaked each new sprite to fall faster (min_speed and max_speed) and shoot more often (shoot_random_wait).

Classified intel

To add a copy of a sprite from one project to another project, one can right-click the sprite and select **save to local file**. The sprite is then saved to a file named Rock.sprite2. which can then be imported to another project.

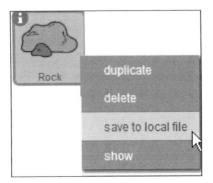

Adding scripts to Spaceship Ammo and Enemy Ammo

The Spaceship sprite fights enemy sprites with Spaceship Ammo, and enemy sprites attack with the Enemy Ammo sprites.

Prepare for lift off

Spaceship Ammo has one local variable, `speed`. The speed variable is how fast this sprite moves. Upon creation, it flies out of the Spaceship sprite and moves straight up until it hits an enemy or the top edge of the Stage.

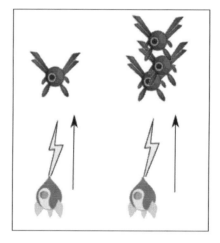

The Enemy Ammo sprite is very similar to the Spaceship Ammo sprite and is different only in direction, hit target (the sprites it can hurt), and costumes.

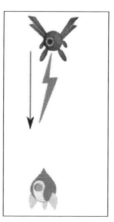

Enemy Ammo moves down, but Spaceship Ammo moves up. Also, Enemy Ammo can hit the Spaceship and Spaceship Shield sprites, but Spaceship Ammo can hit enemy sprites. More interestingly, Enemy Ammo, contrary to Spaceship Ammo, is level-aware: it changes the costume based on the current game level. Due to the similarity between Enemy Ammo and Spaceship Ammo, the Enemy Ammo scripts are included in the starter project.

Engage thrusters

When the game starts, the Spaceship Ammo sprite will only initialize its variables but not participate in the game yet.

To create the code to initialize upon receiving the game_start message, perform the following steps:

1. Start with the **when I receive <game_start>** block.
2. Use **set <speed> to ()**; fill in the value 100.
3. Use **set <power_boost_on> to ()**; fill in the value false.

The final script should look like the following screenshot:

The following steps create the code for each Spaceship Ammo clone:

1. Start with **when I start as a clone**.
2. Add the **go to <Spaceship>** block.
3. Then add the **go to front** and **show** blocks.
4. Add a bit of zest with **play sound <laser>**.
5. Add an **if () then () else** condition block to check whether the **power_boost_on** condition is true.
6. If **power_boost_on** is true, this ammo can destroy multiple enemies. So it uses the **change y by (<speed> * <frame_rate>)** and **repeat until <y position> is greater than ()** blocks; fill in the value 180 in the **repeat until** block.

7. If **power_boost_on** is `false`, the ammo would move up repeatedly until it hits either an enemy or the ceiling. In other words, **change y by (<speed> * <frame_ rate>)** and **repeat until (<y position> greater than (180) or touching <Rock>? or touching <Robot > ? or touching <Monster>? or touching <Mother Ship>?.**

8. After hitting the ceiling or an enemy, delete the clone using **delete this clone**.

The final script should look like the following screenshot:

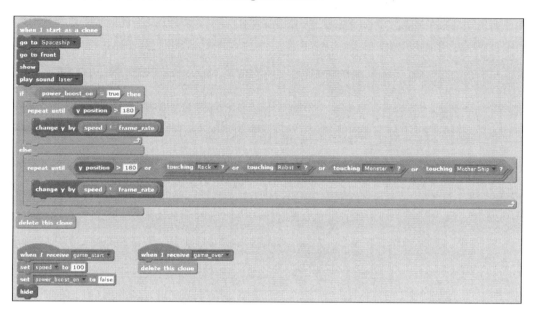

If the game is over, each clone will delete itself. Add the **when I receive <game_over>** and **delete this clone** blocks.

Next, let's add the scripts for the Enemy Ammo sprite:

1. When the game starts, don't show the sprite. Wait for the creation of the clone. Then, add the **when green flag is clicked** and **hide** blocks.

2. Now let's add the script for a clone. Start with **when I start as a clone**.

3. Add the **switch costume to <game_level>** block.

4. Add the **go to x: (pick random () to ()) y: ()** block; fill in the values -240 and 240 for x and 180 for y. Then, add the **go to front** and **show** blocks.

5.   Now add **set speed to (pick random () to ())**; fill in the values 10 and 15.

6.   The effect of repeatedly falling down or moving straight down on the y axis is brought using **repeat until ((y position < -180) or (touching <Spaceship>))** and **change y by ((-1) * (speed * frame_rate))**.

7.   After getting out of the **repeat () loop**, this ammo clone has either touched the stage bottom or the Spaceship. Add **if touching Spaceship and then broadcast ship_hit**.

8.   Finally, delete the clone using **delete this clone**.

Besides hitting the bottom or the Spaceship, an Enemy Ammo clone is also deleted when the current level completes. Add **when I receive <level_up>** and **delete this clone**. The finished script looks like the following screenshot:

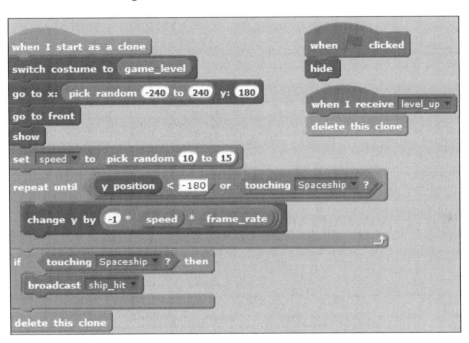

Objective complete – mini debriefing

We finished creating the scripts for Spaceship Ammo as well as for Enemy Ammo. Now you can test each script by double-clicking on the script. If you double-click on the **when I start as a clone** block once, one Spaceship Ammo clone will show at the bottom and flies straight up until it hits the top. For Enemy Ammo, the clones will show at the top and fall down until it hits the bottom or a Spaceship sprite.

Classified intel

Global variables are shared by all the sprites, and local variables are for one sprite or clone. You can think of global variables as values that are posted on the bulletin board for all to see. On the contrary, the local variables are like a letter. When a sprite is cloned, that clone contains its own copy of that letter.

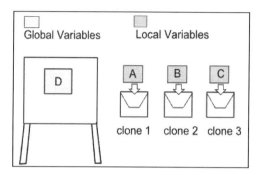

Adding scripts to Shield and Shield Life

Shield protects and is also protected by the Spaceship. Each time the enemy sprite collides into it, Shield will lose one grid of power, displayed by Shield Life.

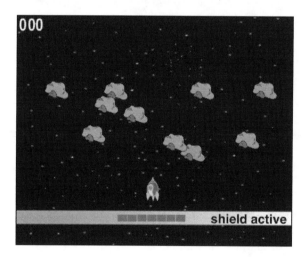

When the power is gone (all red), Shield is destroyed and the game is over.

Shield Life displays the shield power grid by changing its costumes, each at a power grid damage level. The technique to display damage level with costumes is to match the costume number with the number of hits. Scratch costumes start from one, instead of zero, so **costume#1** depicts zero hit, **costume#2** for one hit, and so on.

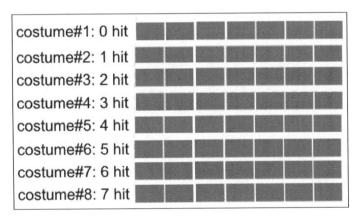

Prepare for lift off

Shield Life has two local variables: num_shield_hits and num_max_hits. The number_shield_hits variable tracks how many hits the Shield sprite has suffered, and the num_max_hits variable tells the maximum number of hits that Shield can take before its complete destruction.

Engage thrusters

The following steps are used to build the scripts for the Shield sprite:

1. Add the **when <green flag> clicked** block, but before the player starts to play, just hide (using **hide**).

2. The next script starts with **when I receive <game_start>**. First, add **switch costume to <normal>**, then **go to x: () y: ()**; fill in the values 7 and -110 respectively. Finally, add **show**.

3. To define the behavior during gameplay, start with **when I receive <shield_hit>**, make it real by adding **switch costume to <hit>**, **wait <frame_rate> secs**, then **switch costume to <normal>**.

4. If the shield is destroyed, the Shield sprite would receive the **shield_destroyed** message. Therefore, add **when I receive <shield_destroyed>**, **switch costume to <destroyed>**, and **stop <other scripts in sprite>**.

The final script looks like the following screenshot:

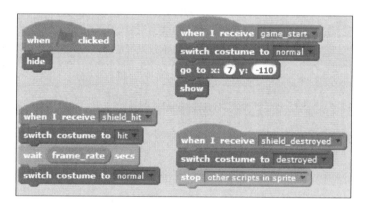

Next, we will create the scripts for the Shield Life sprite.

Before the game starts, this sprite will hide. At the start of the game, it initializes its local variables.

The following steps handle the **<green flag>** click and **game_start** messages:

1. Add the **when <green flag> clicked** block, but before the player starts to play, just hide (using **hide**).

2. The next script starts with **when I receive <game_start>** message. First add **go to x: () y: ()** with the values -51 and -120, then **set <number_max_hits> to ()** with the value 7, and **set num_shield_hit to ()** with the value 0. Next, add **switch costume to <0 hit>**, then **go to front**, and **show**.

During the play, these sprites process four broadcast messages: **shield_hit**, **shield_destroyed**, **life_power_up**, and **level_up**.

The following steps build the required scripts:

1. The first script starts with **when I receive <shield_hit>** and **change num_shield_hit by ()** with the value 1. Then, add **switch costume to (<num_shield_hit>+())** with the value 1. Add an **if () then** condition block. Check whether the number of hits the shield has taken is greater than the number of maximum hits it can, by using the **<num_shield_hit> is greater than <num_max_hits> - 1** block, and then add the **broadcast <shield_destroyed>** block.

2. The last script starts with **when I receive <life_power_up>**, restore the power grid and add **set <num_shield_hit> to ()** with the value 0. Then, update the look using **switch costume to <0 hit>** and **show**.

The finished script will look like the following screenshot:

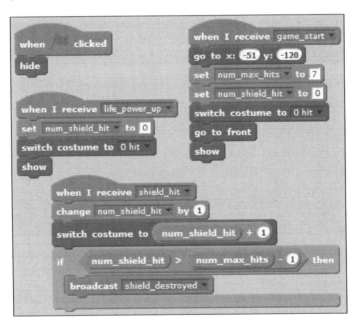

Objective complete – mini debriefing

We added scripts to the Shield and Shield Life sprites. The Shield sprite makes the game more dynamic and interesting, whereas the Shield Life sprite displays the life statistics visually and in a more lively manner.

Classified intel

During the game, a gamer needs to track not only the power level as shown in the Shield Life sprite but also the score. Space Age displays the score on a scoreboard using three sprites, one for each digit. They are complete sprites that work right out of the box. The **Hundredth** sprite displays the hundred's place, the **Tenth** sprite displays the ten's place, and the **One** sprite displays the one's place. Just like the Shield Life sprite, each scoreboard sprite has costumes that matches the shown values, as shown in the following diagram:

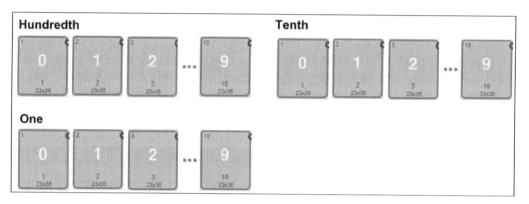

To display numbers from 0 to 9, all the three sprites have costumes ranging from **costume#1** to **costume#10**, with **costume#1** displaying the number **0** and **costume#10** displaying the number **9**.

For example, to display the score 257, the Hundredth sprite would switch to costume 3, the Tenth sprite to costume 6, and the One sprite to costume 8.

Meeting your Game Manager

The Game Manager sprite is the brain of the game. It manages game logic including scoring, level completion, winning, and losing.

When the user clicks on the green flag, Game Manager displays the start page with instructions and a start button. The game starts when the start button is clicked. After the game starts, Game Manager processes the broadcast messages sent from other sprites and decides on the following aspects:

- ▸ The time to move up a level
- ▸ When the game is won
- ▸ When the game is over

At the beginning of each new level, Game Manager engages the user as well as the other sprites in the game. To users, it displays the level-up screen that scrolls up, giving the users time to wiggle their fingers before the next game. To the other sprites, it notifies that this level is over and the sprites then wrap up the current level and prepare for the next one.

Prepare for lift off

Instead of creating the Game Manager scripts from scratch, we will use the complete Game Manager sprite from the starter project and add two new levels to it.

Game Manager is the most complex sprite in this game. The Space Age message flow diagram below shows that Game Manager is at the center of the happenings. It determines and announces each stage of the game play: start, level-up, and termination. Moreover, Game Manager scripts also enables existing levels to be configured and new levels to be added.

Engage thrusters

At system start (**when <green flag> clicked**), Game Manager displays the game rule to the user and prompts the user to play. It also initializes global variables and game levels. This initialization script is included in the starter project so that one can test the other sprites. Let's take a look at its **when <green flag> clicked** script:

1. Display the start page by adding **go to x: () y: ()** with the values 8 and 13, then **switch costume to <Start Screen>**, and **show**.

2. There are two game levels that we will add next. The first one is **set <max_game_level> to ()** with the value 2.

3. We start with Level One by using **set <game_level> to ()** with the value 1.

4. Reset the game score using **set <game_score> to ()** with the value 0.

5. Now add **set <min_enemy_count> to ()** with the value 3. If the enemy count goes below **<min_enemy_count>**, the player moves up a level.

6. Add **set <move_steps> to ()** with the value 20. Add **set <frame_rate> to ()** with the value 0.2.

7. Let's move on to level configuration. First, clear all the entries from the level lists. Add **delete <all> of <enemyTypeList>**, **delete <all> of <enemyCountList>**, and **delete <all> of <levelTimeoutList>**.

8. Use the **Configure Level ()** block to configure each level.

9. For Level One, use **Configure Level: 1 enemyType: <Rock> enemyCount: () timeout: ()** with the values 15 and 20. The enemy type must be exactly the same as the enemy sprite name. Make sure that there is no extra space.

10. For Level One, use **Configure Level: 2 enemyType: <Mother Ship> enemyCount: () timeout: ()** with the values 1 and 30.

The finished script looks like the following screenshot:

Game Manager also has a custom block to start a new level. It's called **Start Level <level_ num>**. It's already included in the starter project so that one can test the other sprites. We do not need to make a change to the Game Manager scripts yet; let's take a look inside the **Start Level ()** block:

1. Add **switch costume to <level_num>**, which is the level banner.

2. Create the scrolling effect using **go to x: () y: ()** with the values -14 and -188, then **show** and **glide 4 secs to x: () y ()** with values -30 and 180 for x and y respectively. Then add **hide**.

3. Now, add **set <current_enemy_type> to item <level_num> of <enemyTypeList>**.

4. Then, add **set <current_enemies_to_create> to item <level_num> of <enemyCountList>**.

5. Next, add **set <current_enemy_threshold> to item <level_num> of <enemyThresholdList>**.

6. Then come the **repeat <current_enemies_to_create>** and **create clone of <current_ enemy_type>** blocks.

7. Add **set <current_enemy_count> to <num_enemies_to_create>**.

8. Lastly, add the **broadcast <timer_start>** block.

The finished script looks like the following screenshot:

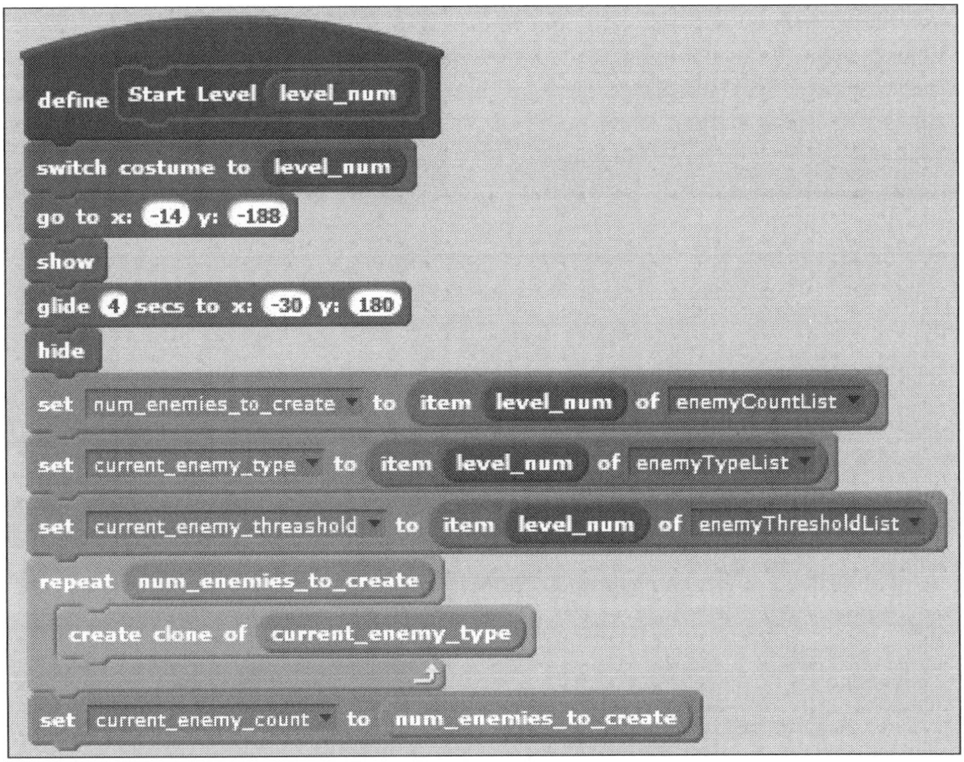

To determine when to move the level up, an intuitive and simple way is to track how many enemies are left. If all the enemies have been shot down, then the level should go up, right? The answer is yes and no. Yes, if the game has very few enemy clones or if you do not use cloning at all. However, for a game such as Space Age, which uses many broadcast messages and clones, tracking the number of surviving enemies is not reliable. You can observe this for yourself by going to the **Data** tab and checking the **current_enemy_count** checkbox. Then, you can observe that the current enemy count does not always go down each time you shoot down an enemy, especially when the enemy clones are close to each other and you fire ammo rapidly.

To help with this problem, Game Manager uses **current_enemy_threshold**. If **current_enemy_count** becomes lower than **current_enemy_threshold** for that level, the game advances to another level.

Game Manager has a **Configure Level ()** block that allows the user to configure existing levels or add new levels. Game Manager stores the configuration of each level in three lists: **enemyTypeList**, **enemyCountList**, and **enemyThresholdList**. The **enemyTypeList** stores the enemy sprite types for all the levels; the **enemyCountList** stores the enemy counts (how many enemy clones to create); the **levelTimeoutList** stores the level timeout.

The **Configure Level ()** block is already included in the starter project so that one can test the other sprites. Let's take a look inside the **Configure Level ()** block:

1. This block is called **Configure Level: <level_num> enemyType: <type> enemyCount: <count> enemyThreshold: <threshold >**. The **<level_num>** input variable is the next level number; the **<count>** variable shows how many enemy clones are to be created for the next level, and **<type>** shows the type of enemy sprite to be created; the **<threshold>** variable shows how low the enemy count has to go before moving up a level.

2. Next, add **<type>** to **<enemyTypeList>**. If the entry is already there, use **update** instead of **insert**. Check condition **if (length of enemyTypeList) is smaller than <level_num>**. If yes, add **insert <type> at <level_num> of enemyTypeList**. Else, add **replace item <level_num> of enemyTypeList with <type>**.

3. Next, add **<count>** to **<enemyCountList>**. If the entry is already there, use **update** instead of **insert**. Check condition **if (length of enemyCountList) is smaller than <level_num>**. If yes, add **insert <count> at <level_num> of enemyCountList**. Else, add **replace item <level_num> of enemyCountList with <count>**.

4. Finally, add **<threshold>** to **<enemyThresholdList>**. If the entry is already there, use **update** instead of **insert**. Check condition **if (length of enemyThresholdList) is smaller than <level_num>**. If yes, add **insert <threshold> at <level_num> of enemyThresholdList**. Else, add **replace item <level_num> of enemyThresholdList with <threshold>**.

The following screenshot shows the final script:

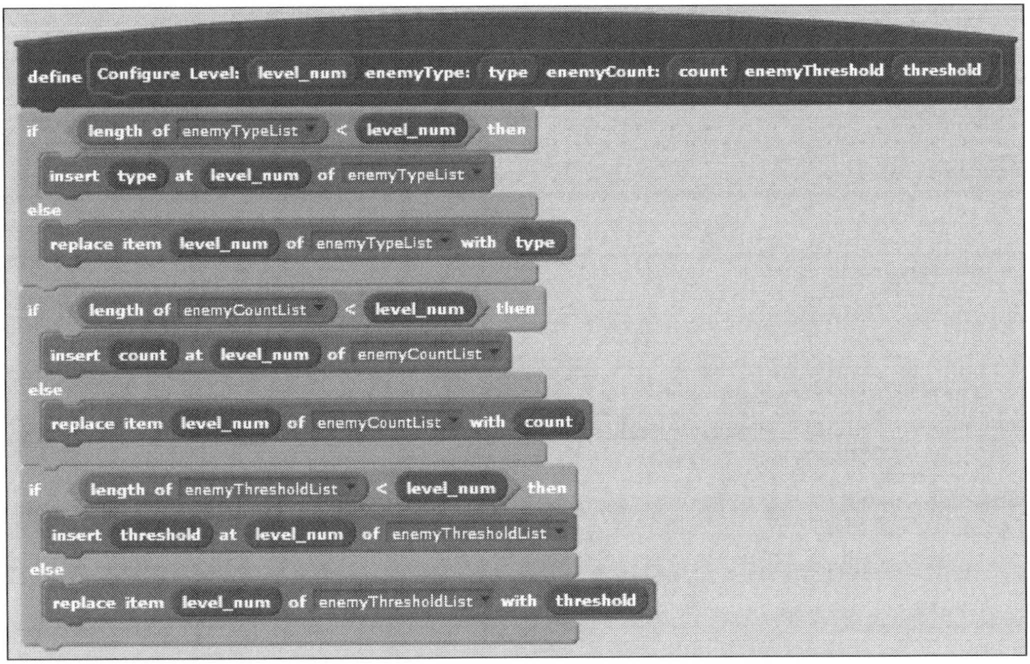

Objective complete – mini debriefing

We have gone over the existing scripts in Game Manager to handle starting a game, starting and ending a level, and finally, configuring a level.

Adding levels – three simple steps

If you have not done so, test the current code. If you are a good gamer, you should ace this and finish both levels in no time. To make the game harder to beat and more interesting, let's add two new levels using Monster and Robot.

Prepare for lift off

For each game level, there are different enemy types, enemy counts, and level timeouts. The enemy type is the name of the enemy sprite, enemy count is the number of enemies to create, and the level timeout is the maximum time each level lasts. The level can move up before the level timeout if enough enemies are eliminated.

With the **Configure Level ()** block, it's very easy to add new levels and we will do just that in this section. The following screenshot shows the complete level list when we are done:

Level: One
Enemy: Rock
Speed: 4 to 8
Time wait to shoot:: 1000

Level: Two
Enemy: Monster
Speed: 5 to 10
Time wait to shoot:: 100

Level: Three
Enemy: Monster
Speed: 6 to 11
Time wait to shoot:: 75

Level: Four
Enemy: Mother Ship
Speed: fly speed
Time wait to shoot:: 75

Essentially, we are going to add level information for the two new levels to the three lists: the enemy type, enemy count, and level timeout lists. According to the following diagram, level one has **15** Rock clones and would advance when current enemy count goes below **3**:

	enemyTypeList	enemyCountList	enemyThresholdList
level 1	Rock	15	3
level 2	Monster	15	3
level 3	Robot	15	3
level 4	Mother Ship	1	1

Engage thrusters

To do so, we need to update Game Manager's scripts. Go to Game Manager's **Scripts** tab to find the **when <green flag> clicked** script, and add the following levels to it:

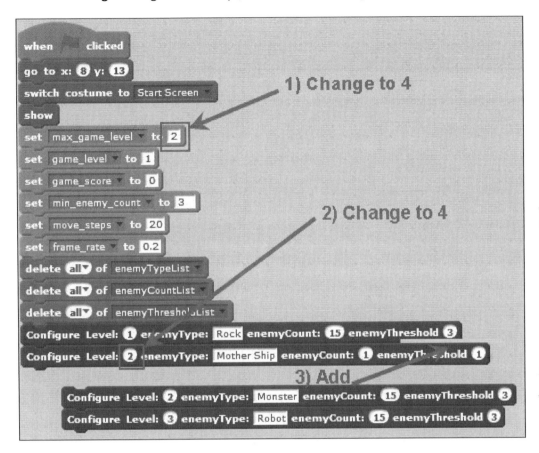

The steps to add two additional levels are as follows:

1. Add **set <max_game_level> to ()** and change value from 2 to 4.

2. Change level 2 to level 4 in the **Configure Level: 2** block to make **Configure Level: 4 enemyType: Mother Ship enemyCount: 1 enemyThreshold: 1**.

3. Add **Configure Level: 2 enemyType: Monster enemyCount: 15 enemyThreshold: 3**.

4. Add **Configure Level: 3 enemyType: Robot enemyCount: 15 enemyThreshold: 3**.

5. Then, drop **Configure Level: 2** and **Configure Level: 3** between the **Configure Level: 1** and **Configure Level: 4** blocks.

Matching the Enemy sprite name exactly

Ensure that the enemyType field exactly matches with the enemy sprite name, including the spaces. Also, make sure that there is no space before or after the name string.

There we have it. We've added two additional levels in three simple steps. The resulting script is as shown in the following screenshot:

```
when   clicked
go to x: 8 y: 13
switch costume to Start Screen
show
set max_game_level to 4
set game_level to 1
set game_score to 0
set min_enemy_count to 3
set move_steps to 20
set frame_rate to 0.2
delete all of enemyTypeList
delete all of enemyCountList
delete all of enemyThresholdList
Configure Level: 1 enemyType: Rock enemyCount: 15 enemyThreshold 3
Configure Level: 2 enemyType: Monster enemyCount: 15 enemyThreshold 3
Configure Level: 3 enemyType: Robot enemyCount: 15 enemyThreshold 3
Configure Level: 4 enemyType: Mother Ship enemyCount: 1 enemyThreshold 1
```

Objective complete – mini debriefing

There, we did it! We have added two levels in three simple steps, check out the *Classified intel* section on updating *Space Age* to have more than seven levels.

Classified intel

The Enemy Ammo and Game Manager sprites come with enough costumes to go up to *seven* levels. This means that you can add up to seven levels with the steps described in this section.

To add more than seven levels, you need to add the matching number of costumes to both the Enemy Ammo and Game Manager sprites. For example, if you are really ambitious and want to have 100 levels in Space Age, you need to have at least 100 costumes for the Enemy Ammo and Game Manager sprites.

Mission accomplished

We have created a first-person shooter game utilizing game design concept and these main Scratch features: More Blocks, broadcast messages, timer, and list. We also learned how to easily add new enemies and levels to Space Age.

Now we are ready to test the complete Space Age game! Let's see if you are a good gamer who can beat his/her own game. Test each level to make sure each one works as expected.

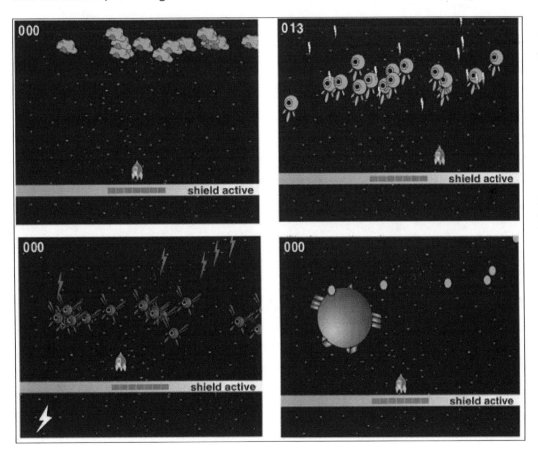

Hotshot challenges

You can take up the following challenges to improve your game:

▶ Add a new enemy by copying the existing enemy sprite and add another level using that new enemy sprite.

▶ Add a new enemy sprite based on the Mother Ship sprite, which flies in a pattern instead of falling straight down. Try updating the pattern.

▶ Add additional power up sprites.

Project 5
Shoot 'Em Up

This project will be the first part of a two-part game example. We are going to build a classic side-scrolling shooter game like Gradius (`http://gradius.wikia.com/wiki/Gradius`). This is an action-packed game that requires fast reflexes and quick responses not only from the player, but also from the computer that runs the game. We will see how much chaos we can create onscreen without the game slowing down to process all the mayhem.

Mission briefing

In this project, we will work on the basic game controls and add enemies and an environment. We will also create a power-up system, so that the player's character can get stronger during the game.

It is necessary for the player to get stronger because in the next project, we will create a challenging boss fight.

Why is it awesome?

This project will contain more different graphical elements than the previous examples. Next to the player character, we will add multiple enemies, several costumes for the player's weapon, and a layered environment consisting of multiple sprites.

We will use these varied graphics for several different purposes. The color of the enemies will show which type they are and what movement pattern the player can expect from them. The weapon costumes will show how powered up the weapon is.

Also with the multilayered background, we will create a **parallax scrolling** effect, giving the game an artificial perception of depth.

Your Hotshot objectives

We will build the game step by step; by first creating a player character, then adding enemies, and finally adding the environment. The following are our objectives:

- ▶ Creating a player character
- ▶ Creating an enemy
- ▶ Adding enemy patterns
- ▶ Shooting those baddies!
- ▶ Creating background images
- ▶ Using parallax scrolling to simulate depth
- ▶ Adding scores and power-ups
- ▶ Tweaking and balancing

Mission checklist

To speed up the process and allow us to focus on scripting, we will use the prepackaged Scratch sprites wherever we can. Only some background sprites will be hand drawn. Start with a new, blank Scratch project. Remove the Scratch cat as usual.

Creating a player character

The most important part of this game is the player character. This is the direct representation of the player in the game. The player can control the character and move it around. The player has to protect the character from harm to win the game.

Prepare for lift off

We will look for an interesting sprite in the Scratch library to use as the player character. The diver looks like an interesting choice since he is lying horizontally and facing right.

A perfect start for a side-scrolling game! The diver can be found in the **People** or **Underwater** category. There are two diver sprites. I choose the orange one, because it stands out better against a blue, watery background.

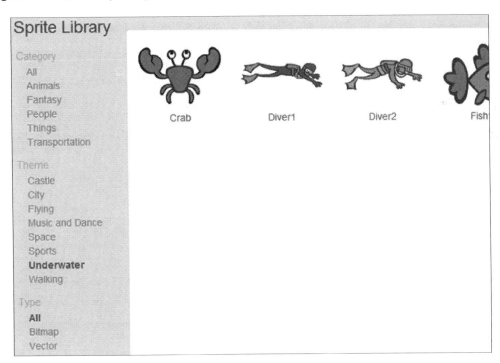

Engage thrusters

After adding the diver sprite to the stage, we can start scripting the player controls. This is a fairly straightforward process, as follows:

1. Start with a **when <green flag> clicked** block.
2. Scale the sprite down with a **set size to ()%** block; enter the value 30.
3. Then, reposition it to the left of the screen using the **go to x: () y: ()** block; enter the value -190 and 0 respectively.
4. Add a **forever** loop.
5. Inside the loop, we will place the keyboard controls. There will be four similar condition checks. One for each of the arrow keys.
6. Combine an **if () then** block with **when <up arrow> key pressed?**.
7. Inside the **if ()** statement, place a **change y by ()** block; enter the value 4.
8. Copy the construction thrice.
9. Add them all together, then place them inside the **forever** loop.
10. Change the arrow buttons checked in the copied **if ()** statements to account for all the four possible directions.
11. Change the direction that the character will face to the corresponding direction when the appropriate button is pressed. Replace the **change y by ()** blocks with the **change x by ()** blocks where appropriate.
12. Change the values in the **change x by ()** and **change y by ()** blocks as shown in the following screenshot:

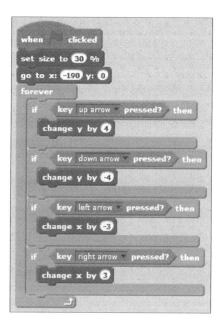

Objective complete – mini debriefing

Click on the script or on the **<green flag>** icon to test whether the script works correctly. With these simple steps, we created a controllable player character. If your character moves in the wrong direction, check again if you changed the script appropriately. The left and down direction should have negative values. Mixing this up can give odd results.

Classified intel

Why didn't we choose to use the much simpler movement script as shown in the following screenshot?

The reason is that the easy way doesn't have quite the same result, and that is because most keyboards have a peculiar way of operating. When you first press a key, the keyboard gives one impulse to the computer, then pauses for a little while. Only if you keep the key pressed, the keyboard will start giving impulses repetitively.

This pause is included to prevent you from accidentally typing a stream of letters when typing. Very useful for text editing but not so much when creating a game where you want responsive controls that react immediately to your input.

With our loop and if key pressed combination, we take control of this procedure that checks whether a button has been pressed and can make sure that the game will respond right away when a button is pressed, without pausing to wait for the next impulse coming from the keyboard.

Creating an enemy

The next step is to add an enemy for the player to dodge or defeat. We will look for another suitable watery character to continue the underwater theme of this game. We will make some changes to the appearance of the character and then write some movement scripts for the character.

Prepare for lift off

Let's search for a suitable enemy for the diver character using the following steps:

1. When we look through the library, we can find several interesting water creatures; crab, fish, shark, and starfish. Let's choose the starfish, because it can easily move in different directions without looking weird.

2. We will change the color of the sprite to be a bit darker than the default bright pink.

3. Go to the **Costumes** editor and choose a dark red color.

4. Make sure that you view the image in **Bitmap mode**. This will make a big difference to the running speed of the game when we create many starfish. You can toggle this with the buttons in the lower-right corner of the editor.

5. Select the Fill tool and fill the starfish with the red color. Recolor both costumes just for the sake of completion.

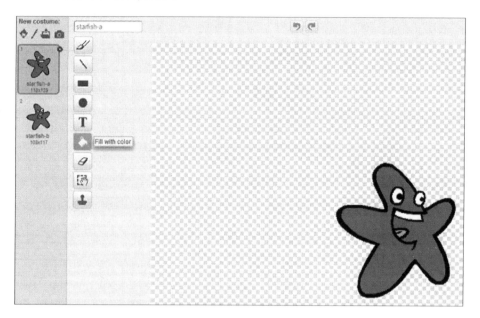

Engage thrusters

The original sprite will be placed on the right side of the screen. From there, we will use the cloning method to generate waves of starfish moving left towards the player character by following these steps:

1. Start with a **when <green flag> clicked** block.

2. Let's click on **hide** to make the sprite invisible when not needed.

3. Also, enter the value 30 in the **set size to ()%** block to make it smaller. It should be about the same size as the diver.

4. Add a **forever** loop to hold the clone generation script.

   We will make the sprite jump to a random location vertically, point in a somewhat random direction to the left, and then spawn five clones.

5. Set up the starting position using the **go to x: () y: ()** and **point in direction ()** blocks.

6. The x value will be 240, the right edge of the stage. The y value will be a random value between -180 and 180, the full y range of the stage.

7. The basic direction of the sprite will be to the left or -90. We will modify that value with a random range. The direction may deviate 30 degrees both ways. So we replace the fixed direction using the **pick random () to ()** block; enter the values -60 and -120 respectively.

8. We also need to change the sprites rotation style to left to right (the bi-directional arrow) in the sprite Properties panel. This makes sure the starfish isn't swimming upside down.

9. Next, repeat the creation of the clone five times by entering the value 5 in the **repeat()** block.

10. We will obviously include a **create clone of <myself>** block.

11. We will enter the value 0.2 in the **wait () secs** block and wait between each cloning process to put some space between the clones.

12. After the cloning process, wait for a random time between 1 and 3 seconds by entering the value 1 and 3 in the **wait pick random () to () secs** block respectively.

13. Put all steps of the cloning process inside the **forever** loop to make it run endlessly.

The following screenshot shows the final script:

Now we are ready to start moving those clones using the following steps:

1. Create a second script starting with a **when I start as a clone** block.

2. Let's first enable **show** to make the cloned sprites visible.

3. The clones' movements will repeat until it touches the edge as seen in the **repeat until touching <edge> ?** block.

4. The clone will move 5 steps each cycle (using the **move 5 steps** block).

5. When the touching condition is met, we will delete this clone by using the **delete this clone** block.

Test the game and you will discover that there is a problem. The clones won't show up or even if it does, only briefly. What is happening? Why are they disappearing so quickly? The answer is easy. We just instructed the clones to delete themselves when they are touching an edge. The clones start their life on the right edge of the stage, so they are immediately deleted after creation.

We can fix this problem by adding another loop to the script as shown in the following steps:

1. Before the **repeat until ()** block, place a **repeat ()** block; enter the value 10.

2. Inside the block, place a **move () steps** block; enter the value 5.

This will ensure that the clones will first move *10 x 5 = 50* steps. This gives them enough room to clear the right edge before starting to check for collision with the edge.

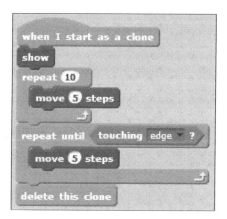

Objective complete – mini debriefing

The first wave of enemies are now happily flying across the screen. We will add a bit more functionality later. The enemies will be able to kill the player character upon touching him, and likewise, they may be killed by the player if he uses his weapon.

But let's first add a few different enemies.

Adding enemy patterns

We will create two more enemy types that follow different attack patterns. The starfish in our first sprite are moving in a straight line one after the other. For the second enemy sprite, we will create a script that causes that enemy to spread out, making it a bit harder to avoid. For the third enemy, we will write a script that makes this enemy type a bit unpredictable, moving in a wavy pattern and turning unexpectedly.

Prepare for lift off

Before we begin scripting, we need two more enemy sprites, which we will create using the following steps:

1. Right-click on the **Starfish** sprite and choose **duplicate**. Do this twice to create two more enemy sprites, including the enemy sprite scripts.

2. To differentiate between the three enemy types, we will recolor the second and third sprites.

3. For the second sprite, we select a blue color and fill the body of the sprite with it.

4. For the third sprite, we select a yellow color and do the same.

The sprites are automatically renamed as **Starfish2** and **Starfish3** as shown in the following screenshot. This is fine for our purposes, so there is no need to manually change the names.

Engage thrusters

We can now modify the script to create varied movement patterns. The basic idea stays the same. We generate a few clones over time that move across the screen independently based on their instructions.

Let's change the script for the blue enemy sprite to make the clones spread out instead of following behind each other:

1. Go to the **Scripts** tab of Starfish2.

2. Add a **turn <clockwise>** block to the **repeat** loop, just before the **create clone of <myself>** block.

3. Take the **pick random () to ()** block, which has the values -30 and 30 respectively, out of the **point in direction ()** block and place it inside the **turn <clockwise>** block.

4. Remove the + operator block.

5. Make sure that the direction the sprite will initially point to is -90 degrees (towards the left side).

6. Change the number of repeats to 3 in the **repeat ()** block.

7. Also change the wait time before the next clone is created to 0.3 in the **wait () secs** block.

The following screenshot shows the final script:

These enemies will spawn a bit slower and in smaller groups than the red enemies. With a small addition to the script, they also have a very different movement pattern. The blue enemies will start moving at different angles. This makes them spread out as they advance.

The yellow enemy will also take the red enemy script as a basis. To make this enemy move even more erratically, we will place a turn command inside the clones instead of placing it inside the original sprite.

We will focus our attention on the clone script first.

1. At the start of the **repeat until ()** block, place a **turn <clockwise>** block.

2. Now we drag the **pick random () to ()** block, which contains the values -30 to 30 respectively, from the **point in direction ()** block in the **<green flag>** script to the newly created turn block inside the clone script.

3. Change the numbers to -10 and 10 to decrease the angle variation.

4. In the **<green flag>** script, we will also change the number of repeats and the wait time just like we did for the blue sprite.

5. Also, remove the remains of the calculation we plundered and make sure the sprite initially points to -90 (left) degrees.

6. Also, change the movement speed in the clone script from 5 to 4.

The following screenshot shows the final scripts:

As a final step in this project, let's make the enemies an actual threat to the player. When an enemy touches the player sprite, it should be *game over* for the player. Now that we have created all enemies, we can easily check for collisions with them.

1. Go to the **Scripts** tab of the diver sprite.

2. We replace the **forever** block with a **repeat until ()** condition block. But make sure to set aside the keyboard control script for reuse.

3. In the condition slot, we check whether the diver is touching any of the starfish sprites. This requires two **or** operators, so we have three condition slots; one for each sprite.

4. Reset the keyboard controls inside the **repeat** loop.

5. To finish off, when the condition is met, this script should stop all scripts by using the **stop <all>** block.

When a starfish touches the diver, the game will freeze immediately by effectively ending the game.

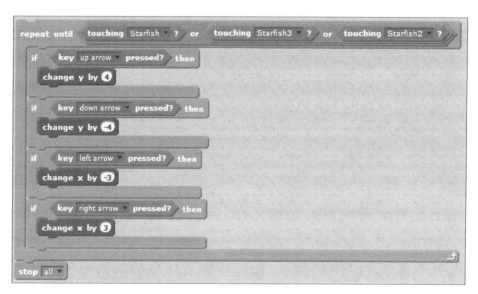

Objective complete – mini debriefing

We now have three similar yet distinct enemies to challenge the player. Run the game with the **<green flag>** button to see all of them go at once.

This project shows that a few simple changes can have big results for your game. It's often not necessary to invent a completely new script for each sprite. Clever copying and reusing of what you already made can save you a lot of time.

Shooting those baddies!

Now that we have enemies, we need to create a way to get rid of them. Let's create a weapon for your player character, which he can fire at the enemies to remove them.

At the end of this project, we will also write a script so that the enemies can hurt the player.

Prepare for lift off

For the weapon, we will again search for a sprite from the Scratch library. With a few changes, this can be turned into a spear for the diver to use.

1. Click on the **choose sprite from library** icon.

2. Browse the **Things** category to search for a suitable projectile.

3. The **Magic Wand** looks like a useful option so we pick that.

Magic Wand

4. Change the name of the sprite to `Spear`.

5. Next, open the **Costumes** editor to make some changes to the picture.

6. Check whether the editor is in **Vector Mode**.

7. First, we use **Select** to select the image and then use **Ungroup**.

8. Then, we can use **Select** to select the yellow lightning bolts individually and delete them by clicking on the *Delete* button.

9. We change the colors to match to that of the diver's more closely. Change the shaft to orange, the tip to yellow, and choose a dark orange or brown color for the outline. Use the **Color a shape** tool to apply the changes.

The modified spear is now ready for duty.

Engage thrusters

We will allow the player to fire a spear from the diver's position when pressing the Space bar. When the spear hits an enemy, the enemy will be removed immediately (and possibly the player will earn a point). But we will work on that later.

1. Switch to the **Scripts** tab and start a new script with a **when <green flag> clicked** block.

2. We will use the cloning technique, so let's first click on **hide** to hide the spear.

3. We also set the size to 30% in the **set size to ()%** block to make it to scale with the diver and starfish.

4. Next, we add a **forever** loop that will contain the cloning process.

5. Inside the loop, we add a **go to <Diver2>** block so that the spear sprite will always follow the diver sprite.

6. We also enter the value 90 in the **point in direction ()** block to make the spear always face right.

7. We add an **if () then** condition to check for player input.

8. We will check when the key is pressed using the **key <space> pressed?** block.

9. If this is true, then we add a **create clone of <myself>** block.

10. Finally, enter the value 0.5 in the **wait () seconds** block and wait so that there is a little delay between the creation of each clone.

The following screenshot shows the final script:

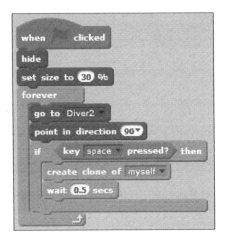

To set the clones in motion, we create a second script as follows:

1. We start with a **when I start as a clone** block.

2. We will enable the **show** block to show the clones which were previously hidden.

3. Next, we add a **repeat until ()** loop.

4. For the condition, we choose **touching <edge>**.

5. So we can delete this clone when it touches the right edge of the stage using the **delete this clone** block.

6. Inside the loop, we place a **move () steps** block to make the spear move forward; enter the value 5 in it.

The following screenshot shows the final script:

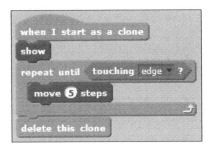

Test the game briefly to see whether the spear behaves as we expect it to. The spear should start from the player position and then move in a straight line to the right until it reaches the edge and is removed.

We can hold down the Space bar, but because of the wait block placed after the clone block, a spear will only be created after every 0.5 seconds.

Now to make the enemies respond to being hit by the spears, we make an addition to their script. This addition should be placed inside the **repeat until ()** block of the **when I start as a clone** script since we will want to constantly check for a hit as long as the enemy clone is around.

1.   We add an **if () then** condition.

2.   We will check whether an enemy clone is touching the spear by using the **touching <Spear>** block.

3.   If that is the case, then we will delete this clone immediately by using the **delete this clone** block.

4.   This script is same for all the three enemy types, so we will add it to all the three enemy clone scripts. Remember that you can drag-and-drop a piece of script on a sprite to copy it.

The following screenshot shows the final script:

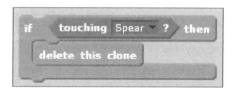

Objective complete – mini debriefing

When we try the game again, the enemies can now be destroyed by the spears.

Creating background images

To create a better sense of movement, we will make a scrolling background. This requires two identical background images that will be sliding horizontally across the stage. As we want to move these backgrounds around, we won't be creating them as actual background images but as sprites instead. Sprites can be moved with scripts, while background images cannot be moved.

Prepare for lift off

Let's create the image first. What we need is something that looks like an underwater view. So the main color should be blue, with a lighter shade of blue to the top resembling sunlight shining on the water surface. I also added a light brown strip to the bottom to resemble sand.

To create this image, I used Photoshop. However, if you don't have an external image editor, you can also create a similar image in Scratch. The most important thing to take note of is to make the image as big as the stage, that is, 480 pixels wide and 360 pixels high.

It's also worthwhile to spend some time lining up the left and right edges of the image, so you won't see the break line when the image starts scrolling. Most image editors like Photoshop have a useful offset option that allows you to slide a set amount of pixels in the image horizontally and/or vertically. It will be very easy to fix the edge line this way.

Unfortunately, the Scratch editor doesn't have this option. In this case, you may want to keep the image simple, using only straight horizontal shapes, so there won't be any height differences. You could also try to cut the image in half and switch the halves around. This way, you can put the edges together and fix them. The cut you made should already be properly lined up.

This step can take some time but mostly relies on your own creative freedom and experience with editing images. Don't worry about it too much and do the best you can. It's not a big problem if you still see an edge at the end. Actually, it would be pretty useful to see the script that we write in action. You could also use the resource file that comes with this project.

Engage thrusters

For the scrolling background, we will need two identical images with slightly different scripts. The easiest way to create this is to write one script first. Then, copy the image including the script and make the necessary changes.

1. Start with a **when <green flag> clicked** block.

2. Define a variable called `speedMultiplier`. Remember that the button to do this is in the **Data** category. This variable should be for this sprite only.

3. Enter `0.5` in the **set <speedMultiplier> to ()** block.

4. Make the image go back 100 layers by entering `100` in the **go back () layers** block. We just use a suitably high number so that the image is placed behind all other sprites on the stage.

5. Then, we position the image to its starting point with the **go to x: () y: ()** block; enter `-240` and `0` respectively. So the center of the image is at the left edge of the stage.

6. We add a **forever** loop, which will contain the movement script.

7. First we need another variable called `scrollingSpeed`. This variable should be for all sprites. We will use it as a base speed value.

8. At each step of the loop, **change x by ()**. The blank slot will take a value that still has to be determined.

9. Here we include a calculation—*scrollingSpeed * speedMultiplier*. We use the multiplier to slow down the background image compared to the scrolling speed of the base. Remember we set it to `0.5` so the background will move at half of the speed.

When the image has scrolled completely out of view, we have to reset it to the right of the stage so that it can scroll in again. To do this, we check where the image is. Also, if it has reached a certain limit, we move it to the right of the stage.

1. We place an **if () then** condition check underneath the **change x by ()** block.

2. Inside the condition, we check whether x position (from the Motion category) is less than -460 by entering `-460` in the **x position < ()** block.

3. If so, then we set x to 500 by entering `500` in the **set x to ()** block.

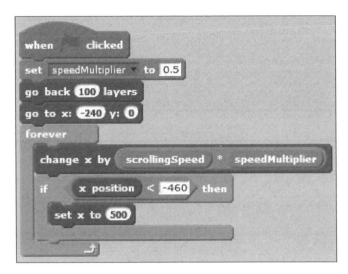

That concludes the first background script. Click on it to test and you will see that nothing happens. We didn't set the scrolling speed yet, so its value is zero, which means there will be no movement. As this variable is universal, we will set it in the stage object. We will use the stage object as a referee, controlling basic values and actions like we did in earlier examples.

1. Click on the **Stage** object and go to the **Scripts** editor.
2. Start with a **when <green flag> clicked** block.
3. Then, we set the scrolling speed to -2 in the **set <scrollingSpeed> to ()** block. We use a negative value because we want the background (and all other objects still to come) to scroll left.

The following screenshot shows the final script:

That was all we needed to add to make the script work. Let's test it again. We'll see that the background sliding towards the left until it is out of view. Then it comes sliding in from the right again.

The only thing left to do is copy the background sprite and make a change to the script. We'll do this using the following steps:

1. Right-click the background sprite and choose **duplicate**.

2. Change the starting value of x from -240 to 240 in the **go to x: () y: ()** block. This will cause the second background to start with its center at the right edge of the stage.

The following screenshot shows the finished script:

Objective complete – mini debriefing

As the two background images start at the opposite edges of the stage and as they are each as big as the stage, they will cover half of the stage area. The other half of both images is out of view beyond the stage edges.

When both the images are activated simultaneously with the **<green flag>** action, they will start moving, following behind each other. Both images are 480 pixels wide. The first image will start with its center point on the left edge (x: -240), showing only the right half of the image. The second image will start with its center point on the right edge (x: 240), showing only the left half of the image. Their borders line up perfectly in the middle when the program starts. Also, as they use the same scrolling speed, they will remain that way, as if glued together. When the image disappears completely out of view, it jumps to the right of the stage, ready to scroll in for another pass. This creates the illusion of a continuously scrolling background.

Using parallax scrolling to simulate depth

To increase the sense of movement and depth, we are going to use a technique called **parallax scrolling**. This means that objects will move at different speeds based on their distance from the viewer. In real life, you can see this phenomenon when you are riding in a train or a car. When looking out of the side window, you will notice that objects that are close to the vehicle seem to be moving past a lot faster than objects that are further in the distance. Objects on the horizon hardly seem to move at all.

This relative movement is what we perceive as depth or distance. It allows us to guess the three-dimensional proportions of a space. We are going to simulate that 3D effect with our 2D sprites to make the scene a bit more realistic and engaging.

Prepare for lift off

First we need some more sprites to use as objects moving past the viewer. Let's create some rocks and seaweed that we can place along the floor of the scene.

1.   Choose a new sprite from the Scratch library. Let's use the **Rocks** sprite.

2.   We need a few different costumes for the sprite. Go to the **Costumes** tab, right-click on the costume, and choose **duplicate**.

3.   Click on the **flip left-right** button to mirror the second costume.

4.   Make two more duplicates of these costumes. Scale both down a bit with the **Select** tool.

5.   Make sure to set the center point at the bottom middle of each costume with the **Set costume center** tool. This will make sure we have better control over the height position of each sprite.

6.   There is no library image for seaweed, so we will have to draw those ourselves.

7.   Click on **paint new costume** to create a new empty costume canvas.

8.   In **Vector Mode**, we draw a circular outline using the **Ellipse** tool.

9.   We fill the ellipse with a lighter shade of green.

10.   Then, we switch to the **Reshape** tool as shown in the preceding screenshot. Some draggable circles show up along the edge of the shape.

11.   Let's move the circles around to twist and stretch the shape until it resembles seaweed. We can also add more circles by dragging the edge where there is no circle yet. Dragging the outline will cause a new circle to be created. Double-clicking on a circle will remove it.

The result should look something like the following screenshot:

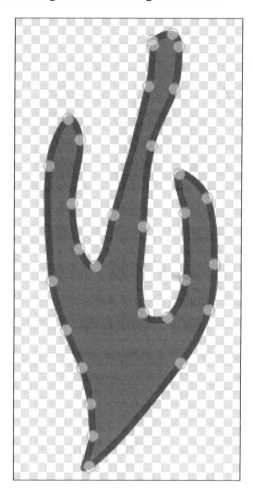

Once we are happy with our first seaweed drawing, we will create another with a slightly different shape and color.

Six different costumes should be enough to create a nicely varied background as shown in the following screenshot:

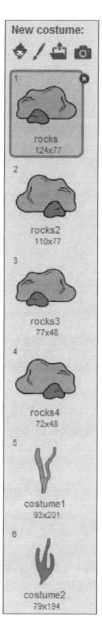

Engage thrusters

Let's move on to the scripting. We will use the cloning method again to create multiple objects from a base sprite shown as follows:

1. As usual we start with a **when <green flag> clicked** block.

2. First, we click on **hide** to hide the original sprite from view.

3. Then, we make it go to front to place it on top of everything else using the **go to front** block.

4. Next, we make it go back five layers by entering 5 in the **go back () layers** block. This is to make sure that the sprite will be at the depth where we want it to be. If the sprites are not layered properly, the parallax effect will look weird.

5. We position the sprite at its starting place with a **go to x: () y:()** command; enter 240 and -150 respectively.

6. This sprite also needs its personal `speedMultiplier` variable, just like the background images.

7. After creating the variable, we set its value to 2.

8. After this, we will start the **forever** loop, which will spawn the clones.

9. We add the **wait () secs** block.

10. For the empty slot, we pick the random numbers 1 and 5. These values give good results.

11. We also change the height to a random number between -170 and -130.

12. Also, we switch to a random costume, numbered 1 to 6.

13. After all these randomized choices are made, we can create our clone by using the **create a clone of <myself>** block.

That concludes the base sprite script. Next we will create a clone script. This will control how the clones will move, just like in the previous examples.

1. We first need to define a variable called `position` only for this sprite. This variable will store a virtual x position value. We use this method to allow a value to go beyond the borders of the stage.

2. We will start a new script by using the **when I start as a clone** block.

3. We will set the position to `300` in the **set <position> to()** block. This is beyond the right border of the stage.

4. Then, enable the **show** block to show the cloned sprite.

5. We will move the clone inside a **repeat until ()** loop.

6. We first change the position variable by **scrollingSpeed * speedMultiplier.**

7. Then, we set x to **position** using the **set x to ()** block.

8. To fill the condition slot, we check when the position is less than -300 by entering `-300` in the **position < ()** block.

9. When that happens, we can delete this clone by using the **delete this clone** block as it is beyond the left edge of the stage.

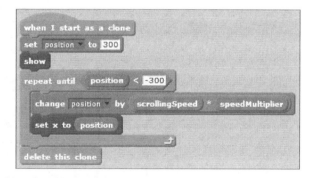

Our first scrolling sprite is now finished. Test the script and we will see that the rocks and seaweed move a lot faster than the background image.

To make full use of the effect, we need a few more layers of objects though. We will create a few more background objects moving at different speeds:

1. Let's copy the **Rocks** sprite twice.

For the first copy, we edit the script in a few places.

2. We make the sprite go back 10 layers instead of 5 by entering `10` in the **go back ()
   layers** block.

3. We enter `80` in the **set size to () %** block to make the sprites a bit smaller.
   These objects are a bit further in the distance.

4. We will emphasize by placing them a bit higher on the stage. We change its
   starting y value to `-100`.

5. These objects will also move a bit slower because they are more distant,
   so we change the value of `speedMultiplier` to `1.5`.

6. We also need to change the random height range to correspond with the
   new basic height. A value between `-90` and `-110` should be okay.

For the second copy, we make similar changes with the following values:

- Enter `15` in the **go back ()layers** block
- Enter `60` in the **set size to ()** block
- Change the starting value of y to `70`
- Change the value of `speedMultiplier` to `1`
- Enter the values `-60` and `-80` for the height range

The parallax background is now ready to go as shown in the following screenshot:

Objective complete – mini debriefing

We added a lot of graphical spectacle in this project, but after the initial effort it took to create the sprites, the scripting is fairly simple. All sprites behave the same. They just use different values based on where they are on the screen. You could even add more layers if you wish. Just keep in mind that all those clones require the computer's attention. When there are too many, you will notice that the game starts slowing down and skipping frames.

Something you might want to try is adding to or changing the costumes. The intensity of the effect depends a lot on the kind of images used. More horizontal images can increase the perception of depth in the scene while vertical objects in the foreground will increase the sense of speed.

Classified intel

A nice add-on is to create large silhouette shapes in the foreground. These objects should use a script similar to the scrolling background images. Like those background images, they will also need two identical sprites to scroll seamlessly.

First, we need to create the image. This will be a hand-drawn image as big as the stage. Let's draw a rocky floor in the Bitmap mode. The floor can contain a few outcrops and spires that obscure a part of the stage. This makes the complete scene more interesting. But we need to be careful about not obscuring too much of the important stuff like the diver and the starfish.

After creating the foreground images, we can drag-copy the script from the background to the new sprite.

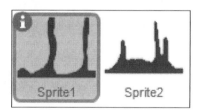

We make a few additions to this script that we take from the parallax scrolling script:

1. The images should be in the **front** layer.

2. The `speedMultiplier` value should be quite high, somewhere between 2.5 and 4 works well; enter `4`.

3. Check whether the starting x positions for both foreground images are correct; enter `-240` and `240` respectively.

4. It's also possible to add multiple costumes that are chosen randomly on each loop. We can add a **switch costume to ()** block inside the **if ()** statement, after the x position in the **x position < ()** block is reset. This functionality is taken from the parallax scrolling objects.

The following screenshot shows the final script:

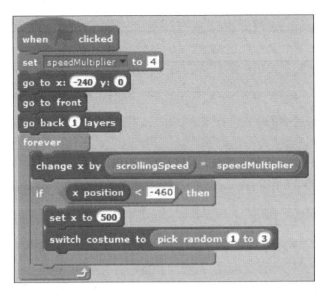

Adding scores and power-ups

To prepare for the upcoming boss battle (next project), it's a nice touch to power up the player character. A power-up system also offers a better reason for shooting enemies apart from the need for survival.

Engage thrusters

We will assign a score value to each enemy type. The player can increase the score by shooting the enemy of the corresponding type. When the player has defeated enough enemies, the spear will be powered up in some way.

1. We have three different enemy types, so we will first create the following three new variables to hold the scores. These variables are available for all sprites.

   ❑ scoreRed

   ❑ scoreBlue

   ❑ scoreYellow

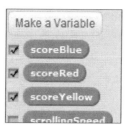

2. Click on the checkboxes in front of the new variables to make them visible on the stage. This way we can keep track of our scores.

3. At the start of the game, we set the values of these variables to 0 as shown in the following screenshot. The best place to do this is inside the stage object.

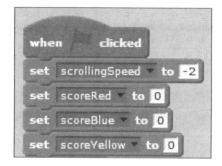

4. Next, we will add a point to the correct variable when an enemy is defeated. We already built a script to check when an enemy is touched by a spear sprite.

5. Just before we delete this clone, we only need to change the correct variable by 1 point in the **change <scoreRed> by ()** block as shown in the following screenshot:

It should be obvious that the scoreRed variable is meant for a red starfish. For the other two colors, we would use scoreBlue and scoreYellow variables respectively.

Now that the score values are increasing as enemies are defeated, we can use those values to increase the power of the spear. Each score value/color will have a different effect on the spear. These effects are as follows:

- The `scoreRed` value will influence how quickly the player can shoot another spear
- The `scoreBlue` value will determine when the spear will be upgraded to a new costume
- The `scoreYellow` value will increase the number of spears shot simultaneously

Let's start scripting the scoring system into the spear sprite. We will tackle the `scoreRed` functionality first. As the `scoreRed` value increases, spears will be spawned at a faster rate. We put a limit of 30 on the value to prevent the spawn rate from increasing to absurd levels.

1. We start this piece of script with an **if () then () else ()** condition block.

2. We use this block to check whether `scoreRed` is less than 30 by entering 30 in the **scoreRed < () block**. We now allow the script to calculate the spawn rate.

3. If this is true, we calculate the spawn rate based on the `scoreRed` value as follows:

   1. First, divide the `scoreRed` value by 30.

   2. Then, deduct the result from a base value of 1.5.

   3. We wrap this calculation in a **wait () secs** block to cause the delay between spawns.

The order of the preceding calculation operators is very important. The operator blocks will be processed from the innermost block to the outer blocks. The result is the number of seconds we have to wait for a new spear to appear.

1. Take the **wait () secs** block and place it inside the **else** bracket to create a minimum spawn time of 0.5 seconds when the `scoreRed` value exceeds 30.

2. Place this piece of script where the **wait 0.5 secs** block was, right underneath the **create clone of <myself>** block.

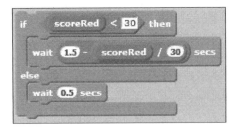

Next, we will handle the `scoreBlue` effect. For this effect, we need to draw a second costume as follows:

1. We switch to the **Costumes** tab of the spear sprite and use **duplicate** to create a copy of the costume.

2. We recolor the second costume in blue tones using the **Color a shape** tool.

3. Naming is important here. We name the first sprite as `basic spear`. The second sprite will be called `ice spear`.

4. Go back to the **Scripts** tab to write a script for switching between these two costumes.

5. We start with an **if () then ()** block to check the `scoreBlue` value. An **else ()** block is not needed in this case.

6. We will enter `29` in the **scoreBlue > ()** block.

7. Inside the condition check, we place a **switch costume to <ice spear>** block.

8. We place this **if ()** statement inside the **forever** loop. It's not relevant if the Space bar is pressed for this functionality.

9. When we change the appearance of the sprite, we also need to make sure that it's set to its basic appearance at the start of the game. We add a **switch costume to <basic spear>** block at the start of the script.

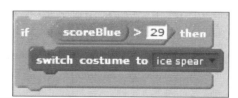

The script for the `scoreYellow` value is the most complicated. Not only do we need to create multiple clones when the score reaches a certain value, but we also need to reposition and angle the clones so they don't overlap on exactly the same spot.

When the score reaches 15, we will start creating two spears at once. We will angle them outwards a bit, so they move forward in a V shape.

When the score reaches 30, we will create three spears at once. One spear will move straight ahead, while the other two will move outward in a V shape.

1. Let's grab another **if () then () else ()** block.

2. Place the **create clone of <myself>** block inside the **else ()** bracket. This will be the default condition for creating one clone when all other conditions fail. This happens when the score is still smaller than 15.

3. Inside the condition block, we check if `scoreYellow` is greater than 14 by entering 14 in the **scoreYellow > ()** block.

4. If that is the case, we will create two clones at an angle as follows:

   1. First, we enter 15 in the **turn <counter clockwise> () degrees** block to turn the sprite upwards a bit.

   2. Then, create your clone by using the **create clone of <myself>** block.

   3. Next, enter 30 in the **turn <clockwise> () degrees** block to angle the same distance downwards.

   4. Again create your clone by using the **create clone of <myself>** block.

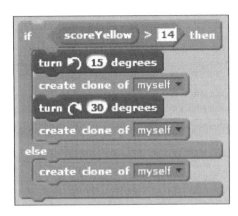

We leave this script for a moment before we place it in its proper spot.

Now on to scripting what happens when the `scoreYellow` value reaches 30.

1. Again, we need an **if () then () else ()** condition block. The quick way to get what we want is to right-click on the piece we just wrote and then on **duplicate**.

2. Then, we change the value to 29 instead of 14.

3. We add another **create clone of <myself>** block at the start of the **if ()** bracket to create a clone that will move straight ahead.

4. We change the position of the other two clones to spread them out a bit using the follow steps. This way they won't overlap at the start of their movement, which looks a bit nicer.

   1. Add **change y by ()** with value 10 to move the upward angled clone up a bit.

2. Then, add **change y by ()** with value -20 to move the downward clone down an equal distance from the original position.

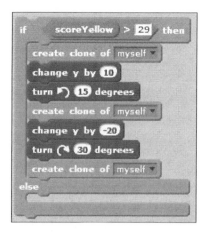

5. Remove the **create clone of <myself>** block from the **else ()** bracket.

6. Replace it with the other **if () then () else ()** condition script.

That completes our scripting for the `scoreYellow` value. The completed result will look as shown in the following screenshot. Make sure that all blocks are sorted in the correct order or the script might behave strangely.

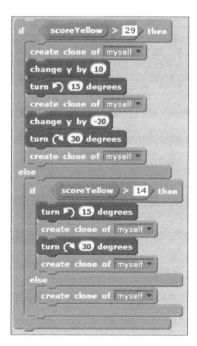

Objective complete – mini debriefing

Test the script to see the scores increase as you shoot enemies. Also note how the behavior of the spear changes as you reach certain score values.

The following is a screenshot of the entire stack of scoring scripts we just built. It looks quite intimidating when viewed as a whole, but because we broke it down into separate steps, it became a lot easier to deal with.

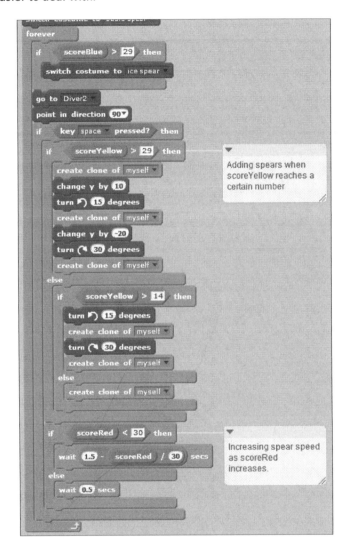

If you have trouble staying alive while testing this script, detach the **stop <all>** block from the diver script. This will prevent the game from stopping when the diver is touched by a starfish.

Classified intel

The order in which the condition checks for the `scoreYellow` value are placed is very important. Since the score is increasing from 0 upwards, we first need to check the highest value (> 29), which is the last condition to be achieved. When this condition is not met, the script will then check if `scoreYellow` has reached 15 yet. And if that's not the case either, it will default the basic, innermost, else condition.

If we switched these checks around, the **>29** condition would never be reached because the **>14** condition would resolve and throw us out of the loop before we reached the other condition check.

Tweaking and balancing

To finish this project, we will add a few more details to prepare for the next project. In the next project, we want to add a boss fight to this game; but when should the boss appear? I've decided to make this a timed event. The player should survive for a certain amount of time, shooting enemies along the way to increase the power of the spear. After 90 seconds, the starfish will disappear and a boss monster will appear.

You may have also noticed that the scrolling images tend to stick to the sides of the stage before disappearing. This is a feature of Scratch to prevent you from completely losing sight of sprites. To get rid of these lingering sprites, we use a visual trick to obscure them.

Engage thrusters

Let's first work on the time limit to complete our game. We will use the built-in timer to count the seconds until the boss appears.

1. Go to the **Stage** object to add some scripts.

2. We first reset the timer (using the **reset timer** block) to start counting from 0 when the game starts.

3. Then, we let the script wait until the timer is greater than 90 by entering 90 in the **wait until timer > ()** block.

4. If the condition is met, we use the **stop <all>** block for the moment. The level is finished. We will change this action with a script for the boss's appearance in the next project.

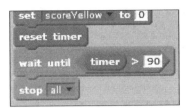

To get rid of the lingering images, we will draw curtains similar to what you would see on a theater stage. This narrows the effective stage area somewhat, but that's not a problem, and the sprites can safely stay behind the curtains, out of view.

1. We paint a new sprite. This sprite will be as big as the stage.

2. Click on the **zoom out** icon to see the entire stage in the costumes editor.

3. We make sure that we are working in the Bitmap mode.

4. With the Rectangle tool, we draw two black vertical strips at either side of the stage area. Finding the right width to obscure the sprites can take a bit of testing and changing the size of the strips.

We add a short script to correctly position the sprite at the start of the game using the following steps:

1. Start with the **when <green flag> clicked** block.

2. Enter 0 and 0 in the **go to x: () y: ()** block respectively.

3. Enable the **go to front** block. This makes sure that the curtains are on top of everything else.

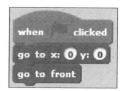

Objective complete – mini debriefing

With these additions, we conclude this project. There is still more work to do, but what we have created in this project already makes for an enjoyable game. Adding the timer gives us a clear endpoint for the game and emphasizes the game goal—gather as many points as possible before the timer runs out.

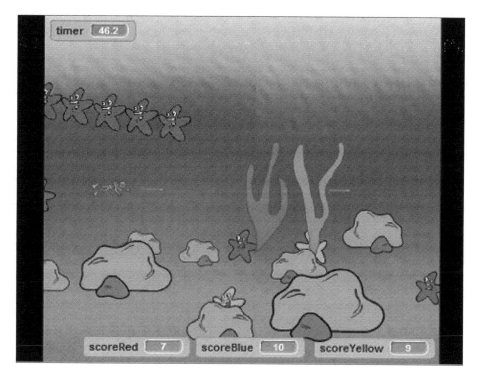

Mission accomplished

We created a dynamic action game with many different elements. Not only did we create a player character, enemies, and a weapon but we also spent some more time on making an interesting moving environment. The environment doesn't really add to the gameplay, but it can add a lot to the atmosphere of the game.

We saw how cleverly copying sprites and changing their scripts can gain us a lot of action and variety within a short time. The hardest part in this kind of game is to maintain balance. We want to create a dynamic environment where a lot is going on at once. The player needs to feel he can win the game. We also need to keep in mind that all those clones flying around can be hard on the computer processor. At some point, the game will slow down noticeably. We need to balance all these factors to create an enjoyable game experience.

Hotshot challenges

Speaking of balancing, you might want to change some of the values we used.

Perhaps you want to use different score limits to make it harder or easier to power up the spear.

You could also change the attack patterns of the starfish—play around with the numbers and instructions, and discover what patterns you can come up with.

Perhaps you have also noticed that we haven't actually done anything gamewise with the `scoreBlue` value. We changed the appearance of the spear when a certain score is reached, but this doesn't actually make any difference to the game. How will you use this new ice spear?

Project 6
Building a Worthy Boss

In this project, we will add another stage to the game that we created in the previous project. Having a good shootout is a lot of fun, but it can't really end without a challenging boss battle. We are going to create that boss battle in this project.

Our boss won't be quite as big and impressive as the following R-Type example (http://en.wikipedia.org/wiki/R-Type), but it will offer any budding space hero a serious challenge:

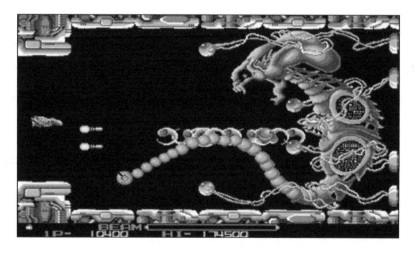

Mission briefing

We will work with some new elements that haven't yet played a part in previous projects. We will look at sending messages between different objects, and create a temporary script that will help us to make it easier to test our work in this two-part game.

Why is it awesome?

No shooter game is complete without a good boss fight. Not only should this be a memorable experience for the players, but it should also create a spectacular encounter that is a very focused and enjoyable process.

Creating a boss is quite different from creating general enemies. The boss is more resilient, so it will stay on screen longer. It requires more attention to its appearance, and the way it moves about the screen often plays a very big part in the gameplay.

Your Hotshot objectives

We will first set up the new elements in this project. When that's done, we continue creating the boss character and its behavior. The objectives are listed as follows:

- Sending a message
- Adding a test script
- Creating the boss
- Creating attack pattern 1
- Creating attack pattern 2
- Creating attack pattern 3
- Making the boss more impressive
- Defeating the boss

Mission checklist

This project continues from the previous one. So to start with, we load the end result of that project.

Sending a message

Sometimes, you don't want a script to start working right from the start of the game. For such cases, you can trigger a script by sending a message, instead of just starting it when the **<green flag>** button is pressed. This way, the script will stay dormant and inactive until it receives the right message. You can actually compare this to someone yelling a certain order that the script has to respond to. In this section, we will postpone the appearance of the boss monster until certain game conditions are met.

Prepare for lift off

Messages are part of the **Events** category. Let's go there and see what we have to work with. Near the bottom of the list are three message blocks; one starting block (with the curved top) that can receive a message, and two broadcasters immediately below that can shout a message to all the scripts.

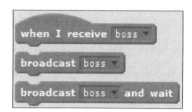

Engage thrusters

We will use these messages to differentiate between the two states of the game. The player can either fight waves of enemies or the boss. Depending on the case, certain scripts have to be made active/inactive:

1. We go to the **Stage** script to set up the broadcasts.

2. First, we throw away the **stop <all>** block. This is just a temporary means of ending the game.

3. In its place, we will use the **broadcast ()** block.

4. We have to create another message using **New Message**. This can be any kind of word or even a single letter or number:

5. To make clear what we are calling it, let's name it boss. This message should summon the boss's state in the game.

6. Before we get there, we also need to summon the waves. So we create another **broadcast** message.

7. This will hold a new message named waves.

8. We place this block right after the **reset timer** block that signifies the start of the game.

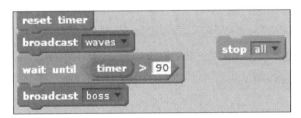

To make use of these broadcasts, someone (or something) has to listen to them. The important sprites that need to respond to the messages are the Starfish enemies and the boss, which are yet to be created:

1. We click on the **Starfish** sprite to switch to its **Scripts** tab.

2. We detach the script from the **when <green flag> clicked** block and throw away the block.

3. In its place, we attach a **when I receive <waves>** block.

4. Now this script will wait for the message instead of starting when the **<green flag>** is clicked on.

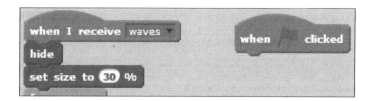

To stop and remove the Starfish enemies when the boss phase of the game is reached, we need to add a third script as follows:

1. Start with another **when I receive ()** block.

2. We now choose the other message called **boss**.

3. When this message is received, we first hide the sprite (using **hide**).

4. Then we use **stop <other scripts in sprite>** to stop the starfish from working.

5. We can copy this script to the other two starfish enemies.

6. We also need to replace the **when <green flag> clicked** block with a **when I receive <waves>** block, just like the first enemy.

The final script will look like the following screenshot:

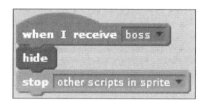

Objective complete – mini debriefing

When we test the game again, we won't notice any difference. Starting the game will still spawn enemies wave after wave, provided we set up everything properly. If we can survive until the timer reaches 90 seconds, we will see a change. At this point, the **boss** message will be broadcast. The enemies will respond by disappearing.

The diver can still move about, and the background will keep scrolling. Other than this, nothing exciting happens. We will change that in the rest of this project.

Adding a test script

Before we dive into the excitement of creating the boss enemy, let's first do something smart and create a script that helps us to test the boss that we create.

Prepare for lift off

As you may have noticed while testing the game, waiting 90 seconds for the boss to appear is a rather long time. We could just decrease the wait time in the script, but that has a few drawbacks.

It would be more difficult to test the wave phase of the game, since the timer runs for such a short time.

We run the risk of forgetting to change the timer before finally publishing the game.

A better option is to create a separate **temporary script** that we can throw away when we have finished the game without any risk to all our hard work.

Engage thrusters

We will add this script to the **Stage** sprite. This is often the best place for these kinds of control scripts.

When a certain button is pressed, we will change the ordinary flow of things, as follows:

1. Start a new script with a **when <b> key pressed** block. We can use any available key. In this case, "b" stands for "boss", as a handy reminder about what we are trying to do.

2. We set the three score values (using **set () to ()**). This is similar to the **when <green flag> clicked** script next to it.

3. Instead of supplying a fixed number, we will use **pick a random number between () and ()** and fill in the values 1 and 30 respectively. This way, we fake having scored some points during the game, so we can see the effects of the upgraded spear on the boss.

4. Then we use **broadcast <boss>** to start the boss phase immediately.

The final script will look like the following screenshot:

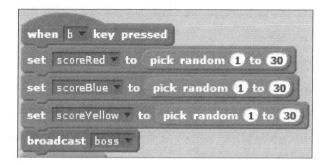

This is all that is absolutely necessary for this script. As you can see, the timer is still running and will eventually reach 90. This would cause the boss message to be called again. We don't want that as it could cause strange results. So, we will take a few precautions to prevent the timer from ever reaching 90.

Stopping the timer altogether would be a great option, but unfortunately Scratch doesn't allow that. The precautions to be taken are as follows:

1. We attach a **forever** loop after the **broadcast** block.
2. Inside the loop, we place an **if () then** block.
3. The condition will check whether **timer > ()** with value 80.
4. If this is the case, we sneakily use **reset timer** so that it will start over from 0.

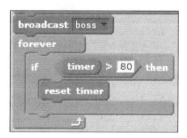

Objective complete – mini debriefing

After we start a new game, we can press the *B* key to immediately jump to the battle against the boss. We make sure the spear has some random upgrades so that we can see the effect. We also make sure the timer that's set for the usual game flow doesn't bother us.

We can now quickly skip to and test the boss fight without first having to play through a wave of enemies.

Creating the boss

With all the preparations out of the way, we can start working on the boss fight. We will first create a new sprite to work with. In the following paragraphs, we will add functionality to this sprite to make it a worthy boss.

Engage thrusters

We only need to add one new sprite for the boss. Let's choose an interesting creature that's obviously different from the starfish we used already. It should still fit the watery theme of this game.

Gobo, the new Scratch mascot, is a good candidate. He looks somewhat like a sea creature and is very recognizable:

1. Click to choose a sprite from library icon.

2. Select the **Fantasy** category to narrow down the list.

3. Gobo can now be easily found and selected. We click on the sprite and then on the **OK** button.

The following screenshot illustrates the preceding process:

This adds the sprite to the stage. We won't make any visual changes to it. However, we will add some scripts to it to work on the way it behaves:

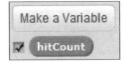

To control the behavior of the script, we will create a few variables.

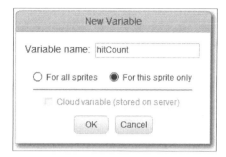

All these variables are local to a single sprite, so we have to make the proper settings.

1. We need a few different variables. These variables are set to **for this sprite only**.

   ❑ `hitCount`: This variable determines the number of hits the boss can take before being defeated.

   ❑ `speed`: This variable determines how fast the boss will move across the screen.

   ❑ `turnStep`: This variable determines how many degrees the boss will turn between each step. This will be used in one of the attack patterns that we write.

2. We also create a list to hold the broadcast messages for the attack patterns.

3. We name the list `attack patterns`.

4. We fill the list with the following three items/words:

   ❑ `pattern1`

   ❑ `pattern2`

   ❑ `pattern3`

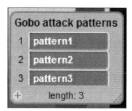

With these variables created, we can write a script that sets up all the required values at the start of the game.

1. We will start this script with a **when I receive <waves>** message block, because this message triggers the game to start after changes have been made in the previous project.

2. Next, we hide the sprite (using **hide**).

3. We also use **set size to () %** with value 40, so it isn't too big compared to everything else.

4. Then we use **set hitCount to ()** using value 0.

5. We use **set speed to ()** with value 6.

6. Then we use **set turnStep to ()** with value 5.

7. We make the sprite face left with **point in direction ()** using value -90.

8. To conclude the script, we move it to its starting point with **go to x: () y: ()**, filling in values 200 and 0 respectively.

The finished script looks like the following screenshot:

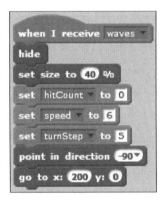

The boss sprite will remain in this static, invisible state until the boss event is triggered with the boss message. So let's create the following script to trigger the boss' behavior:

1. We start with **when I receive <boss>**.

2. The next thing we do is show the boss sprite (using **show**). We already set up everything else.

3. Then we pick an attack pattern. We use a message to trigger the correct script to do this.

4. Since the pattern has to be a random choice between three options, we create an assembled script block based on the attack pattern list and a random number.

5. In any case, we use **broadcast ()** to send a message.

6. The empty space should be filled with **item () of <attack patterns>**.

7. To pick the item from the list, we use **pick random () to ()**; fill in the values 1 and 3 respectively.

8. This will trigger the first random attack pattern to start.

9. We then start a condition loop to check whether the boss has been defeated yet.

10. Attach a **repeat until ()** block.

11. The condition to check for will be **if hitCount = ()** with value 50. (This number can be changed to make it easier/harder to defeat the boss.)

12. Inside the loop, while the enemy hasn't been defeated yet, we will check if it touches the spear sprite using **touching spear**. Technically, this will be a clone of the spear sprite but for the script that doesn't make a difference.

13. When an enemy is hit by a **spear** sprite, we will use **change <hitCount> by ()** with value 1.

Remember how we created an upgraded spear, but didn't actually do anything with it? Let's change that here:

1. We add another check inside the **touching** check, which is an **if () else ()** block in this case.

2. Here we check whether the enemy touches the gray color using **touching color <gray>**. This refers to the light gray tip of the upgraded spear.

3. If so, we use **set speed to ()** with value 4 to temporarily slow down the enemy when hit.

4. If the color is something else, that is to say, not the upgraded spear, we use **set speed to ()** with value 6.

5. To allow some time between hit checks, we wait for 0.01 seconds using **wait () seconds** before running the entire loop again.

The finished script will look like the following screenshot:

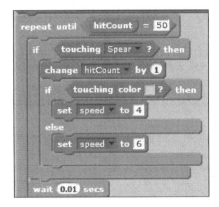

This game isn't much of a challenge if the boss can't hit the player back. So, we will add a small script that ends the game when the player collides with the boss sprite as follows:

1. We click on the **Diver** sprite in the **Sprites library** to see its script.
2. Notice that we already created a hit condition for touching the **Starfish** sprite using the **touching** block. We just need to add one more touch condition.
3. We grab an **or** operator and a **touching <Gobo>** block.
4. Place the new **touching** block in the right slot of the operator.

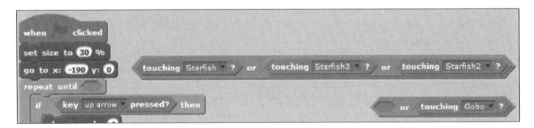

5. Then place the entire earlier construction in the left slot.
6. Now we place this string of four touch conditions in the **repeat until** condition slot.

That's all that we need to do to add a collision effect with the boss to the game.

Objective complete – mini debriefing

That concludes setting up the basic properties of the boss. It will disappear and appear on the screen when required, and it will attempt to start an attack pattern. Of course, it won't actually move because the message receivers and movement patterns haven't been written yet. At this point, we could check whether the hitCount value goes up when we hit the boss with a spear. Shooting a static enemy is a lot easier for testing.

Check the checkboxes for hitCount and speed to see the values change when testing this game.

Creating attack pattern 1

To make this fight more interesting, let's start writing the **attack patterns**.

Prepare for lift off

The thing with attack patterns is figuring out an interesting movement pattern first and then finding a way to create a script that moves the sprite according to that pattern. For this game, we will create three very distinct movement patterns.

The first one will be to move the boss in a pattern similar to the number 8. The number 8 will be lying horizontally, so the boss sprite will appear to be bobbing back and forth and weaving around the player character.

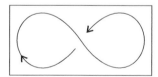

Engage thrusters

We will start this pattern when the correct message is called. Since this is the first pattern that we make, we have named it pattern1.

1. We add a new script starting with **when I receive <pattern1>**.

2. Then we use **set rotation style <all around>** so that the sprite can move about freely and make loops as it goes.

3. We move the sprite to the center of the screen with **glide 1 secs to x: () y: ()**; fill in the values as 0 and 0 respectively.

4. Then we point the sprite using **point in direction ()** with value -135. This points it to the bottom-left.

5. We add a fixed **repeat ()** loop to repeat the pattern, which is shown in the screenshot number 8, `four` times.

6. Inside this loop are four more **repeat** loops that describe each part of the complete pattern.

7. With the first one, we repeat `20` times (using **repeat**) to **move speed steps**. This moves the sprite in a straight line towards the bottom-left.

8. Then we start turning around in a circle. We use **repeat () / turnStep** times with value `270`.

9. At each step, we make the sprite turn clockwise using **turn <clockwise> turnStep degrees**.

10. We also use **move speed steps** to move the sprite in a circle, instead of around its own center point.

11. After this, it's back to a straight line. We can duplicate the earlier script component for this (using **duplicate**) as it works in exactly the same way. Since the sprite has rotated, it will now move in the bottom-right direction.

12. Finally, we make another turn. This is very similar to the first turn, so we can also use **duplicate** to make a copy of this script.

13. In this case, we have the sprite move counterclockwise. So, we replace the **turn <clockwise>** block with the **turn <counterclockwise>** block. That finishes a complete figure-8 move.

14. Once that has been repeated four times, we will pick another random pattern. It might pick the pattern that is shown in the scrrenshot number 8 again, or it could be one of the other two patterns that we will write next.

15. To finish the script, we duplicate the broadcast attack pattern's message construction from the boss message script.

Objective complete – mini debriefing

Creating movement patterns requires a bit of planning. First, we have to think about what would be an interesting move to make. Then, we have to figure out a way to turn that pattern into a script. This often requires some calculation and experimentation.

Since these scripts stand on their own and don't influence other scripts directly, you can't really break anything. Don't be afraid to try a few things when designing something like this. It often takes several tries before you get the result that you want.

Creating attack pattern 2

Having only one pattern isn't all that exciting. So let's quickly continue with creating a second one.

Prepare for lift off

Attack pattern 2 will be quite different from attack pattern 1. We let the boss first pick a corner of the screen. We will use a new kind of script method for this called a `switch` case.

It then zigzags across the screen, forcing the player to keep moving about to avoid being hit.

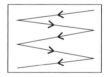

Engage thrusters

This script structure follows the same pattern as the first one. We start with receiving a pattern message. In the end, we let the script take another random pattern.

The interesting part takes place in the middle:

1. First, we use **set rotation style <left-right>** so that the sprite stays upright while moving. It looks better with this pattern.

2. Then we create another variable named `switch` (by choosing **variable only for this sprite**). We are going to use this as a random selector for the corner that the boss sprite will initially move to.

3. Enter 1 and 4 in the **set <switch> to pick random () to ()** block respectively.

4. Then we create four **if ()** statements called "cases" in this type of construction. Each case holds a different instruction and only one case can be valid each time:

   ❑ The first case is **if switch = () then glide () secs to x: () y: ()**. The values for the top-left of the stage are -200 and 150 respectively.

   ❑ The second case is **if switch = () then glide () secs to x: () y: ()**. The values for the top-right of the stage are 200 and 150 respectively.

   ❑ The third case is **if switch = () then glide () secs to x: () y: ()**. The values for the bottom-right of the stage are 200 and -150 respectively.

   ❑ The fourth case is **if switch = () then glide () secs to x: () y: ()**. The values for the bottom-left of the stage are -200 and -150 respectively.

   ❑ Once a corner is chosen, we make the sprite point in direction -100 to angle it just off the horizontal line.

5. Then we start a fixed **repeat** loop that will run 500 times.

6. In each cycle, we move using the **move () steps** block. Due to the angle, we just set the sprite to move horizontally a lot and vertically a bit.

7. We also check when it reaches the side of the stage and prevent it from getting stuck with an **if on edge, bounce** block.

These two blocks inside the loop will cause the boss sprite to move in a zigzag pattern across the stage.

Objective complete – mini debriefing

We now completed our second movement pattern. We changed the rotation style and created a list of starting points for the script to choose from. When the proper starting point and direction are set, we can smoothly move the enemy and have it bounce off the edges to create a zigzag pattern. Just one more to go and we have a complete boss fight (well, almost).

We can test the game now, but sometimes the movement of the boss will freeze when the third attack pattern gets selected. We can also test each attack pattern separately by just clicking on the proper script stack instead of running the entire program with the **<green flag>** button.

Creating attack pattern 3

To finish off all the attack moves for the boss, let's create a third attack pattern script.

Prepare for lift off

For this attack pattern, we are going to use an interesting mathematical formula called a **sine wave**. You might recognize this pattern from mathematics or from a radio wave readout. This pattern causes the sprite to move up and down in a regular curved wave pattern.

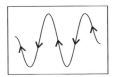

It looks very good and can be quite hard to dodge if you're not careful. It serves as a perfect "killer" move to close this part of the tutorial with.

Engage thrusters

This third attack pattern script starts and closes in exactly the same way as the other two. We start with receiving the message `pattern3` and close by picking a new random pattern from the list, as follows:

1. For this pattern, we also use **set rotation style <left-right>**, since it looks better when the sprite is facing straight ahead.

2. We then use **glide 1 secs to x: () y: ()** and set it to the middle-right corner of the screen, filling in the values `170` and `0` respectively. This will be the starting position.

3. We use **point in direction ()** to make the sprite face left; fill in value -90.

4. Then we add a **repeat ()** loop that will run 500 times.

5. This pattern requires a slower horizontal speed, so we **move speed / () steps** each cycle of the loop.

The finished script will look like the following screenshot:

Now we get to the interesting part. We will use a sine wave formula to determine the vertical position of the sprite based on its horizontal position. This is why we needed to slow down the horizontal movement. At regular speed, the movement would be way too fast and bouncy.

1. So after moving horizontally, we use **set y to ()**. This slot will be filled with a formula that is constructed from different parts.

2. First, we take the x position and place it in the left slot of the () * () block. In the right slot, we enter the value as 0.5. The resulting number determines how frequently the sprite completes a full wave (up-down and back to center). The higher the number, the shorter the wave.

3. Then we take this result and multiply it by 4 (using **multiply**). This number determines the overall speed of the wave motion. It's an optional number. It's not necessary to complete the formula, but it gives us more control.

4. Then we use the mathematical **sin** function on this result. This is what effectively causes the wavy pattern.

5. Finally, we multiply the whole by 150 (using **multiply**). This part determines the amount by which the wave deviates from the center line. This number is literally the maximum vertical distance from the center line.

6. After completing the formula, we just have to check whether the sprite is on edge and bounce if this is the case (using **if on edge, bounce**). The finished script will look like the following:

7. Double-check how the sine formula is assembled. If these blocks are mixed up and are running in the wrong order, we might get strange results. The calculations start from the inner blocks and progress towards the outer blocks.

Objective complete – mini debriefing

This concludes our last attack pattern. We used a sine wave formula to create a smooth, waving pattern for our boss sprite. Now we can fully test the boss enemy's movement. Let's test it a few times to see how it looks. If desired, you can experiment with the different values for the movement patterns. The sine wave can especially change a lot if you play around with the numbers for a bit. Just keep in mind the previous explanation to estimate what changing a certain number will do to the wave.

Making the boss more impressive

The boss creature is now a serious threat to the player. You can never be sure where it will go next, so it will be difficult to hit. The player runs the risk of bumping into it and prematurely ending the game. The boss still looks a bit too plain for a boss creature; let's fix this with some visual spectacle.

Engage thrusters

We will add a clone script to the basic sprite. Contrary to the starfish clones, this one will not have any in-game effect. It will just be used to make the game look a bit more spectacular.

1. First, we add a **create clone of <myself>** block inside the **repeat until** loop of the **when I receive <boss>** script. We place it just at the end of the loop.

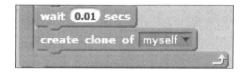

2. Then we start a new script with a **when I start as a clone** block.

3. Next we add a **repeat until ()** block.

4. For the condition, we construct **size < ()** (built-in variable from the **Looks** category) and place it inside the slot; fill in the value as 10.

5. During each loop, we use **change size by ()** (with value -5), making the clone smaller.

6. We also use **change <color> effect by ()**, changing its color with value -10. This will create a rainbow effect.

7. Then we use **wait () secs** to slow the process down so we can actually see it happening; fill in the value as 0.1. Remember that computers work very fast.

The finished script will look like the following screenshot:

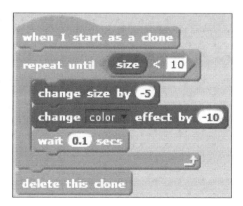

Objective complete – mini debriefing

The boss now shows an impressive colorful tail while moving. Since the clones don't actually move but shrink over time, they show a trailing path behind the boss sprite.

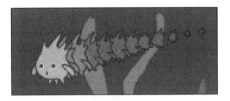

Classified intel

To give the visual effect some kind of function in the game, we can expand the script for it. An easy way is to shorten the tail as the boss creature accumulates more hits. This could show to the player how the enemy weakens as and when it gets hit.

Here is how we could add such an effect. All that is needed is to shorten the pause time so the clones are generated closer together. Instead of a fixed number we add a calculation based on the current hitCount.

1. We grab the – and * operators.

2. To the left of the – operator, we insert a base value of 0.1.

3. The right slot is filled with the * operator.

4. The product will be **hitCount * ()**, with value 0.01.

5. We place this calculation inside the **wait () secs** slot.

6. Now, as the hitCount variable grows, the wait time shortens by 0.01 seconds per hit to be exact. Perhaps this number doesn't show enough of an effect. So feel free to play around with it and try larger numbers.

7. Start the game. Press *B* to skip to the boss battle and see the effect.

Defeating the boss

When the boss has had enough, it should disappear and declare the player victorious. Adding this step will conclude the tutorial and finish the game.

Engage thrusters

We will yet again expand the script of the boss sprite. For this final step, we won't create a completely new script, but we will add to the main boss script that already exists. This is the one that starts with the **when I receive <boss>** block.

When the condition in the **repeat until ()** loop is met, the script will exit the loop. When this happens, it means that the boss has received the described number of hits and should be defeated. We will write the following instructions for this defeat script:

1. After the **repeat** loop, add two **say () for () secs** blocks; fill in the value 1 in the second empty slot for both the blocks.

2. First we will have the boss say "I give up" by filling in I give up. in the first empty slot of the first block.

3. Then we will have the boss say "You win" by filling in You win! in the first empty slot of the second block.

The finished script will look like the following screenshot:

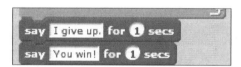

After that, the boss should also disappear with a bit of spectacle.

1. We add a **repeat ()** loop after the **say** blocks; fill in the value 30.

2. Inside this loop, we use **change <color> effect by ()** (with value 25) to make the boss sprite change its color repeatedly.

3. We also add **change size by ()** to make it shrink; fill in value -1.

4. Then we use **create clone of <myself>** to create the clone trail behind the boss.

5. Now we will use **wait () secs** to slow down the process to a visible level; fill in value 0.03.

6. After this fixed loop has finished executing, we will hide the boss (using **hide**).

7. Finally, we can safely use **stop <all>** to conclude the game.

The finished script will look like the following screenshot:

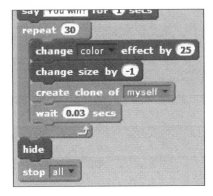

The game is now done! When the player manages to trigger this script, it means that he has won the game.

Objective complete – mini debriefing

This last step is a small but important part to actually finish the game. Without it the game would go on forever, or until the player is hit. That would not be a very nice prospect.

We embellished the end a bit with a message and an effect to the boss to make winning the game more satisfactory.

Mission accomplished

This game has quite a lot going on and it uses a lot of different sprites. It can especially be hard to manage all these different elements. Keeping track of layers to simulate depth can be a challenge. With a bit of thought and planning, we can make it work.

Just remember the relevant information for each object. Think about what it needs to do and what it needs to know in order to do it. This way you can decide whether you need variables; whether these variables need to be made available to all the sprites or you can keep them only for a single sprite.

Then it's just a matter of turning desired actions into script commands like we did with the movement patterns. First, we thought of what the movement should look like. Then we wrote a script to describe that movement.

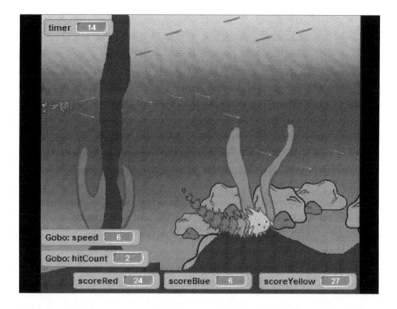

Hotshot challenges

This game leaves a lot of room to expand or change it. You could focus on the graphics to change the look of the game.

- ▸ You could add more variation in background elements.
- ▸ You could also add more/different enemies.
- ▸ You might change all the graphics of the game, and change it from an underwater to a space theme, for example.

More work can be done on the script side as follows:

- ▸ You can play around with the values for the movement patterns and the hit-points of enemies to find that perfect difficulty balance.
- ▸ You can also add new patterns. Try thinking of a move you find interesting, then figure out a good way to script that movement pattern.
- ▸ You can also change the effects for the boss creature.
- ▸ Likewise, you can add a "death" effect to the starfish and the diver.

Project 7
Creating a Level Editor

When developing a game, you may have already noticed that you will repeat certain tasks and operations over and over. This process can get slightly boring, and we don't like to do boring stuff. Making the game should be as much fun as playing. That's why this project deals with using the computer to automate repetitive tasks. We will make preparations and write scripts in such a way that the computer can easily repeat them and still create surprising results.

Mission briefing

This project will form the basis for a classic **dungeon crawl** adventure game. We will build a game similar to **Gauntlet**. The image below shows the box art for this famous swords and sorcery adventure game. More information about this game can be viewed at `http://en.wikipedia.org/wiki/Gauntlet_%28arcade_game%29`:

The basis for such games is the level design. We could work for hours inventing and drawing interesting level designs. But with some realistic planning, we can also use the calculation power of the computer to generate interesting levels for us. This second approach is what we will use in this project.

We will also create a controllable character and a game goal. The final result of this project will be a basic maze game. The next project will build on this base to make it a more challenging game.

Why is it awesome?

Based on simple tiles, we will dynamically create a multitude of levels. As we have the computer generate the levels based on random numbers, the amount of variation is nearly endless.

This kind of approach does require a bit of planning beforehand, so we don't accidentally generate something that will get the player stuck. But this planning and design is half the fun of creating a level editor in this way, and as an added bonus, the levels will keep surprising not only the players but also us, as developers of the game.

Your Hotshot objectives

The plan for the game involves drawing the level tiles; creating a script to generate the levels; and then adding a character, item, and goal to turn the level into a game. We will be covering the following tasks:

- Planning the level map
- Drawing the level tiles
- Preparing the tiles in Scratch
- Creating a level generator
- Creating a character
- Creating a goal
- Adding a bomb item
- Adding the bomb effects

Mission checklist

To create the **map tiles** for the game, it could be useful to use an external image editor, such as Photoshop or GIMP. These editors offer accurate grids and rulers, which are lacking in the Scratch drawing tool. These grids can make it a lot easier to draw accurate map tiles.

If you want to design your own map tiles, it could be useful to have some paper and pencils at hand. This way you can create quick sketches to test ideas before you take an extra effort to create anything digitally.

Planning the level map

Before we start building anything, let's take a moment to think about how this automatic level building is going to work and what we need to do to build it.

Engage thrusters

We intend to create a maze-like level design viewed from the top, similar to the look of the conventional maps. We want to create varying levels dynamically, so we should break the stage up into tiles that can each contain a different graphic. All these tiles placed side by side will create the complete level.

Now for the math involved. We know the entire stage is 480 pixels wide and 360 pixels high. So the tiles have to be of a size that can easily divide the stage in equal segments without any leftover space. It's also useful if the tiles are square. This isn't mandatory, but it makes drawing tiles a bit quicker since it allows to rotate tile designs and still fit them within the same space. Refer to the following screenshot of the stage:

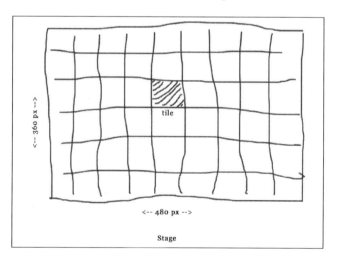

Let's summarize these requirements:

▸   The stage is divided in equal sized tiles

▸   The tile width and height should be equal (square)

▸   Tiles should fill the stage sitting side by side without any leftover space

We can now consider a few different sizes for the tiles. We want the tiles to be small enough to generate enough variation. However, we don't want to make them too small because that would require all the other elements (fitting within the maze) to be very tiny and hard to see.

Let's check how tiles of 80 x 80 pixels would work:

- ▸ **480/80**: It would be six tiles wide. That could work nicely.
- ▸ **360/80**: It would be four and a half tiles high. Oh, but that doesn't work quite so well. We would end up with half a tile row being cut off.

How about 60 x 60 pixels tiles then? Let's check this as follows:

- ▸ **480/60**: It would be eight tiles wide. So far so good.
- ▸ **360/60**: It would be six tiles high. Hey, that might work nicely!

Can we make the tiles even smaller? Perhaps, 40 x 40 pixels. Let's check this:

- ▸ **480/40**: It would be twelve tiles wide
- ▸ **360/40**: It would be nine tiles high

These smaller tiles could work too, but they might leave the game character and other items to be a bit too small. So let's decide on using tiles that are 60 pixels wide and 60 pixels high.

Once that's settled, we can consider the design of the tiles themselves. What's important in a maze? What does it consist of? A maze consists of passageways and walls. So we only need two different kinds of "space". Open corridors through which the player character can walk and solid walls that block his movement. So we can easily do with a simple black and white scheme. We use white for passageways and black for walls.

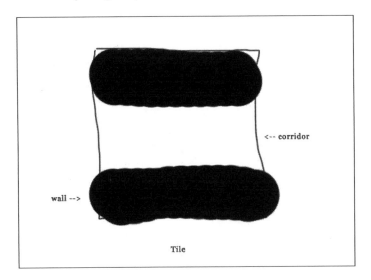

Each tile can be broken down further into smaller segments. We can then color each segment either black or white to indicate it is a wall or an open space. Since the tile will be 60 x 60 pixels, it makes sense to create a grid that is three segments wide and three segments high. Each segment will then be 20 x 20 pixels in size. This holds for nine tiles within a tile.

Objective complete – mini debriefing

After thinking about this design by making some sketches and calculations, we have a good idea about how we want to design the level generator. Sketching ideas before you start to work can be really useful in discovering problems early, such as the size of 80 pixels high not working for the stage height.

It might seem more work to design and plan ahead, and you might be eager to just dive right in and see what happens. However, a little thought beforehand can save you a lot of time. When we design all our tiles, we will be able to create a maze similar to the following screenshot:

Drawing the level tiles

Now that we know the structure of our tiles, we can work on the specific designs. We will create a series of tiles with different pathway designs to use as building blocks for the level generator.

Prepare for lift off

This step can be done with an external image editor, such as GIMP or Photoshop. The step-by-step explanation assumes you have such a tool available. GIMP is available for free.

If you don't want to bother with other tools besides Scratch, the *Classified intel* section of this task will explain how you could go about drawing the tiles in the Scratch image editor.

Engage thrusters

To start drawing the tiles, we first open the image editor of our choice. We will draw twelve different sprites to create a complete set of interesting tile options. Please create the images in the following order, because this will be important later on when we create the script for the tile generator:

1. Create a new canvas 60 pixels wide and 60 pixels high.

2. Then, make the grid visible and if necessary, set its spacing to **20 pixels**. That easily divides our canvas into 20 x 20 pixels segments.

3. We can first fill the entire canvas with a white background to create an open space. Since the Scratch stage is white too, this step is optional. A transparent space works just as well.

4. Our first tile will be a straight vertical corridor.

5. Use the **box select** tool to draw a selection rectangle around the left column.

6. Then, we can click on the **fill** option to fill the selection with black.

7. Repeat these steps for the right column and our first tile is done.

8. Save the image with the name `tile1` in an easy-to-find location. We will later import it into Scratch.

Our first image will look like the following screenshot:

 Notice how the gridlines of the editor are used to divide the tile into nine segments.

We go on to creating the second tile. This will be a horizontal corridor. To create the tile, we perform the following steps:

1. Erase the black fills we drew earlier.

2. Then, select the top row and fill it with black color.

3. Do the same for the bottom row.

4. That's one more tile done. Save this image as `tile2`.

Our horizontal and vertical corridors should look like the following screenshot:

The third tile will be a corner and we create by performing the following steps:

1. First click on the **erase** option to erase the image again.

2. Then reselect the bottom row and click on the **fill** option to fill it with black color.

3. Also, select the left column and and click on the **fill** option to fill that too.

4. As a final step, select the upper-right segment and make that black too.

5. This creates a corridor running from top to right (or vice versa).

6. Save this image as `tile3`.

To speed up the process, let's not redraw the entire image. As you might expect, there are three more corner tiles we can draw; but instead of drawing, we can just rotate the image as follows:

1. Select the entire canvas and click on the **rotate** option to rotate it by 90 degrees.

2. This will create a corner from right to bottom. Save this as `tile4`.

3. Repeat the rotation for the next two tiles.

The following screenshot shows all four corner tiles:

Now we have to think of another kind of corridor. How about a T-section? For this, perform the following steps:

1. First click on the **erase** option to erase the image to have a blank canvas again.

2. Select and click on **fill** to fill the left column with black color.

3. Also, fill the upper-right segment and the lower-right segment. This creates our first T-section.

4. Save this image. This would be named as `tile7`.

5. This tile can also be rotated three more times as follows; so rotate the tile and save each image:

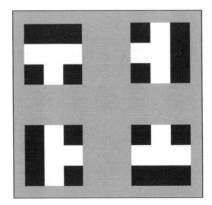

The last two images are unique. Perform the following steps:

1. The eleventh image will be a regular crossroad.

2. Start again with a blank canvas.

3. Select and color each of the corner segments.

4. Then, save the image.

5. The last image will be an open square.

6. Save the last image with the name `tile12`.

The following screenshot shows the crossroads and the open square tiles:

The open square tile is the only image where we have to fill the tile with a white background. The reason for this is that if we leave the image blank, Scratch would treat it as a 0 x 0 size image. That would cause problems for the script we will create later.

Objective complete – mini debriefing

That concludes our set of images. We drew twelve variant images that can fit seamlessly together when placed side by side. The images are simple yet effective for your game. There can be no mistake about which spaces are clear and which block movement.

Classified intel

If you want to create the tiles with the Scratch editor, this is how you could proceed. Please keep in mind that this approach will be less accurate and can leave gaps and overlaps between tiles. Perform the following steps to create the tiles:

1. Click on the **Paint new sprite** icon to create an empty sprite.

2. Look at the image editor and notice the checkered grid in the background. Each square is 4 x 4 pixels in size. This at least gives you a guide to work with for the size of your tile segments.

3. Increase the magnification to **800%** to get a better view and draw with more precision:

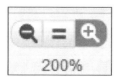

Note the cross hair at the center in the following screenshot. This should remain the center point for the tile, so always calculate distances from there outward:

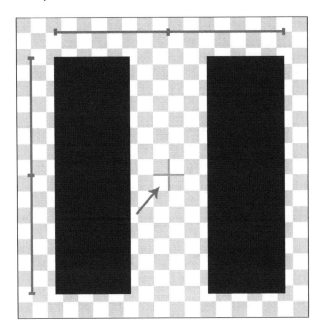

It's easiest to first create a bounding square centered on the cross hair by performing the following steps:

1. Select the **Rectangle** draw tool.

2. Select bright red for color.

3. Make sure to have the **border draw** option selected.

4. Then, count an eight-square distance diagonally from the cross hair to figure out where to start drawing.

5. Drag a rectangle while holding the left mouse button and the *Shift* key to draw a square. Make sure to end the draw operation on the eighth square diagonally in the opposite direction.

6. This bright red border will define the space to draw in.

7. Click on **Duplicate** to duplicate the costume eleven times to have a basic setup to work with.

8. Then, draw black-filled rectangles in each costume to define the walls.

9. Here also, the last tile should be completely filled with white.

10. To remove the red borders, select the **transparent fill** color. Then, use the **Fill** tool and click on the red borders. This will effectively remove the borders.

Preparing the tiles in Scratch

Now that we have a set of tiles to use, it's time to import them into Scratch to be scripted.

Prepare for lift off

Make sure you remember where you saved the tile images. It's often useful to save images to the same folder where you have the project file. That way, you have to search less and you can access them easily.

Engage thrusters

We will create a new sprite from the first uploaded image. Then, we will add costumes to the sprite for all the other images:

1. Click on the **Upload sprite from file** icon to open the Explorer window.

2. Find the image named **tile1**, select it, and click on **Open**, as shown in the following screenshot:

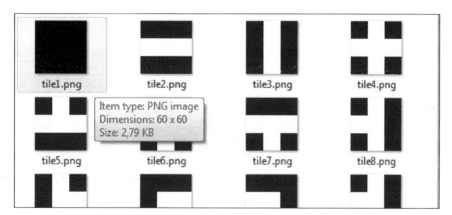

The image will load as a new sprite and be visible in the sprite editor. Now we can add the other costumes as follows:

1. Click on the **Upload from file** icon in the sprite editor.

2. Select all the remaining sprites and click on **Open**.

3. This loads all the other images as costumes. We might have to rearrange them in the numbered order if the upload process mixes these up.

4. Let's check each image to see if the cross hair is in the middle of each one. This is important for scripting.

5. Also, check under each costume if each image is indeed 60 x 60 pixels in size.

6. Rename the sprite to `tileGenerator` to make clear what this sprite is meant to do.

Objective complete – mini debriefing

This concludes the graphical element of our tile generator. The next step will be to add a script that will use the tiles to stamp images on the stage, creating a complete level map.

Creating a level generator

We will add a script to the sprite we just created that selects a costume at random and copies it onto the stage. With a double `for` loop, we will make sure the tile generator steps around the entire stage, so no space is left blank.

Prepare for lift off

To set up this game, we will create a small control script in the **Stage** object to set everything in motion as follows:

1. Start a new script with the **when <space> key pressed** block.

2. Attach a **broadcast** message to this.

3. For the message, type **createMaze**:

This message will trigger when a new maze should be generated. It can be activated by pressing the Spacebar key and at a later stage, through the script when the player completes a level.

Engage thrusters

With the basics out of the way, we can start with the fun stuff; drawing levels automatically. We will draw the level from the lower-left to the upper-right of the screen using the following steps:

1. Go to the **script** tab of the **tileGenerator** sprite.

2. Start a new script with a **when I receive <createMaze>** block.

3. When the script receives this message, click on the **clear** option to clear the stage.

4. Next, we need a few variables. These are available to all sprites.

5. Create **tileSize** to save the width and height of the tiles.

6. Create **xIndex** to save the column in which we are drawing.

7. Create **yIndex** to save the row in which we are drawing:

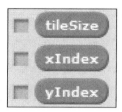

8. Then, set the size and index by selecting **set \<tileSize\> to \<60\>**, **set \<xIndex\> to \<0\>**, and **set \<yIndex\> to \<0\>**.

9. Then, we have the **show** block to show the sprite, so it can start stamping its costumes on **Stage**.

10. Add the **repeat \<6\>** loop to repeat the stamping operation for each row on the stage (*360/60 = 6*).

11. Inside the first loop, immediately place another one, **repeat \<8\>**, to repeat eight times. This one is for each column. (*480/60 = 8*):

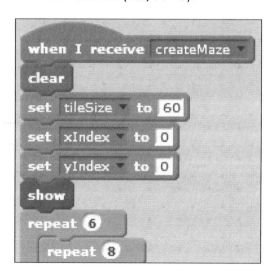

Basically, we make the **tileGenerator** sprite go to a new position on the stage repeatedly. What should be filled in on the blanks requires some calculations. We will leave those until the end of this step, so we can test the results while working on that formula as follows:

1. Insert a **go to x:() y:()** block inside the innermost **repeat** block.

2. When the sprite is positioned correctly, pick a random costume with **switch costume to pick random <1> to <12>**.

3. Then, we are ready to make a stamp on the stage.

4. After this, set the **change <xIndex> by <1>** block to count the first loop.

5. After the closure of the first loop, but before the second, reset the **set <xIndex> to <0>**.

6. Also, set the **change <yIndex> by <1>** block to count the iterations of the second loop.

7. When that's all done, we can add the **hide** block to safely hide the sprite again.

8. As a final step, add the **broadcast** block with a new message saying <**startGame**> as follows; this message will notify all other game objects to get ready for a playthrough:

With the basic structure of the script done, we still have to figure out where to place the **tileGenerator** sprite before we stamp an image. This requires some calculations based on the number of repeats the loops are currently at. To save these values, we use the **xIndex** and **yIndex** variables as counters. Perform the following steps:

1. First, we can assume that **tileSize * xIndex** shifts the sprite right across the width of the stage without leaving gaps between stamps. The **tileSize * yIndex** formula shifts the sprite up across the height of the stage.

2. However, *0 * 60 = 0* would be the center of the stage. We don't want to start at the center. We need to start at the lower-left corner. So we have to adjust the starting value. We need to subtract half the stage width or height from the coordinate value. So, the formulas will become **tileSize * xIndex – 240** and **tileSize * yIndex – 180** respectively.

3. Complete the formula and test this. The tiles will be placed nicely beside each other; but when the drawing completes, we still see a problem. The entire map is offset to the lower left and a wide blank strip is showing along the top and right-hand side of the stage.

4. This offset is caused because the center point of the sprite is placed in the middle of it, and this is the point that gets aligned to the coordinates in the calculation. So we have to add an offset for half the width or height of the tile to shift all the tiles towards the upper right a bit. The complete formulas will be as follows:

$$tileSize * xIndex - 240 - tileSize / 2$$

$$tileSize * yIndex - 180 - tileSize / 2$$

The following screenshot shows the formulae:

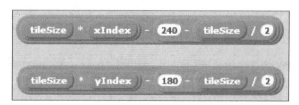

This fixes our offset problem. The maze is now correctly aligned with the stage boundaries.

Objective complete – mini debriefing

This one script is all that is needed to create a new interesting level each time the Space bar key is pressed. Try it a few times to see what kind of designs the computer comes up with. Due to the randomized costume selection, you'll notice that the paths through the maze will be different each time.

Classified intel

You might notice that in many cases, the paths will be relatively short with walls blocking the passage at fairly short distances. This is because each tile has an equal chance of being selected by the randomizer. However, some tiles, the straight corridors especially, contain more wall segments than open passageways.

We can manipulate the random selection of tiles to favor the ones that are more open. We already made sure that the more closed tiles are at the front of the costume list while the more open paths are towards the end with the open square closing the list.

We use this knowledge to perform a calculation on the random selection which favors higher numbers over lower ones. We calculate this using the following steps:

1. Instead of **pick random (1) to (12)**, set the value from 1 to 144.

2. From the resulting number, take the square root.

3. As a final step, use the **round** block to round the number to a whole, so it points to a specific costume again:

Why does this work? This is because the square root of the higher numbers in the extended range resolve to a higher value more often. For example, only square root of 1 and 2 rounded off will resolve as 1. But all the numbers from 133 up to 144 will resolve as 12. That means 12 chances to come up with costume 12 and only 2 chances to come up with costume 1.

Creating a character

To make use of our generated maze, we will need to include a character the player can control. We'll use the default Scratch cat as the protagonist and add all the required control script to make it move through the maze.

Prepare for lift off

If we haven't left it on the stage from the start, we have to add the Scratch cat as a new sprite as shown in the following steps:

1. Click on the **Choose** sprite from the library icon.

2. Search for the **Scratch cat** option, select it, and click on **OK**.

The Scratch cat will be loaded for use in the game. Next, we will add a script to it to make it interactively controlled by the player.

Engage thrusters

Let's first set up the broadcasts that will trigger the cat sprite to take proper actions. We need two of those events. The first one is very simple and will be repeated in all game objects as follows:

1. Start a new script with **when I receive <createMaze>**.

2. To this, add the **hide** block to hide the sprite as shown in the following screenshot:

   This makes sure all other sprites are hidden when the **tileGenerator** sprite runs. They will remain hidden until we call them to do something later. The cat sprite will be activated right after the maze is created.

3. Create a second broadcast script with **when I receive <startGame>**.

4. After this, we will place a **function** block. So now is a good time to introduce functions.

   With a function, you can describe a certain operation that is repeated many times during the program. Instead of describing the steps required each time they are needed, just point to the function and tell the computer to perform those actions. Using a function can save space in the running program, because we set specific sets of actions aside as separate scripts. This will also make the general flow of the program easier to understand.

5. Click on the **More Blocks** category. This is where we can define and use functions.

6. Click on the **Make a Block** button, as shown in the following screenshot:

7. A pop up will show where we can name the new function block. Let's name it `findStartPosition`.

8. We don't need options. So just click on **OK** to create the new function block.

Note how a new starting block (with a curved top) will appear called **findStartPosition**. This is the start of the script where we can write all the steps the function should take as shown in the following screenshot:

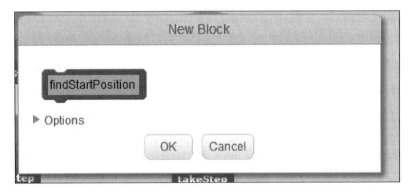

We want to place the cat in an open hallway and not in a wall. To test if the cat can move to a certain position, we will move it and check if it then collides with a wall. If it does, we will move it another tile segment and test again. We repeat this process until we can place the sprite. Now perform the following steps:

1. Make a list for this sprite, called **xySave**, to store the coordinates. This list will be used later to help move the sprite.

2. Between the **startGame** receiver and the **findStartPosition** block, make sure to create a **delete <all> of <xySave>** block to start with an empty list, as shown in the following screenshot:

3. Continue to define the function we just created. Such a definition is just like a normal stack of script blocks. It can be called whenever we use the function block.

4. Our first addition to the **define findStartPosition** script is to create the **set size to (15) %** block to make the sprite fit inside the maze.

5. Then, move it to the upper-left corner with a **go to x: (-230) y: (170)** block.

6. Add a **repeat until** block to check for collisions with the walls.

7. In the condition slot, place a combination of **not touching color <black> ?**. Use the **eyedropper** option to pick the color.

8. The action to repeat will be to use the **change x by (20)** block, making the cat step to the right.

9. After the cat has found its starting position, use the **add x position to <xySave>** (the built-in variable).

10. Then, set the **add y position to <xySave>** (the built-in variable).

11. Make the sprite **go to front** to make sure it isn't covered by other sprites.

12. Finally, make the **show** sprite.

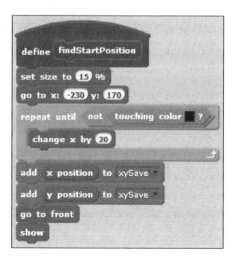

We can then add the basic movement controls. As we have to keep in mind that the cat shouldn't be allowed to walk through walls, we have to perform a check before each move. This check will be the same for each step we take.

We will create another function to define this repeated collision check. Regardless of the key pressed or the direction the cat will move in, the check will stay the same.

To set up the keyboard controls, we create four-key pressed script, as we have done in earlier examples. For each directional key, we point the cat in the right direction as follows:

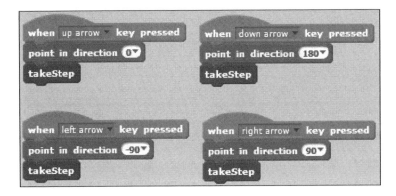

When the cat is facing the correct direction, we can make it try to take a step forward. We create a function to describe this move attempt. If the way is clear, the cat will move. If it's blocked by a wall, the cat will stay where it is. Perform the following steps:

1. Click on the **More Blocks** category.

2. Then, click on the **Make a Block** button.

3. Name the new function as takeStep and click on **OK** without selecting options.

Another starting block will appear called **define takeStep**. This is the start of the script where we can write all the steps the function should take. Perform the following steps:

1. To the **define takeStep** block, add set the **replace item <1> of <xySave> with x position** block (the built-in variable).

2. Then, add the same for the y position; by setting the **replace item <2> of <xySave> with y position** block (the built-in variable).

3. Then make the cat move twenty steps by setting the **move (20) steps** block. This corresponds to one tile segment, as we calculated earlier when planning the maze tiles.

4. Add an **if () else ()** statement to check for collision and decide what action to take depending on the result.

5. In the **if** condition, check for **touching color <black> ? or touching <edge> ? then** block.

6. If the cat does collide with either one of those, reset it to its original position with a **go to x:() y:()** block.

7. Fill the slots with the **item <1> of <xySave>** and **item <2> of <xySave>** block with x and y positions respectively.

8. If the cat didn't collide with a wall, we can save the new coordinates.

9. Set the **replace item <1> of <xySave> with x position** block.

10. Set the **replace item <2> of <xySave> with y position** block.

We could leave it at that point, because the cat is now in a new valid position. However, the movement will look very jumpy this way. So we will improve that by adding a few scripts to create fluid movement which are as follows:

1. Reset the cat to its previous position by setting the **move (-20) steps** block.

2. Then, we will make the **glide (0.4) secs to x:() y:()** block.

3. In the slots, we will use the freshly saved coordinates, **item <1> of <xySave>** and **item <2> of <xySave>**:

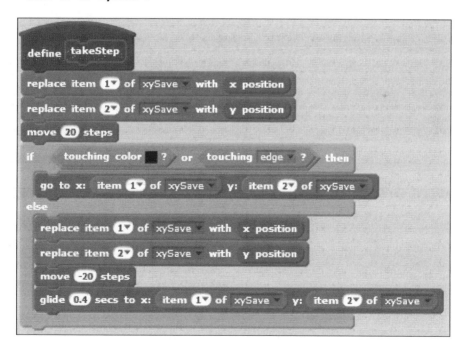

That completes our main player control scripts. The cat sprite can be moved freely through the corridors of the maze but it won't be able to cross a wall.

Objective complete – mini debriefing

With this step, we have probably completed the most difficult part of the script. We used the new **Make a Block** option to create functions that make script a little easier to read and can save work or excessive copy-pasting when creating complex operations.

The beginnings of a game can be visible now; the cat can be moved through the maze.

Creating a goal

Now that the cat can explore the maze, it needs a challenge. It's a good idea to give it a specific goal to search for.

Prepare for lift off

We will draw a sprite that will be the goal for the cat to reach. What this goal will look like is not really important. The important thing is that it is exactly 20 x 20 pixels in size, so it will fit a tile segment perfectly.

I choose to represent the goal as a "magical" warp panel consisting of bright, blue rings. You can create the same or design your own goal sprite.

Once done, name the sprite as `exit`. This will give us the following screenshot:

Engage thrusters

This sprite will have the same two broadcast listeners as the cat to start working. When the maze is drawn, we will hide the sprite, and when the game starts, we will show it by performing the following steps:

1. Drag the **when I receive <createMaze>** script from the cat and drop it on the **exit** sprite to copy it there. That's the first half done.

2. Then, start the second script with a **when I receive <startGame>** block.

3. First, move the **exit** sprite to the lower-right with **go to x: (230) y: (-170)** block.

4. Then, add a **repeat until** loop.

5. Check for the condition **not touching color <black> ?**

6. As long as we will collide with the black walls, we will set the **change x by (-20)** block to move the sprite on the left-hand side.

7. After it has found a free space, we can set the **show** block the sprite:

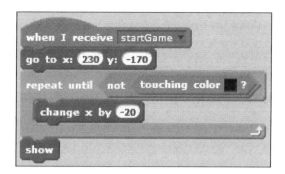

Do these steps look familiar? They should. It's effectively the same script as the cat is using in the `findStartPosition` function, barring the use of the list. Since the **exit** tile doesn't move, we don't need to save its position.

To let the player know when he or she has reached the exit and has won this (part of a) game, we add some feedback to the cat sprite. We will add a few additional actions to the `takeStep` function as follows:

1. At the end of the function, add an **if () then** statement to make a check after each time the cat moved.

2. We will check if the cat has reached the exit point with the help of the **touching <exit> ?** block.

3. If the cat responds, it will show **(Yay! On to the next level.)** and set the **for (2) secs** block.

4. After that, we will set the **broadcast <createMaze>** block to trigger the drawing of a new maze. This will also trigger the cat and allow the exit to reset as follows:

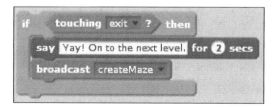

This is starting to feel more like a game already.

Objective complete – mini debriefing

With this simple addition, we brought a feeling of gameplay to the program. Before this step, it was more like a movement simulator or a keyboard test, but now, there is actually something to achieve. All it required was copying a script, writing another script that we might just as well have copied and changed, and writing a simple collision check and effect.

Some steps in programming can be really difficult, but once the basics are set it's quite easy to add improvements.

Adding a bomb item

We try to get the cat to the exit of the maze, but we soon run into a problem. Most likely, all the passageways are blocked and turn out to be dead ends. There is no way to reach the exit, because the cat can't move through walls.

How could we solve this issue? Let's make holes in the walls. We will add a bomb item that the player can use to blast holes in the walls. That way, they can always reach the exit.

Prepare for lift off

We draw another new sprite that resembles a classic cartoon-style bomb with a sparkly fuse. It's easier to draw the item a bit bigger than is needed and later, scale it down with a script.

This drawing can be made with the Scratch drawing tool, by performing the following steps:

1. First, create a black-filled circle.
2. Then, select the **Fill** tool.
3. Select white color for the foreground and black for the background.
4. Point and click on the upper-right of the circle to create a white highlight. This makes the circle look round.
5. Then, select the **Brush** tool and make sure the color used for drawing is black and the line isn't too thin.
6. Draw a short curve at the top of the ball to make a fuse.
7. Then, change the color to yellow.
8. Draw a dot at the tip of the fuse to light it.

The following is a nice looking bomb in just a few steps:

We also need a way to make the holes in the walls. Since those are stamped onto the stage, we can't really remove any elements. They are just a drawing on the canvas. What we can do is stamp over them with white. For this, we create another sprite to use as a stamp. In this case, it is important that the sprite is exactly of the right size, so it will fit the maze segments.

We can create this sprite in an external image editor as we did for the tiles. What we need is the four-way crossroad tile without the black corners (`tile11`). We can easily copy and adapt this tile.

If we need to draw the tile with Scratch, we can follow the same procedure as described earlier for drawing the tiles:

1. First, create a 60 x 60 pixels red outline.

2. Then, fill the middle row and column with a white **Rectangle** option.

3. When done, fill the red outline with the transparent color to remove it:

It might be easier to first fill the entire space with white and then draw invisible squares in the corners using the transparent color.

Once our **hole** stamp is done, we can start scripting. Let's not forget to name the bomb sprite as bomb and the hole stamp as `hole`.

Engage thrusters

Let's first write the scripts to place the bomb:

1. We can copy the **createMaze** listener script from another sprite.

2. To this script, add a **set size to () %** block as follows:

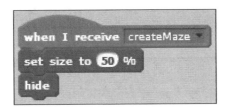

I used 50 for the value, but if your sprite was drawn bigger or smaller, you might need another value. Just experiment until the bomb fits the maze.

Then, we add another keyboard control to place a bomb using the following steps:

1. Start the script with a **when <b> key pressed** block.

2. We will make the bomb sprite to go to the cat by setting the **go to <cat>** block.

3. Then, set the **show** block to show the bomb sprite.

4. We have a countdown to detonation with a few messages as follows:

   - **say (3) for (1) secs**
   - **say (2) for (1) secs**
   - **say (1) for (1) secs**

At this point, we need another message for the explosion event. For this, perform the following steps:

1. Add a **broadcast <>** block and create a new message called **createHole**.

2. Then, go on to make the **say (KABOOOOM!) for (0.5) secs**.

3. When it has exploded, we can set the **hide** block to hide the bomb sprite again:

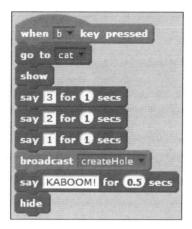

The next step is to create scripts for the `hole` sprite. This will mainly respond to the **createHole** message we just added. Perform the following steps:

1. First, copy a **createMaze** listener to this sprite as well but not the one we just edited for the bomb, because this sprite shouldn't change in size.

2. Then, create a second script to receive the **createHole** message, starting with a **when I receive <createHole>** block.

3. Set the **go to <bomb>** block.

4. The hole will add a **broadcast** block to broadcast another message for later use. Name this new message **kaboom**.

5. Then, set the **wait 0.1 secs** block to create a small delay for the effect.

6. Add the **show** block to the sprite.

7. Add the **stamp** block to stamp it onto the stage. Any black segments underneath the sprite will now be overwritten.

8. Then, add the **hide** block to hide the sprite again:

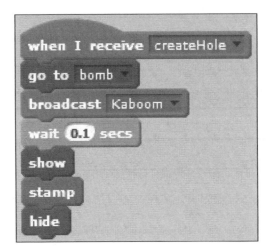

If placed correctly, the bomb item should now blow holes into the black walls. Once the walls are removed, the cat is free to move on.

Objective complete – mini debriefing

We just created a sprite item to be used by the player and a functional effect to make the item work. Stamping over the stage can be an easy and effective way to change the level design. It can be used as a player instrument, as in this case. However, you could also use it for automated changes and challenges in the game, such as opening and closing doors and throwing temporary hazardous effects into the level.

Adding the bomb effects

The player can now easily create a way through the maze. If something is in the way, just blow it up. That does make the game slightly easy. So let's add another challenge in the form of a points system and a way to get hurt when using the bomb.

Prepare for lift off

We need another sprite for an explosion effect to follow the detonation of the bomb. The size of this sprite doesn't have to be exact, but it's a good idea to keep it roughly the same size as a tile, 60 pixels wide and 60 pixels high.

We can draw this sprite in Scratch easily as follows:

1. Click on the **Paint new** sprite icon.

2. Select the **Circle** tool and draw a filled yellow circle. Press the *Shift* key while dragging the cursor to make it perfectly round.

3. Next, switch to the **Fill** tool and select yellow for the foreground and orange for the background.

4. Also, select the **circular gradient** option.

5. Then, click the middle of the circle to fill it with a gradient, which is bright in the middle and gets darker towards the edges.

6. Name the new sprite as `explosion`:

That completes our **explosion** graphic.

Engage thrusters

When the player places a bomb, he/she has to make sure that the cat will move out of the blast radius, or it will hurt and cost them points.

We will first create the explosion effect as follows, so that we can estimate our next step:

1. Start again with copying the plain **createMaze** listener, without any size alterations.

2. Then, start a new script with a **when I receive <Kaboom>** listener.

3. When the explosion sprite receives this message, we will set the **go to <hole>** block.

4. Then, add the **set size to (0) %** block to make it infinitely small.

5. Reset the **set <ghost> effect to (0)** block to make the sprite solid.

6. Then, add the **show** block to the sprite. At this point, it will not be visible, because its size is set to 0 percent.

7. Then, add a **repeat (20)** loop to make the sprite grow in size.

8. At each step, add the **change size by (5)** block. So by the end of the loop, it will be at *20*5 = 100* percent size.

9. Set the **change <ghost> effect by (5)** block. This will slowly make the sprite transparent again as it grows until it becomes invisible.

10. After the loop is done, add the **hide** block to hide the sprite again as follows:

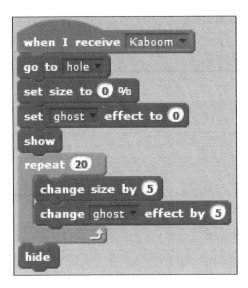

There is a difference between the **ghost** effect and the **show** or **hide** blocks. The **ghost** effect can make a sprite invisible, but it will still play a part in the program. You, as a viewer, just can't see it, but the computer and other sprites can. When hiding a sprite, it is completely removed from the program. It can't be detected by anything or have any effect while hidden.

Now that the animation of the explosion is complete, we can go on to the points system. This will also function as the scoring system that determines whether the player loses or wins the game. Perform the following steps:

1. First, click on the **Make a variable** button, select **for all sprites**, and then type points.

2. Let's also create a variable called level to keep track of how many levels the player has completed.

3. Both these variables may be visible on the stage. So check their checkboxes, as shown in the following screenshot:

4. In the **Stage** object, add a block to the existing script by adding the **set <points> to (0)** block when the Space bar key is pressed.

5. Also add the **set <level> to 0** block, as shown in the following screenshot:

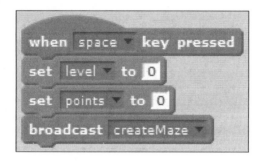

6. Then, move on to the **tileGenerator** sprite. Here, set the **change <level> by (1)** and **change <points> by (100)** blocks, as shown in the following screenshot, each time a level is created:

7. Then go on to the **cat** sprite, which will get the most additions to its scripts.

8. To change the **points** value, we will make a new block called **changePoints**.

9. In this case, we will add an option to add a number to the function. This will be called **number1** by default, which is fine. Refer to the following screenshot:

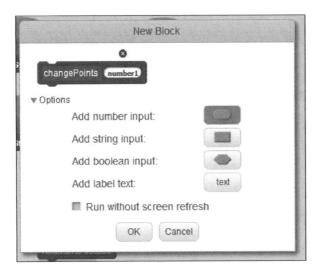

10. When the function runs, set the **change <points> by number1** block. This is the value that we will add into the function each time we use it.

11. Add an **if () then** statement to make a check.

12. Check **if points < 0**.

13. When that's the case, the sprite containing the function will show the **say (No more points. Game over!) for 2 secs** block.

14. We will then set the **stop <all>** script to end the game, as shown in the following screenshot:

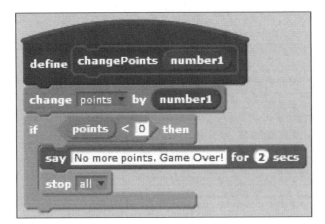

We will make use of the **changePoints** function in the **startGame** listener as follows:

1. We will expand this script with a **forever** loop.

2. In this loop, place an **if () then** statement.

3. Check if the cat touches the explosion by setting the **if touching <explosion> ? then** block.

4. If it does, set the **changePoints (-10)** block. This is where we tell the function the number it should use.

5. After the function has completed, the cat will say **Ouch! That hurt. Let's try again.** in **say () for (2) secs** block.

6. Then, we will call the **findStartPosition** function block to reset the cat to its starting position:

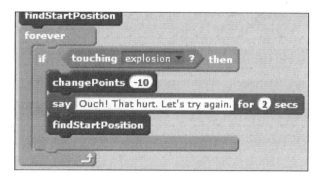

A nice addition is to not only deduct points when the cat gets hit but also to pay a price when placing a bomb. That way the player can't place infinite bombs and blow up the entire level. Perform the following steps:

1. First drag the `define changePoints` script to the **bomb** sprite to make a copy there. Unfortunately, the Scratch functions aren't universal across all sprites.

2. Switch to the **bomb** sprite to add some blocks there to use the **changePoints** function.

3. In the **key press** script, add a **changePoints (-10)** block to deduct ten points each time the player places a bomb:

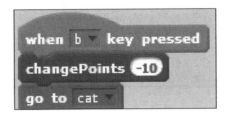

That's all we needed to do to create a points system and a hazard for the cat. If you wish, you can play around with the point values to change the difficulty of the game.

Objective complete – mini debriefing

With limited resources, this game has become more challenging. It's now possible to lose the game. We also keep track of how much the player has accomplished by showing the level number and number of points scored.

Mission accomplished

On building this project one step at a time, we slowly changed it from a rather dry calculation exercise, to a simulation, and then to a game. We have seen that small additions can have big effects on how the game feels. Refer to the following screenshot:

Having the computer generate elements of a game automatically can keep it surprising each time, even for us as developers. It can be fun just to see what the machine "thinks" of next.

Adding a goal can give the player something to work for. Adding danger to a game can greatly increase the engagement of the player because there is something to lose.

In this project, we also touched on some valuable new scripting techniques, such as using functions to separate scripts into readable pieces. Using the stamp tool to draw and change the level also offers some interesting options.

Although we have the basics of a game now, it still isn't too exciting exploring this maze alone. In the next project, we will add more items and enemies to turn this maze exploration into a real quest.

Hotshot challenge

Since this is just the halfway point for this game example, there isn't too much you can add at this stage that won't be covered in next project. If you enjoy drawing, you might like to add prettier graphics. The following are some ideas to get you started:

- ▶ The cat only uses one frame at this stage. You could try to give it a walk animation using both frames that are in the sprite.

- ▶ You could also add more costumes to the cat sprite for more fluid animation.

- ▶ Another improvement would be to redraw the maze tiles. Just keep in mind that we check collision based on color, so try to keep it simple if you choose to use more colors in the walls.

- ▶ You can also choose to separate the visual graphics from the functional ones, as we did with the karts in the racing game earlier. This way, you can go all out with the drawings while still being accurate with the scripts.

Feel free to add to the game and move in a different direction than described in the next project. It's your game after all.

Project 8

Dungeon Crawl

This project will continue where we left off in the last project. Our maze game is interesting but still not all that engaging. It's quite easy to reach the exit and accumulate points. We are going to add more features to offer the player a challenging experience.

Mission briefing

We will add enemies to the game as well as items. This gives the player more things to look out for than just the level exit. The player has to avoid enemies or try to kill them. He/she can do this using the bomb or one of the other items that we will include in this project. The following gameplay screenshot from Gauntlet II will be the inspiration for what we will create in our project:

Why is it awesome?

No questing game is complete without enemies and items. These are the things that change a simple exploration game into an exciting adventure. Every player likes to boast how they just barely avoided the menacing ghosts to achieve victory, or how they found a great treasure in the unlikeliest of places.

We will add a variety of elements to the maze. Each one will behave differently and offer a different challenge or opportunity for the player. Some earlier scripts can be reused, but we will adapt them to suit our purposes.

Your Hotshot objectives

We will add two types of enemies and items to the game. Each one of them will behave differently. The objectives for this project are:

- ▶ Adding a knight
- ▶ Adding a ghost
- ▶ Creating a sword
- ▶ Creating a bow and arrow
- ▶ Tying up loose ends

Mission checklist

This project will continue on from the last one. So the first thing we have to do is load our previous project, the Maze game. You can load your own project or use the example project that's included with this book.

Adding a knight

We will add our first enemy to the maze. This will make it harder for the cat to move through the maze freely. The player has to choose his path wisely or risk getting caught.

Prepare for lift off

We will use the **Knight** sprite from the Scratch library.

1. Click on the **Choose sprite from library** icon.
2. We search for the **Knight** sprite. It's in the **Fantasy** category.
3. We click on the sprite to select it, and click on **OK** to use it in our game.

Knight

Engage thrusters

The knight will behave quite similarly to the cat sprite. It's allowed to move through the hallways, but it can't pass through walls. That means we can reuse a lot of the scripts we've already written for the cat.

1. We drag both the **createMaze** listener script and the **takeStep** function from the cat to the **Knight** sprite to make copies there.

2. Then, we click on the **Knight** sprite to switch to its **Scripts editor**.

3. To the **createMaze** listener, we add a **set size to () %** block and type in 12. This makes the knight fit the maze.

4. At the end of this script, we add a **delete this clone** block.

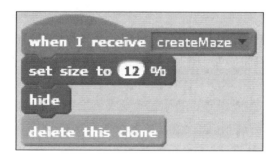

You might wonder about this last step. There aren't any clones to delete, and you would be right. There aren't any clones, not yet at least. However, we will soon write a script to create them.

However, first we will have a look at the copied **takeStep** function. You may have noticed that with the function **xySave**, the list has been copied as well. That's a good thing, because we will need that list. Note that both the **cat** and the **Knight** have their own personal version of the list. When created, it was set to be **for this sprite only**.

We don't need to make many changes to the function. The movement part works perfectly as it is. It's exactly the same way the cat can move. We only need to remove the last part of the script that deals with touching **exit**. The knight is not allowed to escape the level.

1. Grab the **if** statement with the cursor and drag down to separate it from the script.
2. Drag the script part to the left and drop it in the toolbox to remove it.
3. Alternatively, we could also right-click on the part and choose **delete**. This also removes the script.

Now we have to call the function to actually make the knight move. We will also add an interesting feature based on which level we are playing. For each level, the number of knights will be increased by one. So level 1 will have one knight, level 2 will have two, and so on.

1. We create a new script starting with a **when I receive <startGame>** block.
2. Then, we add **repeat ()**.
3. We fill the slot with the level variable to repeat as many times as the level we want to play.
4. Then, we place the sprite with a **go to x:() y:()** block.

We want to pick a random tile on the map, so we have to make a calculation based on a random number. Luckily, we designed the tiles in such a way that the middle segment is always free, so we won't have to check for collisions with walls.

1. For the x position, the formula will be: *tile width * random tile in row – (half the stage width – half the tile width)*. This translates to **(60) * pick random (0) to (7) – (210)**.
2. For the y position, the formula becomes: *tile height * random tile in column – (half the stage height – half the tile height)*. This translates to **(60) * pick random (0) to (5) – (150)**.
3. When that's settled, we can use the **create clone of <myself>** block.
4. Next, we wipe the **xySave** list clean with a **delete <all> of <xySave>** block.
5. We use the **add x position to <xySave>** block.
6. We also use the **add y position to <xySave>** block.

The completed script will look like the following screenshot:

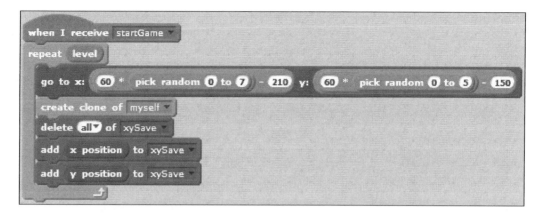

Remember how we already placed a **delete this clone** block at the end of the **createMaze** script? That was to remove any clones that will be created with this script during a game. We are now ready to write a script to move the clones.

1. We obviously begin a new script with **when I start as a clone**.

2. Then, we show the sprite using the **show** block.

3. We add a **repeat until** loop.

4. There we check whether the clone is **touching <explosion>?**

5. Until that's the case, we turn in a random direction with a **turn <clockwise> () degrees** block.

6. We limit the clone to the cardinal directions by entering 90, 0, and 3 respectively in the **() * pick random () to ()** block.

7. Then, we call the **takeStep** function to actually move the clone.

8. We close the script with a **delete this clone** block, which triggers after a clone is hit by an explosion.

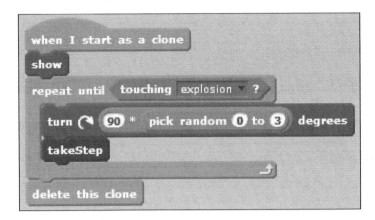

The scripts are now complete and the knight can wander about the maze looking for a suspicious-looking cat.

Objective complete – mini debriefing

We added an enemy that behaves in the same way as the player character. Due to this, we could reuse a lot of scripts, saving us some time. We still had to review each script to make some changes and to check we didn't leave any unwanted behavior, like a knight responding to the exit sprite.

Adding a ghost

Our next enemy will be quite different. It will be easier to script, but offers a bigger challenge to the player. This enemy will be a ghost that is allowed to move through walls freely. Therefore, it can pop up anywhere without restrictions.

Prepare for lift off

We first load a ghost sprite from the Scratch library. To do this, we perform the following steps:

1. We click the **Choose sprite from library** icon.

2. The ghost is also in the **Fantasy** category, just like the knight.

3. There are two options. We select **Ghost2**, because it looks more scary.

4. Press **OK** to add **Ghost2** to the game.

Ghost1   Ghost2

Engage thrusters

Structurally, the scripts for the ghost will be the same as those for the knight and the cat. However, it doesn't need the **takeStep** function, because the ghost can just move all over the place.

1. We can first copy the **createMaze** listener script and the **startGame** listener script from **Knight**. This will shrink the ghost to the right size for the maze and also sets up where it should be placed.

2. Then, we only need to remove the two **add () to xySave** blocks, because the ghost doesn't require them. Other than that, these two scripts will be exactly the same as for the knight.

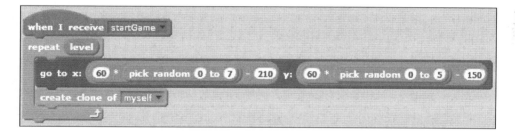

So we can quickly move on to creating the clone script.

1. We start again with a **when I start as a clone** block.

2. Then, we first show the sprite again using the **show** block

3. Next, we use the **point in direction ()** block to determine which way the ghost will move.

4. This direction can be completely random, so we fill in 1 and 360, in the **pick random () to ()** block.

5. Then, we will add a **repeat until...** loop.

6. We check again for **touching <explosion>?** like we did earlier with the knight.

7. As long as everything is well, we will use the **move 2 steps** block.

8. As a precaution, use **if on edge, bounce**, so the ghost doesn't get stuck on the stage edge.

9. We conclude this script with a **delete this clone** block for the case where the ghost does get hit.

That's our second enemy done.

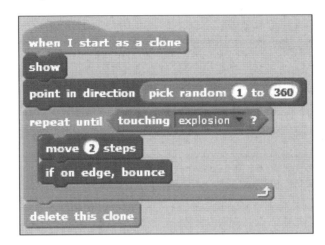

Objective complete – mini debriefing

In this step, we see that more complex scripts don't always mean a more dangerous enemy. The script for the ghost is simpler than that for the knight. However, the ghost poses a much bigger danger to the player because it can move through the walls. If the player isn't careful, he/she can be easily driven into a dead end.

Creating a sword

Now, let's create an additional weapon to make it easier to get rid of the enemies lurking in the maze.

Prepare for lift off

We will create a sword sprite which we can draw ourselves.

1. So, we start by clicking on the **Paint new sprite** icon.

2. In the editor, we start by choosing a **brown** color and the **Rectangle** tool.

3. We draw two rectangular boxes forming a T-shape. This will be the handle for the sword.

4. Next, we switch to a **gray** color.

5. We select the **Ellipse** tool and drag out a long, narrow, oval shape to form the blade. It doesn't look very sharp up close, but at the downscaled size, it will.

6. If you like, you can decorate the sword some more with a pommel, gems or engravings.

7. We name the sprite sword for use in the scripts.

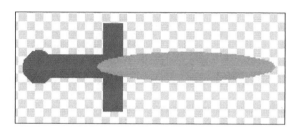

Engage thrusters

The player won't have access to the sword right from the start. It will lie somewhere in the maze. So to use it, the player has to make an effort to go and get it.

1. As the first step, we can again copy a **createMaze** listener script from another sprite.

2. We then create a second script starting with a **when I receive startGame** block.

3. We enter 5 in the **set size to ()%** block to make the sprite fit the maze. Perhaps your sprite should be slightly bigger or smaller depending on how big you made the drawing.

4. We enter 45 in the **point in direction ()** block to place it diagonally.

5. Then, we use the **show** block to show the sprite.

6. We place it on a random free tile with the **go to x:** 60 * **pick random** 0 **to** 7 − 210 **y:** 60 * **pick random** 0 **to** 5 − 150 block.

7. Then, we can use the **wait until touching <cat>?** block.

8. Next, we need to create a new list named `items`. This list will be available for all sprites.

9. In the script, we add **sword** to the **items** list.

10. Then, we use the **hide** block to hide the sprite.

```
when I receive startGame
set size to 5 %
point in direction 45
show
go to x: 60 * pick random 0 to 7 - 210 y: 60 * pick random 0 to 5 - 150
wait until touching cat ?
add sword to items
hide
```

When this script completes, the sword has changed places from inside the maze to the players inventory. When it's in the inventory it can be used as a weapon to defeat enemies. We will add that functionality now.

1. We start another script with a **when <s> key pressed** block.

2. Then, we make a check with an **if...** block. Only when this resolves will we take action on the key press.

3. We check the **if <items> contains sword** block then we make the sprite **go to <cat>**.

4. Then, we need to create a new variable to save the direction the cat is facing. We name this variable `catDir`. It needs to be available for all sprites.

5. We make the sword point in the direction using the **point in direction catDir** block, so it will be facing the same way as the cat sprite.

6. Then, we make it move using the **move 15 steps** block so the sword isn't on top of the cat but a bit in front of it.

7. We use the **show** block to show the sprite.

8. Then, we use the **wait 0.2 secs** block to keep it visible for a short while.

9. We use the **hide** block to hide the sprite again.

We still have to change the **catDir** value to actually make it work. To do that, we add a few blocks to the cat scripts.

1. We click on the **cat** sprite to view its scripts.

2. To each of the **key pressed** scripts, we add a **set <catDir> to...** block after we have changed its direction.

3. We fill the slots with the built-in **direction** variable. This saves the cat's current direction to the variable so it can be used elsewhere.

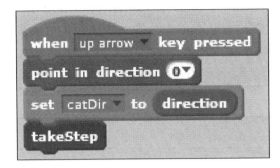

The sword should now function properly. Let's play a game to test it. Firstly, we have to move the cat to the sword to get it. Then we can use the sword with the *S* key. At each key press, it should be stuck out in the direction the cat is facing.

Objective complete – mini debriefing

We have now added a second weapon to the game. We could already use the bomb to remove enemies, but that poses a danger to the cat because the cat can get hurt by the explosion as well. The sword doesn't have that problem and it can be used repeatedly a lot faster. The player has to get very close to an enemy though, so that still poses a risk.

Another benefit of adding this weapon is that it offers another goal to achieve before running for the exit. The player has to weigh the benefit of gaining the item versus moving to the exit straight away. His decision will rely mostly on how many enemies are in the way.

Creating a bow and arrow

As noted, the sword is a very short ranged weapon, which poses a great risk to the player. If an enemy makes a sudden turn, which the knights do very often, they can easily hit the player before he/she has a chance to remove the enemy with the sword.

So as an alternative, we will also create a long range weapon that is much safer to use.

Prepare for lift off

We will create a bow and arrow. This will consist of two separate sprites. We will draw these sprites ourselves.

1. We select the **Paint a new sprite** block.

2. We select the brown color and the **Ellipse** tool.

3. We draw a tall vertical oval shape.

4. Next, we switch the color to **transparent**.

5. Still using the **Ellipse** tool, we will take three bites out of the brown shape to form the limbs of the bow.

6. Then, we will choose the light gray color.

7. We select the **Line** tool and draw a straight vertical line connecting the tips of the bow limbs. This will be the bow string.

8. When the drawing is complete, make sure it is centered properly on the costume center. For example, see the following image of how to position the costume center.

9. We name this sprite as bow.

This completes the drawing of a bow. Drawing an arrow is very simple as given in the following steps:

1. We again select the **Paint a sprite** block.

2. We choose the dark gray color.

3. With the **Line** tool selected, we draw a short horizontal line.

4. We name this sprite `arrow`.

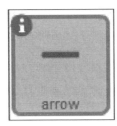

That's all we need to do. We are now ready to script these new sprites.

Engage thrusters

We will first place the bow sprite at a random place in the maze, just like we did with the sword. Because this is effectively the same sequence of instructions, we can easily copy the scripts from **sword** to **bow**:

1. We drag both the **createMaze** and **startGame** listener from the **sword** to the **bow** to create copies.

2. We just need to change the word to add to the items list from `sword` to `bow`.

```
when I receive startGame ▼
set size to 5 %
point in direction 45▼
show
go to x: 60 * pick random 0 to 7 - 210 y: 60 * pick random 0 to 5 - 150
wait until touching cat ▼ ?
add bow to items ▼
hide
```

With that, the placement of the **bow** item is done. It can now be picked up by the cat. To use it, we will add scripts to the arrow sprite, which will be the active part of this weapon.

1. Drag both the **createMaze** listener and the **() key pressed** script to **arrow** to make copies.

2. First, we change the key to be pressed as **a**, for arrow.

3. Then, we check using the **if <items> contains <bow>** block where **sword** has been replaced by **bow**.

4. The following blocks remain the same until the instructions reach the **wait 0.2 secs** block. We don't need that, so we remove it from the script.

5. We replace it with a **repeat until ()** loop to check for collisions.

6. We will check whether the arrow hits many different things, that is, if it is using the **if touching <edge> or touching color <black>? or touching <Knight> or touching <Ghost2>?** block.

7. While the arrow hasn't touched any of the previously mentioned objects, it will repeatedly use the **move 5 steps** block. This will make it fly forward.

8. Once it has touched an obstacle, we will use the **hide** block to hide the arrow. This block is already there.

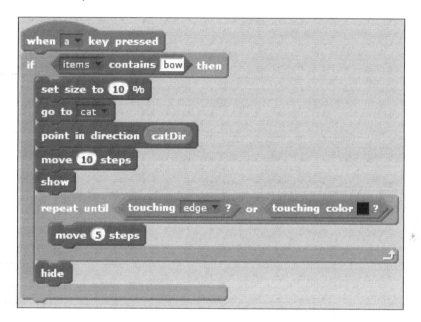

That completes our arrow functionality.

Objective complete – mini debriefing

The player now has two weapons to look for. Once either one of them is picked up and moved to the item list, it can be used by pressing the corresponding key.

When testing the game, we still notice a problem. The enemies won't actually be removed when hit by either of the new weapons. Only the bomb works completely as intended.

We will fix these final issues in the following step.

Tying up loose ends

The game is almost complete. There are just a few final adjustments to be made for all the sprites to interact properly.

Engage thrusters

Let's first solve the issue where the enemies don't respond to being hit by the sword or the arrow. What we are lacking is a collision check for these items. This can be easily fixed by the following steps:

1. We look at the **Knight** scripts.
2. In the **clone** script, we find a collision detection for the **explosion** block. We can add more checks here.
3. We expand the existing condition with the **or touching <sword>? or touching <arrow>?** block.
4. Then, we switch to the **ghost** sprite and add the same blocks there.

That fixes our collision problem, but not all the problems. As you may have noticed, the cat isn't actually harmed when touched by either one of the enemies. That's rather unfair, so let's change that as well.

1. We check the scripts for the **cat** sprite.
2. There we also find a collision check for explosion.
3. We add to this an **if touching <Knight>? or touching <Ghost2>?** construction.

That's more fair now that the cat will be reset and lose points by anything bad happening to it.

While we're reviewing the points system, let's add to that as well. The cat loses points when touched by an enemy. So it should also gain points on hitting an enemy.

1. We copy the **changePoints** function from the **cat** sprite to both the **Knight** and **Ghost2** sprites to be able to use it there.

2. At the end of either of the **clone** scripts, just before deleting the clone, let's reward points for defeating the enemy.

3. For the **Knight** sprite, we award 10 points.

4. For the **Ghost** sprite, we award 20 points, because it is more difficult to hit the ghost.

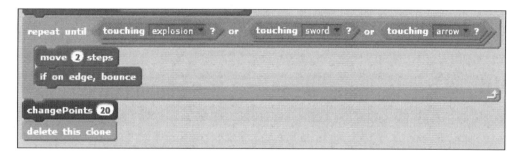

Now to prevent the players from uncontrollably pressing the weapon buttons, let's deduct points again for using a weapon. That way, there is a limit to how many times the weapons can be used. It will encourage the player to make a deliberate choice and not get into a mad killing frenzy.

1. We also copy the **changePoints** function to both **sword** and **arrow**.

2. In either of the **() key pressed** scripts, we call the **changePoints** function, just after we have confirmed the player actually has the item in the inventory.

3. For each use of an item, we deduct 5 points.

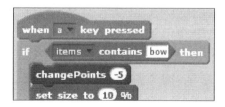

As a final step, we will also reset the items for each new level played. So at each level the player has to collect the items before he/she can use them.

1. We move to the **tileGenerator** scripts, as that's where we set most of the variables.

2. At the top of the list, we add a **delete <all> of items** block to empty the list.

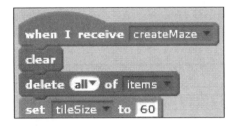

Test the game and see how many levels you can clear before getting defeated.

Objective complete – mini debriefing

We cleaned up the game and tied all the loose ends together. You'll often find that while developing games, you will try and add new features piece by piece. This often requires some rethinking and later adjustments to the parts of the game that we have already (thought were) finished.

Therefore, it's a good idea to keep the way you write games clear and consistent. Set variables at the start of a script. It's even better if you can collect them in the **Stage** object. Using functions also helps to separate different pieces of functionality.

Mission accomplished

That concludes this game. By adding enemies and items, we changed it from a relatively simple exploration game to a challenging search for items and an exit. We copied a lot of functionality already written, making changes only where we needed to create variation.

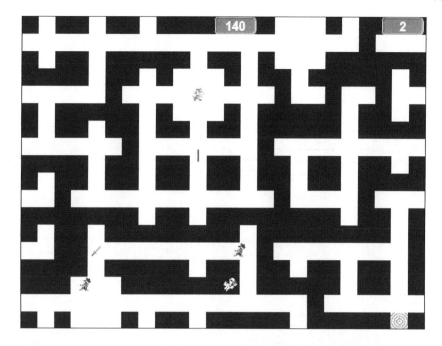

Hotshot challenges

There are still many more things you can add to this game to make it even more adventurous.

- ▶ You may notice that the enemies can kill themselves when they fly into the sword while it's still lying in the maze. Can you think of a way to fix this bug?

- ▶ Perhaps you'd like to improve the graphics or create an actual storyline. This would make the game look different at each level and improve the sense of an adventurous journey.

- ▶ You can also add other enemies or more weapons to use during the quest.

- ▶ Perhaps it's not such a good idea to reward the player points automatically on completing each level. It could be a lot more fun to fight for them. How about including gems and other treasures that are worth points?

Either way, it should be as much fun for you creating the adventure as it is for the players to play it. Be imaginative and make this adventure your own.

Project 9
Hunger Run

In this project, we will build a fast-moving game called Hunger Run. It is an auto-scrolling platform game. Although the art for Hunger Run is inspired by Super Mario, my all-time favorite platform-based game, the game is more similar to Monster Dash (`https://itunes.apple.com/us/app/monster-dash/id370070561?mt=8`).

Mission briefing

In this project, we will create an auto-scrolling platform game called Hunger Run. We will learn to view our game world's spatial space as a 2D grid of fixed-size grid units. On this 2D grid, we will learn how to scroll a player sprite through grid units. Moreover, we will add food sprites to each grid for Marco and Polo. They will run from one grid to another, picking up food as they go. Along the path of their frantic run, they will find food that nourishes as well as poisonous mushrooms that kill.

Why is it awesome?

While creating Hunger Run, we will learn how scrolling works and will also create auto-scrolling platforms that simulate player sprite moving between platforms. Not only that, we will also add food sprites that scroll with the platforms and interact with the player.

Our player sprite might remind you of Mario and Luigi. Marco and Polo are as cool as Mario and Luigi and definitely hungrier than them. They may not have a princess to save, but they have an empty stomach to fill!

Moreover, Hunger Run, just as in *Project 4*, *Space Age*, has a Game Manager sprite that manages the game's lifecycle and level advancement. To display the score, the score sprites are included in the starter project and can be used as they are.

Your Hotshot objectives

To build Hungry Run, we will start with a starter project that includes a complete set of Hunger Run sprites, minus the scripts. We will first understand the mechanics of scrolling and then apply the scrolling concepts to create the platform and food sprites, the scrolling sprites in this game. Next, we will create scripts for the player and Game Manager sprites. The following are our objectives:

- ▸ Understanding scrolling
- ▸ Adding scripts to the brick sprite
- ▸ Adding scripts to the food sprite
- ▸ Adding scripts to the player sprite
- ▸ Adding scripts to the Game Manager sprite
- ▸ Tweaking the game

Understanding scrolling

In this section, we will go over how horizontal and vertical scrolling work conceptually and mathematically.

Engage thrusters

In a horizontal scrolling game, the player sprite is always visible, but the non-player sprites can move in and out of the stage. The non-player sprites in the Hunger Run game include the background sprites (such as bricks) and interactive sprites (such as food items). Even when a sprite moves in and out of the stage, it still exists in the game space. In a 2D scrolling game, the game space can be represented as 2D grids, which consists of 2D unit grids as shown in the following screenshot. Each grid unit is the same size as the stage, 480 pixels in length (L) and 360 pixels in width (W).

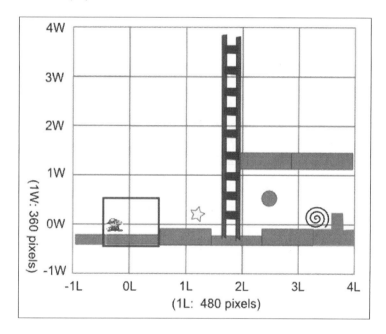

To keep the player sprite visible while scrolling, we keep the player sprite fixed in the grids but move other sprites horizontally or vertically, depending on the direction of the scrolling. To scroll Marco horizontally by N steps, move the other sprites to the opposite direction by N steps using the following steps:

1. To scroll Marco right by N steps, move the other sprites to the left by N steps.

2. To scroll Marco left by N steps, move the other sprites to the right by N steps.

The following screenshot illustrates how to scroll Marco to the right by N steps:

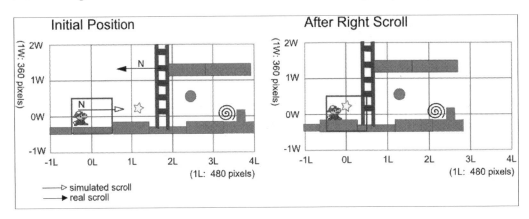

To simulate scrolling Marco vertically by N steps, move the other sprites also in the opposite direction by the same amount using the following steps:

1. To scroll Marco up by M steps, move the other sprites down by M steps.

2. To scroll Marco down by M steps, move the other sprites up M steps.

The following screenshot illustrates scrolling Marco up by M steps:

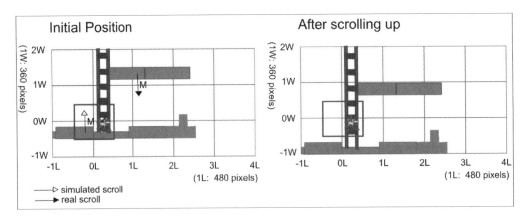

Since Hunger Run game is a side-scrolling game, lets simplify our matrix grids to a row, as shown in the following screenshot. There are five grids shown; Marco is in grid at index **-1** and the star is in grid at index **1**.

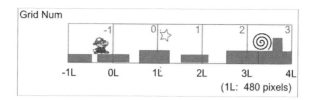

Objective Complete – mini debriefing

We introduced the 2D grids as the game space, which consists of 480 x 360 (in pixels) grid units. Then through illustration, we showed how to scroll the player sprite horizontally and vertically. To scroll the player sprite, simply move all other sprites by the desired scroll steps in the opposite direction. In the next section, we will add scripts to the brick sprite to respond to the scrolling.

Adding scripts to the brick sprite

Brick sprites are the building blocks that form the game platform. In this section, we will show how to clone the brick sprite to form the game platform. Moreover, we will make the platform auto-scroll to make the game faster-paced and more interesting. In Hunger Run, to keep it simple, we will start the game with one brick for each grid. Further, we will create all the bricks at game start to reduce game lag. For real world games with much larger grids and more sprites, the sprites may be created when needed for scalability.

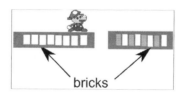

bricks

Engage thrusters

We will create scripts for the following:

- ▶ To respond to game start
- ▶ To initialize a clone's costume and location
- ▶ To scroll automatically
- ▶ To end the game

Perform the following steps to create the code to respond to the game start and create one brick for each grid:

1. Start with a **when I receive <game_start>** broadcast message block.

2. Set the index of the new grid to 0 using the **set <new_grid_idx> to ()** block.

3. Set the index of the minimum grid to 0 using the **set min_grid_idx to ()** block.

4. Set the maximum scrolling amount to 480 and the grid count to 0 using the **set <max_scroll_amount> to (() * (grid_count - ()))** block.

5. Then, for each platform, create a clone and assign it the clone platform index. First start with the **repeat until (new_grid_idx > grid_count)** block.

6. Inside the **repeat until (new_grid_idx > grid_count)** block, place a **create clone of <myself>** block. Then, enter 1 in the **change <new_grid_idx> by ()** block.

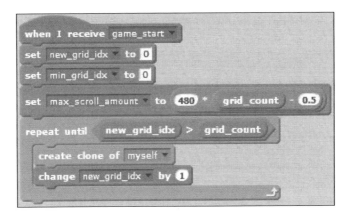

Before building the scripts, let's first look at how to find initial and current positions of the scrolling sprites.

Assume that your game grids look like the following screenshot, all the bricks start with x=0 inside their grid, thus point to the center of the grid. In the grids, however, each brick is at **(my_loc_in_grid + 1/2*grid_width + grid_width*my_grid_idx)**. The Food sprite's initial position is computed in the same way. In the example that follows, brick 1 starts at x=480, and apple starts at x=680.

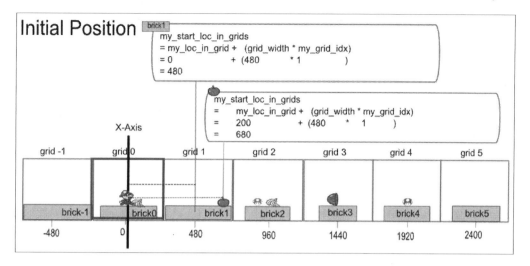

Initial Position

my_start_loc_in_grids
= my_loc_in_grid + (grid_width * my_grid_idx)
= 0   + (480   * 1   )
= 480

my_start_loc_in_grids
=   my_loc_in_grid + (grid_width * my_grid_idx)
=   200   + (480   * 1   )
=   680

Perform the following steps to create code to initialize a clone's look and location:

1. Start with a **when I start as a clone** block.

2. Set my location in the grid to 0 using the **set my_loc_in_grid to ()** block; enter 0.

3. Next, set my start location in grids by using the **set my_start_loc_in_grids to (my_loc_in_grid+my_grid_idx*grid_length)**.

4. Set my grid index to the new grid index using the **set <my_grid_idx> to new_grid_idx** block.

5. Add the **switch costume to ((my_grid_idx + ()) - my_grid_idx)** block; enter 1. We add 1 to **my_grid_idx** because the Scratch costume number starts at index 1 but the grid index starts at 0.

6. Then, enable the **go to x: my_start_loc_in_grids y: platform_y_value** and **show** blocks.

7. Next, add a **forever** block.

8. Inside the **forever** block, add the **set x to curr_scroll_amount + (my_grid_idx * grid_length)** block.

9. Under the **set x to curr_scroll_amount + (my_grid_idx * grid_length)** block from step 6, add an **if (<abs> of x position) > () then** block; enter 350. Then, enable the **hide else show** block. The **<abs> of x position > ()** block is a mathematical method that returns the absolute value of its input. You can try to use numbers other than 350, especially if you wish to create new brick costumes. This value should be between 240 (half of the stage or a grid) and 480. If this value is set too high, you will find that the sprites are "stuck" to the edge of the Stage and follow the player while scrolling. If this value is set too small, then the sprites would disappear suddenly.

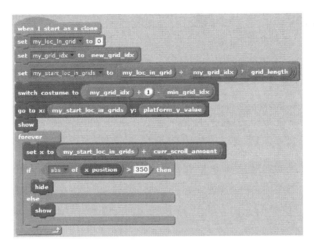

Perform the following steps to create code to scroll automatically:

1. Start with a **when I receive <start_scrolling>** block.

2. Inside the **when I receive <start_scrolling>** block, add a **forever** block.

3. Enter -1 in the **change <curr_scroll_amount> by (() * scroll_speed)** block, and check whether the current scrolling amount is greater than the maximum scrolling amount using the **if (<abs> of curr_scroll_amount > max_scroll_amount)** block. When the maximum scrolling amount is reached, the player has reached the edge of the grids. If so, then broadcast the **broadcast <scroll_max_reached>** block.

Finally, perform the following steps to create the code to end the game:

1. Start with a **when I receive <game_over>** block.
2. Delete the clone using the **delete this clone** block.

Objective complete – mini debriefing

In this section, we created scripts to respond to the game_start message, initialize a clone's look and location, scroll automatically, and end the game.

Adding scripts to the food sprite

For each platform, we will create clones of food sprite. To make the game more interesting, the food clones are randomly placed on its assigned platform and scroll with that platform. If the player sprite eats or touches bad food, then the player dies and the game ends. For all other food types, eating food will earn the player one point.

Prepare for lift off

Before diving into the scripts, we need to take a look at the food sprite costumes, as well as their scrolling mechanism.

The costumes of the food sprite are grouped into bad and good food, with bad food at the front of the costume list. The good_food_start_cos_idx variable defines which costume index is the starting index of good food costumes. We will use good_food_start_cos_idx later in the scripts to determine whether Marco eats a bad food sprite.

As shown in the following screenshot, if good_food_start_cos_idx is set to 3, then food sprites with **Red Mushroom** or **Green Mushroom** costume would be bad. Food sprites with all other costumes are good.

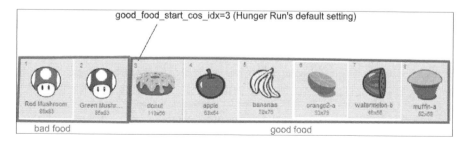

To make the game harder, increase the value of `good_food_start_cos_idx`, say to 4. Then donut would be considered bad as well—if it tastes so good, it has to be bad, right?

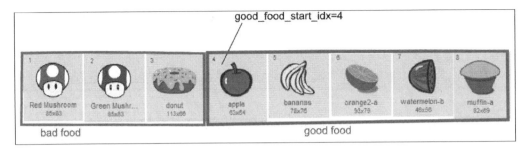

Engage thrusters

We will create scripts for the following:

▶ To handle the **<green flag>** click

▶ To handle the **level_start** message

▶ To initialize the look and location

▶ To scroll

▶ To handle collision with the player

Perform the following steps to handle the **<green flag>** click:

1. Start with a **when <green flag> clicked** block.

2. Next, let's initialize the food variables: `good_food_start_cos_idx`, `new_grid_idx`, `num_food_per_grid`, and `num_costumes`.

   ❑ The variable `good_food_start_cos_idx` is the starting costume ID of the good food group.

   ❑ The variable `new_grid_idx` is for the next platform index to be used for a new clone.

   ❑ The variable `num_food_per_grid` is the number of food clones to create for each platform.

   ❑ Finally, the `num_costumes` variable is the number of costumes the Food sprite has.

3. Enter 3 in the **set <good_food_start_cos_idx> to ()** block.

4. Enter 0 in the **set <new_grid_idx> to ()** block.

5. Enter 4 in the **set <num_food_per_grid> to ()** block.

6. Enter 8 in the **set \<num_costumes> to ()** block.

7. Then, enable **hide** because we only want the clones on stage, not the main sprite.

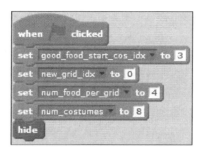

Perform the following steps to handle the `level_start` message:

1. Start with a **when I receive \<level_start>** block.

2. Add a **repeat until (new_grid_idx > grid_count)** block.

3. Inside the **repeat until (new_grid_idx > grid_count)** block, add a **repeat num_food_per_grid** block.

4. Inside the **repeat num_food_per_grid** block, add a **create clone of \<myself>** block.

5. Place a **change \<new_grid_idx> by ()** block following the **repeat num_food_per_grid** block; enter 1.

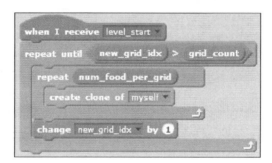

Perform the following steps to initialize a clone's look and location when it starts:

1. Start with a **when I start as a clone** block.

2. Set my grid index to the new grid index using the **set \<my_grid_idx> to new_grid_idx** block.

3. Add a **set \<my_loc_in_grid> to pick random () to ()** block; enter -240 and 240 respectively.

4. Set the startup location in the grids for this clone using the **set \<my_start_loc_in_grids> to ((my_grid_idx * grid_length) + (my_loc_in_grid))** block.

5. Drag out a **if () else ()** block.

6. Update it to be a **if (my_grid_idx < bad_food_start_grid_idx)** block. If this true, then add the **then** and **switch costume to (pick random good_food_start_cos_idx to ())** blocks; enter 8. The costumes with index ranging from good_food_start_ cos_idx to num_costumes are good. The variable bad_food_start_grid_idx controls whether bad food should show in this grid. For example, if the value of bad_food_start_grid_idx is 2, then bad food will show from grid 2 and up. This is to tweak the Hunger Run difficulty level. If bad_food_start_grid_idx is low, bad food would show sooner, thus the game, harder.

7. If the condition in the **if (my_grid_idx <bad_food_start_grid_idx)** block is false, then add the **else** and **switch costume to pick random () to ()** blocks; enter 1 and 8 respectively. The costume selection set includes bad food.

8. Finally, go to the starting location in the grids. Enter -120 in the **go to x: my_start_ loc_in_grids y: ()** block.

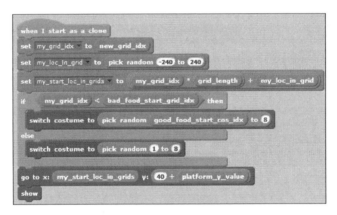

Perform the following steps to scroll with the platforms:

1. Start with a **when I start as a clone** block.

2. Add a **forever** block.

3. In the **forever** block, add the **set x to curr_scroll_amount + my_start_loc_in_grids** block.

4. To check when this clone has gone out of the viewable area, add an **if () then ()** block. Then, update it to be a **if <abs> of x position > ()** block; enter 230. Then, add the **hide**, **else**, and **show** blocks accordingly. Instead of 240, we use 230 to avoid clones getting stuck at the edge because their position never gets larger than 240 or smaller than -240. You can test it out on your own by changing the value to 240 to see the undesirable "sticking" effect.

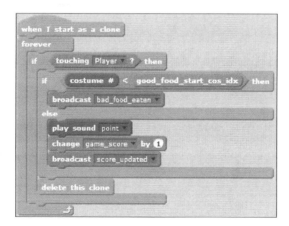

Perform the following steps to handle collision with the player:

1. Start with a **when I start as a clone** block.

2. Add a **forever ()** block. Then, inside the **forever ()** block, add an **if touching <Player> ? then ()** block.

3. Inside the **if touching <Player>? then ()** block, add an **if costume # < good_food_start_cos_idx then ()** block.

4. Inside the **if costume # < good_food_start_cos_idx then ()** block, add a **broadcast <bad_food_eaten>** block. In other words, if the player sprite eats a bad food item, then the food clone sends out a `bad_food_eaten` message.

5. Place an **else ()** block and inside it, add a **play sound <point>** block. Then, place the **change game_score by ()** and **broadcast <score_updated>** blocks; enter 1. In other words, if the player sprite eats a good food item, then they earn one point.

6. Finally, enable the **delete this clone** block to wrap up collision handling.

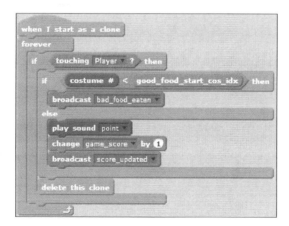

Objective complete – mini debriefing

We have created the code to handle the **<green flag>** click, to handle the `level_start` message, initialize the look and location, scroll, and handle collision with the player. To test the scrolling, you can build a block as shown in the following screenshot, and double-click on it to start auto-scrolling:

Adding scripts to the player sprite

The player sprite in Hunger Run is relatively simple. Its main action is to jump to avoid lethal food.

Prepare for lift off

Open the player sprite and verify that the player sprite has two costumes: **Marco** and **Polo** as shown on the following screenshot:

Engage thrusters

We will create codes for the player sprite to do the following:

▸ To initialize when the game starts

▸ To fall down

▸ To jump

▸ To end the sprite

Perform the following steps to initialize when the game starts:

1. Start with a **when I receive <game_start>** block.

2. Check whether to be Marco or Polo. The user selects the character at the beginning of the game. Add an **if player_name = () then () else ()** block; in **if player_name=()**, enter Marco. If the player's name is Marco, add the **switch costume to <marco>** block. Inside **else ()**, add the **switch costume to <polo>** block accordingly.

3. Enter 120 in the **set <jump_steps> to ()** block.

4. Enter 0.5 in the **set <jump_wait_time> to ()** block.

5. Enter 8 in the **set <fall_speed> to ()** block.

6. Enter 0 and 80 in the **go to x: () y : ()** block respectively.

7. Enable **show**.

Perform the following steps to fall down:

1. Start with a **when <green flag> clicked** block.

2. Enable **hide**.

3. Add a **forever** block. In the **forever** block, add a **repeat until touching <Brick>?** block. In the **repeat until touching <Brick>?** block, add a **change y by () * fall_speed** block; enter -1.

Perform the following steps to jump:

1. Start with a **when <space> key pressed** block.

2. Enable the **change y by jump_steps** block.

3. Enable the **wait jump_wait_time secs** block since sprite will continue to jump. This is to wait between each jump to prevent player from jumping too high.

Perform the following steps to end this sprite:

1. Start with a **when I receive <game_over>** block.
2. Enable the **stop <other scripts in sprite>** block.

The finished scripts are shown together in the following screenshot:

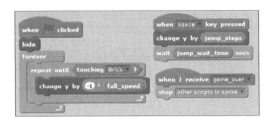

Objective complete – mini debriefing

In this section, we created the code for the player sprite to initialize when the game starts, fall down, jump, and end the sprite.

Adding scripts to the Game Manager sprite

In *Project 4*, *Space Age*, we introduced the practice of adding a Game Manager sprite to handle the game initiation and termination, level up, as well as scoring. Keep the game logic in a centralized location such as Game Manager, which makes it easier to configure and update the game. The Hunger Run starter project also includes a Game Manager sprite.

Prepare for lift off

Verify that the Game Manager has costumes named **Starter Screen** and **Level One**.

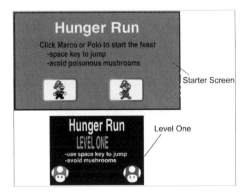

Engage thrusters

We will create the code to initialize the game and determine the game completion or termination.

Perform the following steps to initialize the system:

1. Start with a **when <green flag> clicked** block.

2. Enter 2 and 5 in the **go to x: () y: ()** block respectively.

3. Enable the **switch costume to <Start Screen>** block.

4. Enable **show**.

5. Enter 480 in the **set <grid_length> to ()** block.

6. Enter 0 in the **set <game_score> to ()** block.

7. Enter 0.2 in the **set <frame_rate> to ()** block.

8. Enter 10 in the **set <grid_count> to ()** block. This number should be equal to or less than the number of the costumes in the brick sprite.

9. Enter 3 in the **set <bad_food_start_grid_idx> to ()** block. The bad_food_start_ grid_idx variable is the platform number when bad food can start appearing. For example, if this variable is set to 3, then mushroom can appear starting from grid 3.

10. Enter 0.75 in the **set <scroll_speed> to ()** block.

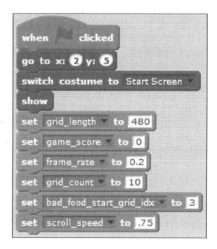

Perform the following steps to initialize the game:

1. Start with a **when I receive <game_start>** block. The game_start message is broadcasted when the **Start** button is pressed.

2. Enter 0 in the **set <curr_scroll_amount> to ()** block.

3. Then, enable **hide**.

4. Enable the **play sound <level_start>** block.

5. Then, broadcast the **broadcast <level_start>** message block.

6. Enter 2 in the **wait () secs** block. This is to give the player a chance to take a breather before the fast-scrolling action.

7. Next, broadcast the **broadcast <start_scrolling>** block. The brick and food sprites will respond by starting to scroll.

To win the game, Marco or Polo has to finish the run without eating bad food. When the last frame has been reached, the brick sprite would send out the **scroll_max_reached** message. To handle the **scroll_max_reached** message, perform the following steps:

1. Start with a **when I receive <scroll_max_reached>** block.

2. Enable the **switch costume to <You Won>** block.

3. Enter 24 and -24 in the **go to x: () y: ()** respectively.

4. Then, enable **show**.

5. Next, broadcast the **broadcast <game_won>** block.

6. Enable the **play sound <triumph> until done** block.

7. Finally, enable the **stop <all>** block.

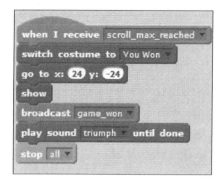

Objective complete – mini debriefing

We have added scripts for the Game Manager sprite to initialize the game and determine the game completion or termination. You can now test Hunger Run and may the odds be ever in your favor.

Tweaking the game

You may have beat the Hunger Run game in no time or you may have failed miserably just like me. Whichever type of gamer you are, you can configure Hunger Run to be harder or easier. We will wrap up this project with just doing that.

Prepare for lift off

The table shows all the configurable items:

Sprites	Variable name	Usage	Value to use for tweaking
Game Manager, Brick, Food	`grid_count`	Number of grids in the game	Lower is easier. When lower, the run is shorter.
Game Manager	`scroll_speed`	The scrolling speed	Lower is easier. Player can avoid bad food.
Food	`good_food_start_cos_idx`	Bad food ratio	Lower is easier. When lower, fewer food types are bad.
Food	`bad_food_start_grid_idx`	Bad food appearance time	Lower is more difficult. When lower, bad food would show sooner.

Engage thrusters

We will demonstrate how to configure these variables: `grid_count`, `bad_food_start_grid_idx`, `scroll_speed`, and `good_food_start_cos_idx`.

Tweaking the number of grids in the game

Perform the following steps to decrease the value of the `grid_count` variable:

1. Go to the Game Manager sprite's **Scripts** tab.
2. Find the **when <green flag> clicked** block, and enter a value lower than 10 in the **set <grid_count> to ()** block.

Perform the following steps to increase the value of the `grid_count` variable:

1. Create additional costumes for the brick sprite. Say we add five more costumes to make a total of 15 costumes.
2. Go to the Game Manager sprite's **Scripts** tab.
3. Find the **when <green flag> clicked** block, and enter 15 in the **set <grid_count> to ()** block.

Tweaking bad food's appearance time

Perform the following steps to adjust the time when bad thing and bad food appears:

1. Go to Game Manager sprite's **Scripts** tab.
2. Find the **when <green flag> clicked** block.
3. To make the game harder, enter a lower value than 3, say 2, in the **set <bad_food_start_grid_idx> to ()** block. Therefore, the bad food would show up at grid 2, instead of grid 3.
4. To make the game easier, enter a higher value than 3, say 5, in the **set <bad_food_start_grid_idx> to ()** block. Therefore, the bad food would show up at grid 5, instead of grid 3.

Tweaking the scrolling speed

Perform the following steps to tweak the scrolling speed:

1. Go to the Game Manager's **Scripts** tab.
2. Find the **when <green flag> clicked** block.

3. To make the game harder, enter a value higher than 0.5, say 2, in the **set <scroll_ speed> to ()** block. Therefore, the bad food would show up at brick number 2, instead of brick number 3.

4. To make the game easier, enter a value higher than 3, say 5, in the **set bad_food_ start_grid_idx to ()** block. Therefore, the bad food would show up at brick number 5, instead of brick number 3.

Tweaking the movement of the player

Perform the following steps to tweak the movement of the player:

1. Go to the player's **Scripts** tab.

2. Find the **when I receive <game_start>** block.

3. To make the game easier, increase the value of the `jump_steps` or `jump_wait_ time` variable. The larger the `jump_steps` variable is, the higher the player sprite will jump.

4. Moreover, we can make the player fall faster after he jumps. To do so, increase the value of the `fall_speed` variable.

Tweaking the bad food ratio

Assume your food sprite costume list is as the one shown in the following screenshot (as included in the starter project):

To make the game easier, reduce the bad food ratio by performing the following steps:

1. Go to the food sprite's **Scripts** tab.

2. Find the **when <green flag> clicked** block.

3. To make the game easier, enter a value lower than 3, say 2, in the **set <good_food_ start_cos_idx> to ()** block. There would be one bad food type.

4. To make the game harder, enter a value higher than 3, say 5, in the **set good_food_ start_cos_idx to ()** block. Then there will be four bad food types.

The result of tweaking the `good_food_start_cos_idx` variable is shown in the following screenshot:

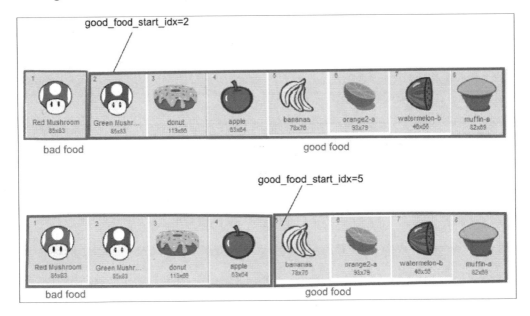

Objective complete – mini debriefing

We have demonstrated how to tweak Hunger Run in the following ways:

- ▶ Tweaking the number of bricks in the game
- ▶ Tweaking the time of appearance of bad food
- ▶ Tweaking the scrolling speed
- ▶ Tweaking the movement of the player
- ▶ Tweaking the bad food ratio

Mission accomplished

We learned the mechanics of scrolling in detail and also created an auto-scrolling platform to simulate the player sprite moving between them. Further more, we added the food sprites that scroll with the platform and interact with the player. Next, we added the game logic that is common to all the sprites of the Game Manager, which controls the top-level game initiation and termination, as well as level advancement. Finally, we ended with several ways to tweak the game for the desired level of difficulty.

Hotshot challenges

The following are your challenges for this project:

- ▸ Update the brick sprite costumes to have gaps between them and add to the game rule that if the player falls through the gaps, then the game ends
- ▸ Add a mode to turn off the auto-scroll and add scripts to allow manual bi-directional scrolling
- ▸ Create a vertically scrolling game based on Hunger Run
- ▸ Make the background cityscape scroll

Project 10

Sprites with Characters

In this project, we will focus on creating costumes for a sprite. We will learn how to create detailed costumes with various methods as well as create animations using costumes.

Mission briefing

In this project, we will leverage many new and impressive features in Scratch 2.0's sprite editor to create costumes for a robot sprite. We will also create movement animation scripts using the costumes shown in the following screenshot:

Why is it awesome?

Better game graphics make any game more enticing and engaging. The Scratch 2.0 Costume editor includes several new and useful features. We will use these new features to spice up our game.

Your Hotshot objectives

First, we will create a simple project, covering the following points:

- ▶ Building the robot wireframe
- ▶ Coloring it as metallic
- ▶ Performing final adjustments
- ▶ Animating
- ▶ Parting with a few tips

Building the robot wireframe

In this section, we will explore various cool and new features in the costume editor. We will create costumes in the Vector Mode. Vector graphics look much smoother in games, especially in the full-screen mode. Moreover, vector graphics can be reshaped easily. The Vector Mode is very flexible and is my preferred mode of creating costumes.

You may wonder why vector graphics appear smoother than bitmap graphics. It's because in vector, the edges of lines and objects become more transparent gradually, fading into the background or layer behind. This effect is called **antialiasing**.

Prepare for lift off

We are going to create a robot costume for our player. The first thing I usually do when creating a detailed costume is start from a simple wireframe, then add color and shade.

Let's create the new costumes and a new project by performing the following steps:

1. To create a new project, navigate to **File | New**.
2. Create a new costume by clicking on the **Paint new costume** icon.
3. On the **Paint Editor** page, switch to the vector mode by clicking on the **Convert to vector** button.

The Vector Mode tools include Select, Reshape, Pencil, Line, Rectangle, Oval, Paint Bucket, Stamper, Layer, and others. We will demonstrate the use of some of these tools.

Engage thrusters

Click on the **costume** tab of the new sprite and then click on the black color to change the primary shade to black. Next, create the parts for the robot costumes using the following steps:

Next, create the parts for the robot costumes using the following steps:

1. Click on the **Oval** tool button.
2. Click and drag on it to make a circle to be the head and a small oval to be one ear.
3. Click on the **Stamper** tool button and click on the ear to make a copy.
4. Drag the copied ear away.
5. Click on the **Select** tool button.
6. Position both ears to the head, as shown in the following screenshot:

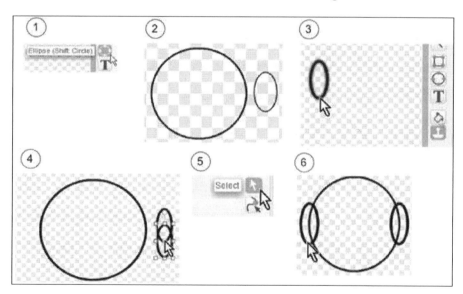

To create the robot's torso, perform the following steps:

1. Click on the **Rectangle** tool button.
2. Drag it to make three rectangles to be the neck, the upper body, and the lower body.
3. Next, click on the **Reshape** tool button.

4. Shape the upper body by moving the vertices.

5. To shape the lower body, still in reshaping mode, click on the lines to add one vertex on each side. To remove a vertex, simply click on it.

6. Move the vertices to shape the lower body like a diamond.

7. Click on the **Select** tool button.

8. Move the three pieces to form the torso, as shown in the following screenshot:

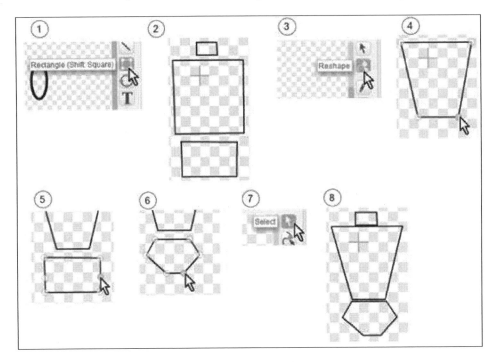

To create arms and legs, perform the following steps:

1. First, use the **Rectangle** tool to make three rectangles; one for an arm, one for a leg, and one for the feet; then use the **Ellipse** tool to create a circle to be a joint.

2. Then, click on the **Reshape** tool button.

3. Click on each vertex to move it and adjust each shape.

4. Next, select all the parts, duplicate (*Ctrl + C* and then *Ctrl + V*), and flip horizontally.

5. Repeat for all other symmetric parts. Then, add each part to the body as shown in the following screenshot:

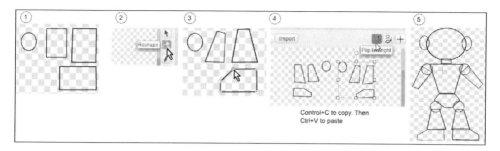

6. Add eyes and hands using the **Rectangle**, **Ellipse**, **Reshape**, and **Select** tool with the technique covered in previous steps. Refer to the following screenshot:

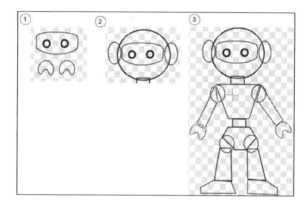

You may want to resize the whole costume. To do so, perform the following steps:

1. Click on the **Select** tool button, and draw a dotted blue rectangle around the whole costume.

2. The selected costume should be inside a white box.

3. Click on any of the corners of the white box to see a double-arrowed icon for resizing.

4. Then, adjust the size of your choice, as shown in the following screenshot:

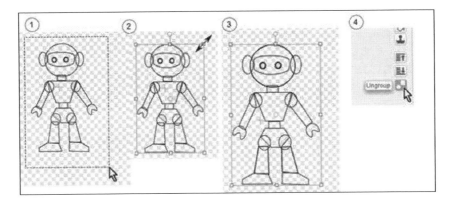

Objective complete – mini debriefing

There, we did it! We have created a robot wireframe, complete with head, arms, legs, feet, and joints. In the next section, we will kick it up a notch by adding color.

Coloring it metallic

For a more realistic look, we will use the **gradient** option. A gradient is a combination of two colors. There are three gradient options, namely horizontal, vertical, and radial.

Prepare for lift off

A horizontal gradient makes the transition color smooth from the left end to the right of a fill-in. A vertical gradient changes the color gradually from the top to the bottom of the fill-in. Lastly, a radial gradient blends the colors from the paint bucket's click and outward. There is also an option to switch back to a **solid fill**, which is the option in the upper-left box as shown in the following screenshot:

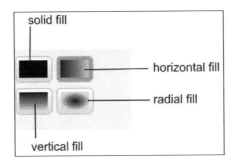

Engage thrusters

Click on the paint bucket. Let's select colors for the primary and secondary shades.

1. Select a color to change the primary shade.

2. Click on the secondary shade box.

3. Select a color for the secondary shade.

4. Click on the primary shade box to switch it back to color.

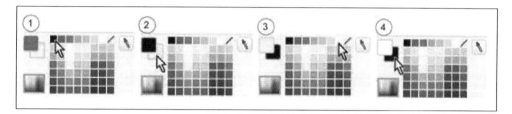

The result should look like the following screenshot:

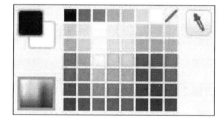

To fill the color for the main body parts, perform the following steps:

1. Click on the **Paint Bucket** tool. Then, select gray and white as the two colors (refer to the steps shown in the *Building the robot wireframe* task). Select **Radial Gradient**.

2. With the paint bucket, click on each circular shape, namely ears, head, and joints.

3. Select **Horizontal Gradient**.

4. With the paint bucket, click on the rest of the shapes as shown in the following screenshot:

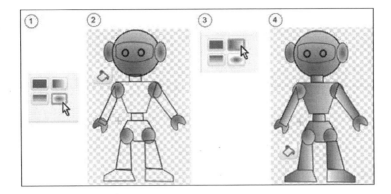

Next, fill the eyes. Note that we want to fill the mechanical eyeballs first. If filling the larger shape first, it'll be difficult to locate the smaller shapes. Fill the colors as shown in the following screenshot:

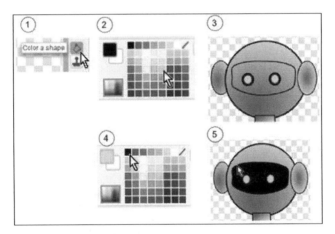

Objective complete – mini debriefing

In this task, we learned how to select two colors to use for a gradient. We used both vertical and radial gradients to color various parts of the robot.

Performing final adjustments

Though we've created the robot frame and colored it, we are not done yet. To make the robot look more natural and three-dimensional, we will adjust the position, including the layer position, of several shapes.

Prepare for lift off

Make sure that the robot shapes are ungrouped.

Engage thrusters

To adjust the head, perform the following steps:

1. Click on the **Select** tool.

2. Select a ear. Press the *Shift* key and click on the **Back a layer** button to send the ear back.

3. Do the same for both ears, as shown in the following screenshot:

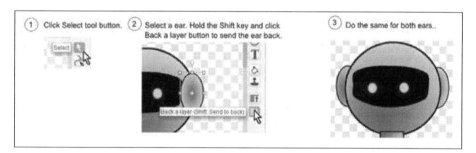

Next, we will adjust the shapes on the upper body:

1. Select an arm joint, press the *Shift* key and click on the **Back a layer** button to send the arm joint back.

2. Select the right arm, press the *Shift* key, and click on the **Back a layer** button to send the right arm back.

3. Do the same for the other joint and arm, as shown in the following screenshot:

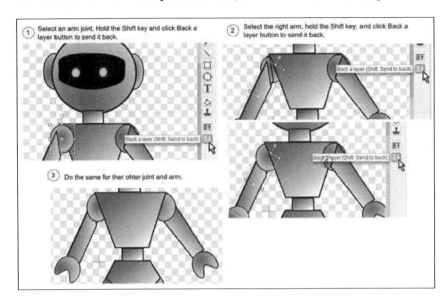

To adjust the legs, we also first select the joint, send it to the back, then select the leg and send it to the back. The details are included in the following screenshot:

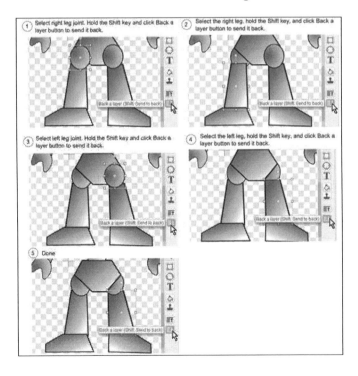

Objective complete – mini debriefing

In this task, we added the gradients and adjusted the layers of the robot costume. As seen in the following screenshot, we are ready to animate it in the next section:

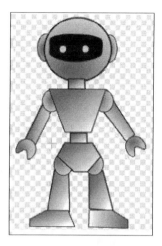

Animating

Animation loops are the scripts to simulate movement more lively by switching costumes. We will create different costumes based on the robot costume we just created.

Prepare for lift off

Make two copies of the robot costumes. Name one as `left arm up` and the other `walk right`.

Engage thrusters

Let's first create a costume called `left arm up`. Duplicate the robot costume and name the copy as `right arm up`. Then, perform the following steps to update the `left arm up` costume:

1. Press and hold the *Shift* key. With the **Select** tool, click on the robot's left arm.

2. While the *Shift* key is still pressed, click on the left hand.

3. Now both the left arm and the left hand are selected.

4. Use the rotation handle to rotate the arm and hand as shown in the following screenshot:

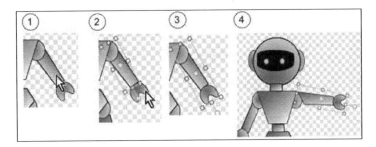

Using the same technique (duplicate costume, then move or rotate body parts), you can easily create costumes that can be used in animation loops. The complete project includes three costumes, namely **robot, left arm up 1, left arm up 2** ,as shown in the following screenshot:

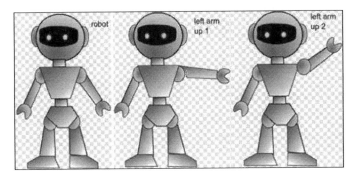

To create an animation loop for the left arm up and down, perform the following steps:

1. Start with the **when <a> key pressed** block.

2. Set the **switch costume to <robot>** and **wait (.2) secs** blocks. Note that the delay is needed for this costume to show long enough for the game player to see.

3. Set the **switch costume to <left arm up 1>** and **wait (.2) secs** blocks.

4. Set the switch **costume to <left arm up 2>** and **wait (.2) secs** blocks.

5. Set the switch **costume to <left arm up 1>** and **wait (.2) secs** blocks.

6. Set the switch **costume to <robot>** and **wait (.2) secs** blocks.

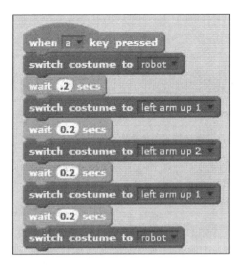

Next, let's update the `walk right` costume to face to the right. First, update the head by performing the following steps:

1. Observe the head and visualize how it should look like if it was facing the right.

2. Use the **Select** tool to move both ears, the visor, and both eyes away from the head.

3. To move the ear to the top, select the ear, press the **Shift** key, then click on the **Forward a layer** button.

4. Verify that the ear is on top and visible.

5. Click on the **Reshape** tool and adjust the visor size.

6. Select unneeded parts and hit **Delete** key to delete the parts.

7. Select and adjust the position of the eye, as shown in the following screenshot:

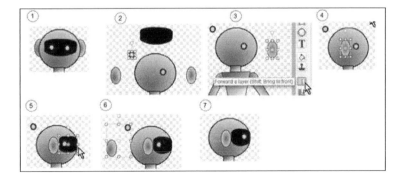

Next, update the rest of the walk right costume, by performing the following steps:

1. To select the robot's right arm and hand together, click on the **Select** button, press the Shift key, and then click on both. There will be a light-gray box around the selected parts.

2. While the robot's right arm and hand are still selected, press and hold the Shift key, and click on the **Forward a layer** button to bring both to the top.

3. To select the robot's right leg joint and the leg together, click on the **Select** button, press and hold the Shift key, and then click on both the robot's right leg joint and the leg. While the Shift key is still pressed, click on the **Forward a layer** button to bring the right leg joint and the leg to the front.

4. Select the **Reshape** tool, and adjust the upper torso and the lower torso accordingly.

5. Click on the **Select** tool.

6. Select the right foot, and click on the **Flip left-right** button to flip it horizontally.

7. Adjust the foot's location.

8. We are done with the costume.

Refer to the following screenshot:

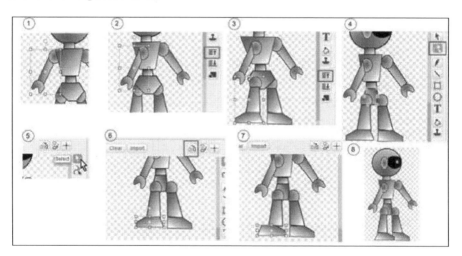

Based on the costume **walk right 1**, you can rotate the robot's arms and legs to create additional costumes such as **walk right 2** and **walk right 3** as shown in the following screenshot:

To create an animation loop to mimic walking to the right, perform the following steps:

1. Start with the **when <b> key pressed** block.

2. Set the **switch costume to <walk right 1>** and **wait (.2) secs** blocks. Note that the delay is needed for this costume to show long enough for the game player to see.

3. Set the **switch costume to <walk right 2>** and **wait (.2) secs** blocks.

4. Set the **switch costume to <walk right 3>** and **wait (.2) secs** blocks.

5. Set the **switch costume to <walk right 2>** and **wait (.2) secs** blocks.

6. Set the **switch costume to <walk right 1>** and **wait (.2) secs** blocks.

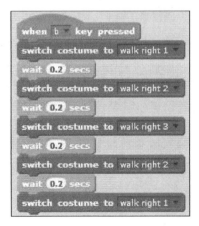

To create costumes for walking towards left, just duplicate each costume and use the **Flip left-right** tool. Refer to the following screenshot:

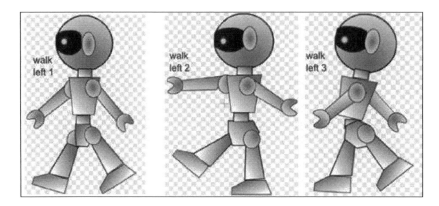

Objective complete – mini debriefing

In this section, we created costumes by duplicating the robot costume and making changes, mostly small changes, to create new costumes to be used in the animation sequence. We also demonstrated how to script animation loops by switching to the next costume in an animation sequence, pause, then to the next, until we get back to the costume that the sequence starts with.

Parting with a few tips

There are a few more tips that are helpful when creating the vector graphic in the **Paint editor**.

Engage thrusters

To view the full canvas, click on the **Zoom out** icon. To work with a smaller shape, use the **Zoom in** icon. There are four magnification levels as shown in the following screenshot:

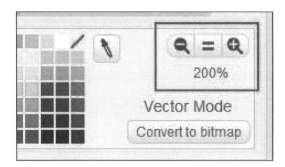

To create a transparent or see-through effect, select the **No Fill** paint (a white box with a red strike across it) as one gradient color, as shown in the following screenshot:

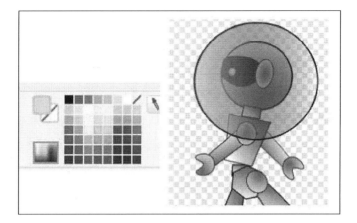

Objective complete – mini debriefing

We have picked up a few more tips that will make the use of the Scratch Paint editor even more pleasant and efficient.

Mission accomplished

We have learned to use the exciting new features in the Scratch Paint editor to make vector graphics.

First, we created the wireframe for the robot costume using the following tools:

- ▶ Shaping tools:

  The tools included in this category are rectangle, ellipse, and reshape

- ▶ Positioning tools:

  The tools included in this category are Forward a layer and Back a layer

- ▶ Grouping tool

Next, we filled the costume wireframe with a metallic color using the following tools:

- ▶ **Paint tools**: We used the paint bucket tool
- ▶ **Gradient tools**: We used the vertical gradient and radial gradient tools

Then, we created additional costumes based on the first costume for animation sequences. Moreover, we created scripts to animate the sprite by switching costumes in a motion sequence. To wrap it up, we closed with several useful tips for creating vector graphics in the Scratch Paint editor as shown in the following screenshot:

Hotshot challenges

Import the robot costumes to an existing game, as shown in *Project 9*, *Hunger Run*, and add missing costumes and animation scripts to mimic walking, running, and jumping.

The robot created in this lesson does not have elbows nor knees. Update it to have them, just like the voodoo dolls shown in the following screenshot:

The New Scratch Interface

With the introduction of Scratch 2.0, some things about the program have changed. In this appendix, we will walk through the website and have a look at the most important elements of Scratch. We will take special note of what has been added or changed.

Mission briefing

We will have a look at the website in general and the different pages we can look at to find information and inspiration. Then we go into the Scratch editor, which is the main focus of this book. We will have a look at how old features have been rearranged and how new features have been added.

Why is it awesome?

It can really slow you down if you want to do something and can't find the proper buttons to do it. By having a good look around, we can prevent unexpected surprises when we are building a project. It's better to take this extra time now and gain a better understanding of how the Scratch interface works than to try and figure everything out on the go. This can prevent frustration later on when we want to focus on building a cool game.

Your Hotshot objectives

We will start from a broad perspective, then dive deeper into the editor, and have a look at the interesting and new features. We will move through the following things in order:

- ▶ Website overview
- ▶ Creating an account and logging in
- ▶ The Scratch editor layout
- ▶ Creating and importing sprites
- ▶ New script block categories
- ▶ Saving and loading projects
- ▶ Sharing the backpack feature
- ▶ Some benefits and drawbacks of the new Scratch interface

Mission checklist

To start our journey, all we need to do is open a web browser and go to the Scratch home page at www.scratch.mit.edu.

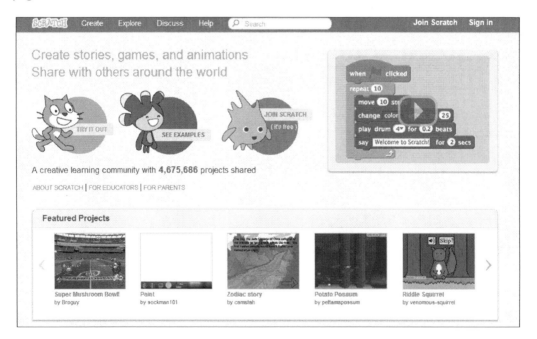

Scratch makes use of the Adobe Flash Player, so you need to have this installed. Many computers already have Flash installed since it's used quite frequently in websites and web games. But if you still need to get it, you can find the installation package at `get.adobe.com/flashplayer`.

Website overview

While opening the Scratch home page, we are greeted by a familiar sight. The main page hasn't changed a lot compared to the previous site. It still shows a sample of recently added or interesting projects from other Scratchers. You can still view/play with these projects by clicking on the images. It might have a few more featured categories than before.

At the top of the site is a row of buttons to other useful pages. We will have a look at the **Create, Explore, Discuss,** and **Help** links to see what they have to offer. We'll look at **Join Scratch** and **Sign In** in the next step of this overview.

Engage thrusters

The **Create** button brings us to the heart of the Scratch website, the Scratch editor. This is where all the magic happens and where we can create projects. We'll have a closer look at the editor and its features later.

The **Explore** button brings us to a greater selection of projects posted by other Scratchers. We can look at featured projects that are currently in the spotlight. This is based on how well-liked a project is in the Scratch community. We can also make a selection based on the artistic category the projects belong to. If we're looking for something really specific, we can search on tag words. We can also switch to a studio overview. These show collections of projects belonging to a specific Scratch member or an event.

The **Discuss** button leads to the Scratch forum. This is the place to ask questions and to find answers. The forum is divided into categories to make it easier to find what you need. Just look for the appropriate general topic first and then search for something specific within that category. There is a link at the top of the forum to search for subjects based on keywords and other restrictions. To post your own question or comment in the forum, you need to be logged in as a member. It's not possible to place anonymous comments.

If you're new to Scratch, you can use the **Help** button. On this page, you will find all kinds of useful information for new Scratchers. The left-hand column offers a range of tutorials and cheat sheets to get you started quickly. The right-hand column offers some more specific and in-depth information. It's useful for teachers and parents, or if you want to know more about the technical side of Scratch.

Objective complete – mini debriefing

With these four buttons, you can get to most of what you need to learn about and playing with Scratch. Scratch is meant to be an easy-to-learn animation and game-building tool, and the website is no different. It helps you find your way in a few minutes. If you want to explore more, you can always dig deeper.

Creating an account and logging in

To make full use of Scratch, it's best to create a Scratch account. This allows you to participate in forum discussions. It also ties your projects directly to your name and allows you to save them online. Any serious Scratcher can't go without a Scratch account, so it's best to get this done early.

Join Scratch   Sign in

Engage thrusters

Click on the **Join Scratch** button to be presented with an application form. You choose a Scratch username. This is the name that will appear publicly on the forum and next to all your projects, so choose wisely. You will be known by that name to the rest of the Scratch community. You also need to type your secret password twice to make sure you don't make any typing errors.

Next, you are presented with some questions about your age and gender. You can answer these truthfully. They are just used for statistics by the Scratch team, so they know in general who is using their program. The most important question is your e-mail address. This is used in case you forget your password.

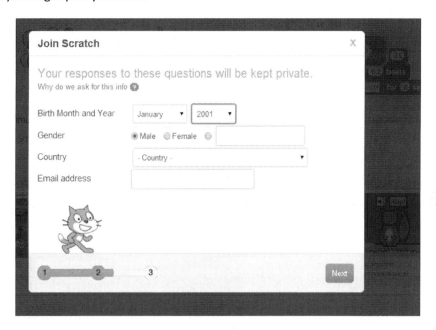

If you filled in everything correctly, the application will conclude with a welcome message. After that, you are automatically logged in with your new account, and a friendly welcome message is waiting for you in your Scratch mailbox.

In case you have quit the website and need to log in again, you can use the **Sign In** button. Here, you fill in your username and password. When logged in, the button will change to show your username and picture. If we click on the button now, some other options will appear. We can view (and change) our profile or have a look at our projects (called **My Stuff**). We can also change account settings, which is basically an option to change your password or e-mail address. Finally, we get the option to sign out again.

Objective complete – mini debriefing

Signing up for a Scratch account is a fairly straightforward process. It's also a necessary step if you'd like to do more than explore a bit or experiment with some one-off project that you have no interest in saving. If you come back to Scratch, sooner or later you would really like to get that Scratch account.

The Scratch editor layout

As an active Scratch designer and programmer, we'll spend a lot of time in the Scratch editor. The entire editor is collected in a single page, with a few options that will open a pop-up window to make a selection. In Scratch 2.0, the editor has changed a bit compared to the previous version. So we'll have a look at what's changed and what has stayed the same.

Engage thrusters

At first, you'll see that the screen is divided in to three sections. There's the **Stage** area, where we view the results of our work. Below that is the **Sprites** area, where we can view and select all our sprites. These are like the actors that take part in our project. Clicking on a sprite highlights it as the active sprite to work with.

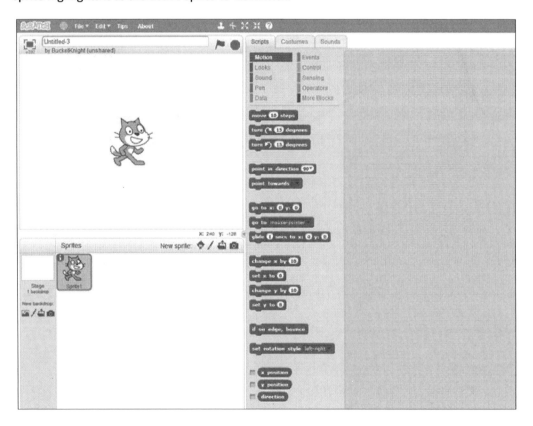

As a new addition, each sprite has a small info button in the top-left corner. Clicking on this button leads to a Properties panel where we can change some general properties such as the name of the sprite, its default direction, and the directional restraints. These used to be in a separate info window above the scripts view. Since changes to these properties are made infrequently, they are now hidden beneath the sprite to save some room.

The way to add sprites has been changed a bit as well. Since the tool is now used online, the importing of existing sprites has been split. We can now choose to load a sprite from the default online library, or we can upload a sprite from our own computer to use online. These uploaded sprites are never directly accessible to other Scratchers, unless you share your project. The option to take a picture with your webcam has been moved to a more obvious location, next to the other sprite-creation icons. This feature was already available, but it used to be hidden under the **Costumes** tab.

Next, let's have a look at the biggest part of the screen, the **Scripts/Costumes/Sounds** editor. This is the part of the editor where we will spend most of our time in either creating sprites and costumes or adding scripts to sprites. Between the editor window and the Stage and Sprites windows, you'll find a thin vertical line with an arrow somewhere around the halfway point. Clicking on this arrow will expand/shrink the editor. This allows more space to create scripts and costumes, or more space to view the project and arrange sprites.

At the top of the screen, there is a menu bar with some general functions, such as saving and loading a project. You'll also find the quick copy, delete, and scaling tools here. Added to that is a useful help button. If you are confused about something, just click on the help button and then click on the part that's confusing you. A help page will pop out that explains a bit about the feature you clicked on.

You can also browse through these help pages manually if you just want to learn more about Scratch. You can open the help menu by clicking the question mark icon at the top of the right bar.

Objective complete – mini debriefing

The Scratch editor still contains most of the familiar features we were used to. Some features have been moved to a more suitable place, either to make them easier to access or to save some space on the screen.

Creating and importing sprites

There are a few places in the Scratch editor where we can create or import images. If you used Scratch before, you will be familiar with them already. What has changed is that you can now draw images in two different ways. It's now possible to create sprites as bitmap images or as vector images. Each of these modes has some advantages and disadvantages.

Engage thrusters

As mentioned before, we can import images from the default library or from our local hard drive. We can do this for the **Stage** object while adding a new sprite, and also in the **Costumes** tab to add a new costume. You'll see that the same icons are repeated thrice in these three locations.

The more interesting addition is the toggle between **Convert to bitmap** and **Vector Mode**. You can find this button at the bottom right of the costumes editor, as shown in the following screenshot. What this does is it switches the created sprite between two different ways of drawing. It also changes how the image is calculated by the computer. This can make a difference to the performance speed while the project is running. Let's look at the differences between these two drawing modes.

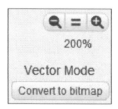

Bitmap mode is what you will be accustomed to from the Scratch 1.4 program. In bitmap mode, sprites consist of pixels. Pixels are little squares that are placed side by side to form an image. An image like this is saved in the computer's memory as rows of pixels using the same color. For example, there are 10 transparent pixels, then two black pixels, then six orange pixels, and so on. The tools to create a bitmap image are similar to using a paintbrush on paper. Wherever you touch the paper with the brush, a clump of color is created. To create sharper graphics, the toolbox also has options to create (filled) rectangles and ellipses. It's also possible to erase parts of the image, pixel by pixel, if necessary.

Vector mode works quite differently. In vector mode, an image is described as curving lines. An enclosed space in between the lines is simply filled with a solid color. The curves and direction of the lines are saved in the computer's memory as math calculations. When an image is fairly simple, with relatively few complex curves, this can save a lot of memory compared to the saving of bitmap images. An advantage of vector images is that they can be reshaped by pushing and pulling the curved lines around. Another benefit is that vector images can be scaled up without a loss of quality. When bitmap images are scaled up, the pixels grow in size and you get to see the jagged edges. Vector images don't have that problem because the entire vector calculation is just multiplied to recreate the image in a bigger size.

When an image contains many different shapes or subtle color differences, like a photograph for instance, vector images don't work very well anymore. An image like that would contain so many curves and little color-filled shapes that the amount of calculations to save adds up. The resulting file would become bigger than a straightforward bitmap.

Objective complete – mini debriefing

Scratch still offers many ways to include images in your projects. There are even a few more options than before. You can get images from elsewhere, take a picture with your webcam, or draw your own images directly in Scratch. The new vector mode offers another way of drawing that can be useful at times. Just keep in mind what kind of an image you want to create, and experiment with both bitmap and vector images to see which one gives you the best result.

New script block categories

Scratch 1.4 contained eight distinct block categories. Scratch 2.0 contains ten.
The new categories are called **Events** and **More Blocks**. Let's have a look at where these new categories come from and what they include.

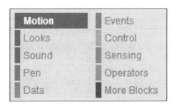

Engage thrusters

The **Events** category doesn't contain anything new. It was split off from the **Control** category to better describe what the blocks contained within do. When we click on the **Events** category, we see that it contains most of the blocks with a curved top. These are the kinds of blocks a script always starts with. They are activated when something happens, or in other words, when an event occurs.

What's left in the **Control** category are loops and conditions. These are the logic blocks that can guide a script along different paths. They control what happens in the project and how it happens.

A new addition to the **Control** category is three blocks that are used to create clones of a sprite. This is a feature that was long missing from Scratch. A clone is a copy of a sprite that behaves the same as the original.

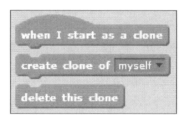

Perhaps you have seen projects with swarms of enemies. In the old version of Scratch, we had to manually copy each sprite. The **Sprites** view would quickly be filled up. This is no longer necessary. Now it's possible to create one basic enemy and then clone that enemy as many times as you want with a simple loop block. There can only be 300 clones on the **Stage** area at any given time, but in most cases, that will be plenty. Just keep in mind that any clones above the maximum amount won't be created.

The **More Blocks** category was introduced from a side project of Scratch. A group of students weren't satisfied with all the options Scratch had to offer already. They wanted to create their own function blocks. So they built an adapted version of Scratch called **Build Your Own Blocks** to include that feature. This feature has now been included in the main Scratch program. So now you can create your own blocks too.

The way this works is quite similar to how you create and use variables. First we click on the **Make a Block** button. Then we can give the new block a descriptive name. We can also include options. These add familiar slot spaces to the block. In this way, we can get variables and other data into the block.

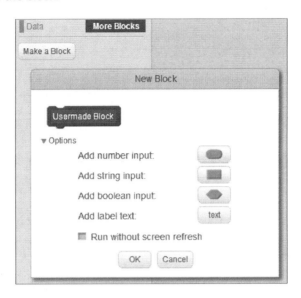

When we are done with this step, a new purple define block appears in the **Scripts** editor. To this block, we can add more script actions, similar to how we create a regular script. You'll also notice that a purple block with our chosen block name has been added to the **More Blocks** category. This block can be put anywhere in any script to trigger the definition block.

This feature is very useful for a combination of actions that is repeated often. Instead of copying whole rows of blocks, we only need to include the self-built function block. The definition has to be written only once, but can be executed many times.

Objective complete – mini debriefing

The new block additions may seem small at first, but they can be very powerful tools to create more impressive projects. Both the cloning and the **Make a Block** option simplify the creation of hordes of enemies. Of course, they can be used for other purposes as well.

Saving and loading projects

When we've done a lot of work on a project, it's a good thing to save it so that we don't lose our progress. This also allows us to continue work later.

Engage thrusters

The good news is that the online Scratch environment saves your progress automatically to the server. So even when we don't take any action ourselves, it's unlikely that we will lose a lot of work. But it can still be useful to save manually as well because the bad news is that Scratch doesn't save different versions. While auto-saving the last saved file, it is overwritten. This can become a problem if you've worked along a path that turns out to be a dead end, or if you (want to) have several variations on a project. In these cases, it's a good idea to save the file manually, preferably with a new name, so we can still access older versions of the project.

In the top menu bar, underneath the **File** button, are the saving options. We can simply click on **Save now** to force an immediate save. This overwrites the project but can be useful if you want to quit for the day and close the browser. If we use **Save as a copy**, we can save a new version of the project. Then there's the option to download to and upload from your computer. These functions are very useful to create local backups of your projects, or if you want to move project files around without having to rely on Scratch accounts and the server.

Objective complete – mini debriefing

There isn't much to say about saving files, other than just save often and be smart about it. It's always better to have a back-up file that you will never look at again than to lose valuable work and time just because you forgot to save your project.

Sharing the backpack feature

Besides sharing entire projects with the community through the Scratch website, it's now also possible to share sprites and scripts between projects easily with the new **Backpack** feature.

Engage thrusters

Previously, when you wanted to reuse parts of other projects, you'd have to open the old project and either import and adapt it in the new one or manually retrace its steps to recreate the scripts. With the introduction of the Backpack feature, this is no longer necessary.

When you are logged in to your account, you will find the **Backpack** feature. This is visible in the Scratch editor as a small bar at the bottom. Click the bar to expand the backpack. This opens a field that behaves similarly to the Sprites window. You can drag sprites from the Sprites window to the Backpack window. The sprite isn't moved but copied, so the original project still contains the sprite as well. What's even better is that you can also copy and hold separate scripts in the backpack. This makes it a lot easier to share scripts among projects. You can simply drag project elements in and out of the backpack. The contents of the backpack remain saved when you log off. If you no longer need to carry them along, just right-click and delete them.

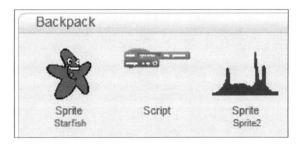

Objective complete – mini debriefing

The **Backpack** feature makes it a lot quicker to work with repeated elements. No longer do we have to recreate the same keyboard control scripts for each game we make. We can just build it once and drop it in the backpack to use in each project that requires them. Before long, you'll have a big library of useful sprites and scripts.

Some benefits and drawbacks of the new Scratch interface

We've looked at many of the new additions and changes to the Scratch interface. A lot of improvements have been made, but there are also some drawbacks to the new environment. These are subjective, based on my own experience, so feel free to disagree. To conclude, I would just like to offer my perspective on my experience with Scratch 2.0 while writing this book.

Engage thrusters

Let's start with the benefits, because these by far outweigh any shortcomings mentioned later. The announcement of the cloning feature got me excited about Scratch 2.0 instantly. As a game designer, it has been my favorite new tool. It just opens up so many opportunities to create better games with Scratch. I hope the example games will demonstrate this.

The **More Blocks** and **Backpack** features are also nice additions. I haven't used them a lot as yet, but I can see their benefit if you're an active Scratcher who creates projects on a regular basis.

Drawing in **Vector Mode** is a nice addition. It offers more variation in the way you can draw your sprites. The only downside is that it can slow down your project if there are many complex vector graphics on stage at the same time. It's a balancing act between drawing enough detail and not slowing the game down when it's running. Unfortunately, there is no clear way to see how the graphics will impact your game until you have made them and are running the program.

The one major drawback I found is that the entire Scratch environment is now online. This means that you always need to be connected to the Internet while working. Many places have Internet access, but you could be in trouble if you wanted to use Scratch while traveling. I can imagine that schools with protected web environments might have some trouble too. Personally, I found that the program can respond a bit slow sometimes if there are more web pages open, or if another program is also using bandwidth.

An offline version of Scratch 2.0 is being worked on, but at the time of writing, this is still in a beta stage. The downloadable 1.4 version of Scratch is also still available. To offer the complete Scratch 2.0 experience, I have only been working in the online environment for this book.

Objective complete – mini debriefing

As you can see Scratch 2.0 offers many interesting features that make it easier to create games. The games that can be made are also a little bit more spectacular. The only drawback I see is its dependence on the Internet, but that issue should be resolved in the future. I hope you enjoy the projects offered in this book and I'm looking forward to see how you will take them further.

Index